SUMMARY OF CHANGES
REVISION OF JOINT PUBLICATION 3-29
DATED 17 MARCH 2009

- Redefines foreign humanitarian assistance (FHA) as an "umbrella" term over the associated humanitarian type activities, to include foreign disaster relief (FDR).

- Establishes foreign consequence management as a related, but separate activity that may require FHA support.

- Establishes the proper sequence and presentation of information by moving the planning and execution processes into the correct order.

- Provides links to topics discussed in greater detail in other publications.

- Updates terminology, definitions, and vignettes.

- Updates the application and usage of medical terms, including health readiness, service, and support.

- Clarifies when to use the Department of Defense (DOD) capabilities for FHA missions.

- Clarifies the application of rules of engagement and the laws of war during FHA.

- Identifies approval authority for FDR missions.

- Clarifies the role of the National Guard State Partnership Program.

- Updates the roles and responsibilities of the Department of State and United States Agency for International Development, to include a significant update to Appendix C, "Department of State and United States Agency for International Development Organizations."

- Updates figures and tables depicting key FHA processes.

- Enhances consistency among other doctrinal publications and DOD and other Unites States Government policies.

Intentionally Blank

TABLE OF CONTENTS

CHAPTER IV
EXECUTION AND ASSESSMENT

APPENDIX

GLOSSARY

FIGURE

Intentionally Blank

EXECUTIVE SUMMARY
COMMANDER'S OVERVIEW

- **Provides an overview of foreign humanitarian assistance (FHA), including foreign disaster relief (FDR).**

- **Explains US policy and legal authorities related to FHA.**

- **Discusses interagency coordination, roles and responsibilities, and principal organizations for FDR.**

- **Covers aspects of planning unique to FHA operations.**

- **Highlights aspects of joint force execution and assessment related to FHA operations.**

Overview

Foreign humanitarian assistance (FHA) consists of Department of Defense activities conducted outside the US and its territories to directly relieve or reduce human suffering, disease, hunger, or privation.

Foreign humanitarian assistance (FHA) activities conducted by US Armed Forces range from steady-state program activities supporting geographic combatant commanders (GCC) security cooperation and related programs to conducting limited contingency operations in support of another United States Government (USG) department or agency. FHA activities include foreign disaster relief (FDR) and other activities that directly address a humanitarian need. FHA operations can be supported by other activities conducted by US military forces or they may be conducted concurrently with other types of related operations and activities such as dislocated civilian support, security operations, and foreign consequence management. FHA operations (including FDR operations) are normally conducted in support of the United States Agency for International Development (USAID) or the Department of State (DOS).

FHA provided by US forces is limited in scope and duration; designed to supplement or complement the efforts of the host nation (HN) that has the primary responsibility for providing that assistance; and may support other USG departments or agencies. Although US military forces are organized, trained, and equipped to conduct military operations that defend and protect US national interests, their inherent, unique capabilities may be used to conduct FHA activities.

The US military normally conducts FHA operations in support of another United States Government (USG) departments or agencies.

The US military also conducts FHA activities in various steady-state programs as part of a GCC's security cooperation program and/or to achieve specific theater campaign plan objectives.

FHA operations involve interaction among many local and international agencies, both governmental and nongovernmental. During FHA operations unity of command may not be possible, but the requirement for unity of effort becomes paramount.

Because Department of Defense (DOD) will normally be in a supporting role during FHA contingency operations, the joint force commander (JFC) may not be responsible for determining the mission or specifying the participating agencies. Appropriate organization, command and control (C2), and, most important, an understanding of the objectives of the organizations involved are all means to build consensus and achieve unity of effort.

Organization and Interagency Coordination

US military forces plan, coordinate, and execute FHA activities at the strategic, operational, and tactical levels to support national security interests as they pertain to geographic combatant commanders' missions.

FHA activities typically depend on a whole-of-government approach for success, whether or not DOD is lead federal agent (LFA). Because of the number of civilian and non-USG actors involved in FHA activities, command relationships outside DOD command structures may not be clearly defined, and unity of effort will be achieved with effective, timely coordination and cooperation.

Presidential and interagency policy and guidance impact mission statements, implied tasks, and plans. The JFC develops a mission statement with clearly identified and achievable objectives. Key considerations in developing the mission statement include the military role in the specific FHA mission and how DOD is to assist other USG departments and agencies, multinational partners, nongovernmental organizations (NGOs), and intergovernmental organizations (IGOs).

The Chairman of the Joint Chiefs of Staff (CJCS) is responsible for recommending military capabilities and relationships for FHA operations to Secretary of

Defense. Once these relationships have been established, the Joint Staff coordinates detailed staff planning under the cognizance of the CJCS.

GCCs direct military operations, including FHA, within their areas of responsibility (AORs). FHA should be done with the concurrence of the chief of mission. GCCs develop and maintain commanders' estimates, base plans, concept plans, or operation plans for FHA. In response to a disaster, the supported GCC structures the force necessary to conduct and sustain the FHA operation, typically forming a joint task force.

Joint Interagency Coordination Group

The joint interagency coordination group (JIACG) is an interagency staff group that establishes regular, timely, and collaborative working relationships between civilian and military operational planners. Composed of USG civilian and military experts apportioned to the GCC and tailored in staff location or title to meet the requirements of a supported GCC, the JIACG provides the GCC with the capability to collaborate at the operational level with other USG departments and agencies. The primary role of the JIACG is to enhance interagency coordination. The JIACG complements the interagency coordination that takes place at the national level through DOD and the National Security Council (NSC).

Non-USG Participants and Organizations

The HN is the nation receiving the assistance, in whose territory the forces or supplies of partner nations organizations or North Atlantic Treaty Organization transit or operate. The HN will coordinate all relief efforts within its territory. US forces conducting FHA do so with the permission of the HN under the guidance of formal and informal agreements.

The United Nations (UN) is an international organization, composed of member nations, chartered to facilitate cooperation in international law, international security, economic development, social progress, human rights, and achievement of world peace. The UN has the lead role in the international community to respond to natural and man-made disasters that are beyond the capacity of national authorities alone.

An IGO is an organization created by a formal agreement (e.g., a treaty) between two or more governments. It may be established on a global, regional, or functional basis for wide-ranging or narrowly defined purposes. These organizations have defined structures, roles, and responsibilities, and may be equipped with the resources and expertise to participate in complex interagency, IGO, and NGO coordination and collaboration. The US maintains formal or informal ties with some of the largest IGOs.

An NGO is a private, self-governing, not-for-profit organization dedicated to alleviating human suffering; promoting education, health care, economic development, environmental protection, human rights, and conflict resolution; or encouraging democratic institutions and civil society. NGOs place priority on addressing humanitarian needs first. In areas of conflict, NGOs' security may be derived solely from their absolute neutrality and humanitarian focus. The extent to which specific NGOs are willing to cooperate with the military can vary considerably.

Increasingly, the private sector resources of the international business community are being utilized to mitigate human suffering associated with disasters. Businesses donate talent or in-kind goods and services to disaster relief and recovery operations in developing countries and wish to ensure that their help is delivered in a coordinated and effective manner. The same is true for foreign disaster response. Many large private-sector companies maintain disaster/crisis response teams that can respond and add value to USG operations.

Interagency Process for Foreign Disaster Relief

The interagency coordination process often is described as "more art than science," while military operations tend to depend more on structure and doctrine. However, some of the techniques, procedures, and systems of military C2 can facilitate unity of effort if they are adjusted to the dynamic world of interagency coordination and different organizational cultures. While most USG disaster responses are coordinated by USAID, through the Office of United States Foreign Disaster Assistance (OFDA) Director, for certain unique or large-scale disasters, the USAID

Administrator may work with the NSC to convene interagency meetings.

Planning

Needs Assessment during Foreign Disaster Relief

HN, USAID, IGOs, NGOs, and USG departments and agencies conduct needs assessments on the extent of the disaster or emergency. Needs assessments also include determining the capabilities and resources of various relief organizations, including military. Analysis is an essential component of the relief process. Needs assessments and capabilities are analyzed to update and resolve differences, determine outstanding requirements, and reasonably anticipated future needs.

Based upon outstanding needs and requirements, the HN may request international assistance. NGOs and IGOs may also appeal to the international community and donors for funding and assistance. The military may receive, normally through OFDA, request for assistance to provide humanitarian assistance support, subject to the policies of the USG.

Understanding the Operational Environment

The nature of the operational environment (OE) obviously impacts the conduct of FHA operations. Important elements of the OE considered during planning and executing FDR operations include the type of disaster involved (including underlying causes), the prevailing security environment, and the system of international relief at work. Joint intelligence preparation of the operational environment will assist in developing this understanding and applying it to planning and execution.

There are three types of OEs when providing FHA: permissive, uncertain, and hostile. The type of OE will have direct impact on the decision to conduct the FHA operation, as well as many planning aspects. Regardless of the OE, force protection will remain of paramount concern to the JFC.

Relief System

An assessment of the situation should include a description of the relief organizations (NGOs, IGOs, HN, and private sector), foreign governments and military forces, UN agencies, or any other pertinent element already involved in the FHA effort, what relationship exists among them, and the effectiveness of the organizations in place. Depending on the type of operation, DOS or USAID will be critical in mapping this system and identifying key players in multiple organizations.

Mission Statement Development

A critical task for the GCC is developing the FHA military mission statement. The mission statement must provide specific direction for attaining the desired end state via clear and attainable military objectives. The GCC normally coordinates the mission statement with the LFA. GCCs consider several factors in developing the mission statement, to include the military force's role in assisting relief agencies, the OE, and security considerations.

Force Planning

In FHA operations, the joint force structure must provide for the means to coordinate and communicate with the numerous military, civilian, US and foreign organizations involved in the overall FHA effort. Effective liaison among these organizations will help reduce organizational conflicts and redundant relief efforts.

Execution and Assessment

Deployment

The joint deployment process consists of four phases: planning; predeployment activities; movement; and joint reception, staging, onward movement and integration (JRSOI). JRSOI can be the most challenging phase in FHA operations. Supported GCCs are responsible for JRSOI within their AORs. Challenges arise when the operational area has been severely impacted by the incident or disaster and US forces have had no presence or routine access to the operational area.

Sustainment

FHA operations are logistic intensive and will most likely include significant engineering requirements. Therefore, the overall logistic concept should be closely tied into the operational strategy and be mutually supporting.

Command and Control

FHA operations must include responsibility for air, land, maritime, space, and special operations forces. It is especially necessary to delegate authority to establish supply or transportation priorities. Delegation speeds decision making and reaction to changes in life-threatening situations faced in many FHA operations. Although there is no command relationship between military forces and other USG departments and agencies, UN agencies, NGOs, IGOs, affected country elements, and foreign governments, clearly defined relationships may foster harmony and reduce friction between participating organizations.

Assessment

The JFC should evaluate task performance and measure effects and determine the progress of operations toward achieving objectives. Measures of effectiveness assess changes in system behavior, capability, or OE. Measures of performance measure task performance. Well-devised measures can help the commanders and staffs understand the causal relationship between specific tasks and desired effects.

Intelligence

Intelligence and information gathering in FHA operations should be broadly focused and include collection concerning political, military, paramilitary, ethnic, religious, economic, medical, environmental, geospatial, and criminal indicators.

NGOs and IGOs should not be perceived as providing intelligence to the military. Consideration should be given to answering the information requirements of adjacent task forces as well as theater- and national-level requirements. Classification and releasability standards for intelligence and sensitive information should be determined early in the planning process and reviewed as the operation proceeds.

Information Sharing

Information sharing is critical to the efficient pursuit of a common humanitarian purpose. Although many different groups and authorities can (and should) work in parallel, a collaborative information environment (CIE) facilitates information sharing. Constructing a CIE is not primarily a technology issue—effective, low-cost, network equipment and data management systems exist today, and more are being developed.

Protection

Even in a permissive environment, the joint force can expect to encounter banditry, vandalism, and various levels of violent activities from criminals or unruly crowds. It is imperative that the joint force be trained and equipped to mitigate threats to US personnel, resources, facilities, and critical information.

CONCLUSION

This publication provides joint doctrine for the planning, execution, and assessment of FHA operations.

CHAPTER I
OVERVIEW

"The earthquake relief effort in Pakistan created a remarkable construct: a relationship between states and peoples significantly improved at every level of society. Flexibility and the ability to quickly build a team from vastly different organizations were the characteristics that enabled mission success. The "soft infrastructure" composed of interpersonal relationships and in-country connections was invaluable. The humanitarian assistance to the people of northern Pakistan set the example for interagency and international cooperation in the face of a complex humanitarian disaster and furthered US goals in the area of operations by facilitating favorable interactions between US personnel and the inhabitants of the region."

**United States Humanitarian Assistance/Disaster Relief
Keys to Success in Pakistan
Joint Forces Quarterly, 1st quarter 2007**

1. General

a. Foreign Humanitarian Assistance (FHA)

(1) FHA consists of Department of Defense (DOD) activities conducted outside the US and its territories to directly relieve or reduce human suffering, disease, hunger, or privation. These activities are governed by various statutes and policies and range from steady-state engagements to limited contingency operations. FHA includes foreign disaster relief (FDR) operations and other activities that directly address a humanitarian need, and may also be conducted concurrently with other DOD support missions and activities such as dislocated civilian support, security operations, and foreign consequence management (FCM). FHA operations (including FDR operations) are normally conducted in support of the United States Agency for International Development (USAID) or the Department of State (DOS).

(2) **FHA provided by US forces is limited in scope and duration; designed to** supplement or complement the efforts of the host nation (HN) that has the primary responsibility for providing that assistance; and may support other United States Government (USG) departments or agencies. Although US military forces are organized, trained, and equipped to conduct military operations that defend and protect US national interests, their inherent, unique capabilities may be used to conduct FHA activities.

(3) The National Security Council (NSC) coordinates foreign assistance policies and programs among all USG departments and agencies. DOS is the lead federal agency (LFA) for developing and implementing foreign policy. DOS's Bureau of Population, Refugees, and Migration (PRM) is the LFA for refugee matters. DOS also supports the foreign affairs activities of other USG departments and agencies. USAID is the principal agency for US bilateral and multilateral development assistance to foreign countries. Together, DOS and USAID are the principal agencies for providing US humanitarian assistance (HA) overseas.

(4) The objective of the HA provided by DOS and USAID is to save lives, alleviate suffering, and minimize the economic costs of conflict, disasters, and displacement. HA is provided on the basis of need according to principles of universality, impartiality, and human dignity. It is often organized by sectors, but requires an integrated, coordinated, and/or multi-sectoral approach to be most effective. Emergency operations will foster the transition from relief through recovery to development, but they cannot and will not replace the development investments necessary to reduce chronic poverty or establish just social services.

b. **US Military FHA Operations.** The US military normally conducts FHA operations in support of another USG department or agency, including FDR operations to alleviate suffering of foreign disaster victims. The US military also conducts FHA activities in various steady-state programs as part of a geographic combatant commander's (GCC's) security cooperation program and/or to achieve specific theater campaign plan (TCP) objectives.

(1) **Support Activities.** Some activities that may be conducted include providing logistical support, such as the transportation of humanitarian supplies or personnel; making available, preparing, and transporting nonlethal excess property (EP) to foreign countries; transferring on-hand DOD stocks to respond to unforeseen emergencies; and conducting some DOD humanitarian demining assistance activities.

(2) **Concurrent Operations.** FCM may be conducted concurrently with FHA activities.

c. **Unified Action**

(1) FHA operations involve interaction among many local and international agencies, both governmental and nongovernmental. Unified action is the synchronization, coordination, and/or integration of the activities of governmental, nongovernmental, and international entities with military operations to achieve unity of effort. Unity of effort is the coordination and cooperation toward common objectives, even if the participants are not necessarily part of the same command or organization, which is the product of successful unified action. Unity of effort in an operation ensures all means are directed to a common purpose. During FHA operations unity of command may not be possible, but the requirement for unity of effort becomes paramount.

(2) Because DOD will normally be in a supporting role during FHA contingency operations, the joint force commander (JFC) may not be responsible for determining the mission or specifying the participating agencies. Obstacles to unified action include differing objectives and modes of operation, competing missions, inadequate structure and procedures, incompatible communications, overly restrictive security classifications, cultural differences, and bureaucratic and personnel limitations. Appropriate organization, command and control (C2), and, most important, an understanding of the objectives of the organizations involved are all means to build consensus and achieve unity of effort, regardless of role. The reciprocal exchange of information, including the establishment of liaison officers (LNOs), is also a critical enabler in ensuring unity of effort.

(3) The joint force will work not only with interagency partners during FHA operations, but also with multinational organizations including the HN, intergovernmental organizations (IGOs), nongovernmental organizations (NGOs), partner nations (PNs), and the private sector. The tenets of multinational unity of effort (i.e., respect, rapport, knowledge of partners, patience, and coordination) applied during an FHA mission cannot guarantee success; however, ignoring them may lead to mission failure.

For further details on unified action, refer to Joint Publication (JP) 1, Doctrine for the Armed Forces of the United States, *and JP 3-08,* Interorganizational Coordination During Joint Operations.

d. Humanitarian principles are central to establishing and maintaining access to affected populations whether in the context of a natural disaster, an armed conflict, or a complex emergency (e.g., a natural disaster that occurs during an armed conflict). Four principals are generally recognized by humanitarian organizations: humanity, neutrality, impartiality, and independence. The principles of humanity, neutrality, and impartiality were endorsed by the United Nations (UN) General Assembly Resolution 46/182 in 1991. The principle of independence was added in 2004 under UN General Assembly Resolution 58/114.

(1) **Humanity.** Human suffering must be addressed wherever it is found. The purpose of humanitarian action is to protect life and health and ensure respect for human beings.

(2) **Neutrality.** Humanitarian actors must not take sides in hostilities or engage in controversies of a political, racial, religious, or ideological nature.

(3) **Impartiality.** Humanitarian action must be carried out on the basis of need alone, giving priority to the most urgent cases of distress and making no distinctions on the basis of nationality, race, gender, religious belief, class, or political opinions.

(4) **Independence.** Humanitarian action must be autonomous from the political, economic, military, or other objectives that any actor may hold with regard to areas where humanitarian action is being implemented.

e. **Related Terminology.** The following terms and descriptions are important to form a basis for understanding FHA operations:

(1) **Foreign assistance** is assistance to foreign nations ranging from the sale of military equipment to donations of food and medical supplies to aid survivors of natural and man-made disasters. US foreign assistance takes three forms: development assistance, HA, and security assistance.

(2) **Development assistance** refers to programs, projects, and activities primarily designed to promote economic growth and improve the lives of the citizens of developing countries while furthering US foreign policy interests in expanding democracy and promoting free-market economic growth.

(3) **HA** is generally referred to by non-DOD agencies as aid and action designed to save lives, alleviate suffering, and reduce the economic and social impact of disasters and humanitarian crises. This immediate life-saving assistance includes the provision of food, water, emergency shelter, and medical aid.

(4) **Security assistance** is a group of programs by which the USG provides defense articles, military training, and other defense-related services by grant, loan, credit, or cash sales to further national policies and objectives.

(5) **Foreign disaster** is a calamitous situation or event that occurs naturally (such as earthquakes, storms, droughts, volcanic eruptions, wildfires) or through human activities (such as industrial explosions or fires, civil strife, infectious disease), which threatens or inflicts human suffering on a scale that may warrant emergency relief assistance from the USG or from foreign partners.

(6) From a DOS and USAID perspective, **humanitarian protection** refers to the measures to safeguard the rights of populations of concern by seeking to prevent or end patterns of violence or abuse; alleviate the trauma and related effects of violence or abuse; identify and promote durable solutions; foster respect for refugee, humanitarian, and human rights; and ensure that humanitarian actions uphold human dignity, benefit the most vulnerable, and do not harm affected populations. In practice, protection can be measures to ensure the safety of women, children, the elderly, and disabled; ensuring that all people have access to assistance and services; providing adequate lighting in a refugee camp; ensuring order at a food distribution; providing identity documents to all individuals; providing refugees access to education, livelihood assistance, and legal services in asylum; and monitoring the physical, social, and economic conditions to which people return after displacement, among many other examples.

(7) **North Atlantic Treaty Organization (NATO) Terminology.** US forces conducting FHA as part of a NATO operation should be cognizant of the following NATO terms:

(a) **HA,** as part of a military operation, is the use of available military resources to assist or complement the efforts of responsible civil actors in the operational area or specialized civil humanitarian organizations in fulfilling their primary responsibility to alleviate human suffering.

(b) **Humanitarian operation** is an operation specifically mounted to alleviate human suffering where responsible civil actors in an area are unable or unwilling to adequately support a population. It may precede, parallel, or complement the activity of specialized civil humanitarian organizations.

(c) **Civil emergency planning** is NATO planning to collect, analyze, and share information on national planning activities to ensure the most effective use of civil resources for use during emergency situations, in accordance with alliance objectives. It enables allies and PNs to assist each other in preparing for and dealing with the consequences of crisis, disaster, or conflict in accordance with alliance objectives.

(d) **Civil-military cooperation** is coordination and cooperation, in support of the mission, between the NATO commander and civil actors, including national population and local authorities, as well as international and national organizations and agencies.

2. Legal Authority and Policy

a. A basic tenet of fiscal law is that expenditure of public funds may be made only when expressly authorized by Congress. The law surrounding FHA consists of statutes, annual appropriations, policies, regulations, and directives that may be confusing. The staff judge advocate (SJA) should be involved in planning for FHA operations as early as possible.

b. **United States Code (USC).** Statutory authority for USG departments and agencies to provide FHA is contained in the **Foreign Assistance Act (FAA) of 1961,** as amended, in Title 22, USC. This legislation provides a blueprint for USG engagement with other nations. The FAA designated DOS to provide policy guidance and supervision of programs created within the FAA. Various sections of Title 10, USC, and Title 22, USC, provide specific authorizations for various types of assistance. In addition, the annual DOD appropriation acts provide funding levels for various authorizations. Taken together, these provisions are very narrow in scope and generally still require prior coordination with DOS and/or USAID. Other sections of the FAA may provide authorization for expenditures by other USG departments and agencies that may involve joint force distribution or coordination. One example is international development accounts, which permit donations of foodstuffs by the US Department of Agriculture on an emergency basis.

c. **Department of Defense Directive (DODD) 5100.46,** *Foreign Disaster Relief (FDR),* **establishes policy guidance for FDR operations.** FDR is assistance that can be used immediately to alleviate the suffering of foreign disaster victims. This policy does not prevent a local military commander with assigned forces at or near the immediate scene of a foreign disaster from taking prompt action to save human lives. In cases in which this authority is invoked, the commander should obtain the concurrence of the HN and chief of mission (COM) of the affected country before committing forces. Also, the combatant commander (CCDR) shall follow up as soon as possible, but no later than 72 hours after the start of relief operations, to secure Secretary of Defense (SecDef) or Deputy Secretary of Defense approval for continuing assistance. Figure I-1 depicts causes of foreign disasters and various types of FDR.

d. Chairman of the Joint Chiefs of Staff Instruction (CJCSI) 3214.01, *Defense Support for Chemical, Biological, Radiological, and Nuclear Incidents on Foreign Territory,* establishes guidance for FCM operations. This instruction applies to DOD support to FCM operations as part of the USG response to chemical, biological, radiological, and nuclear (CBRN) incidents abroad.

For further details on FCM, refer to JP 3-41, Chemical, Biological, Radiological, and Nuclear Consequence Management.

See Appendix A, "Legal Issues," for detailed legal considerations and information.

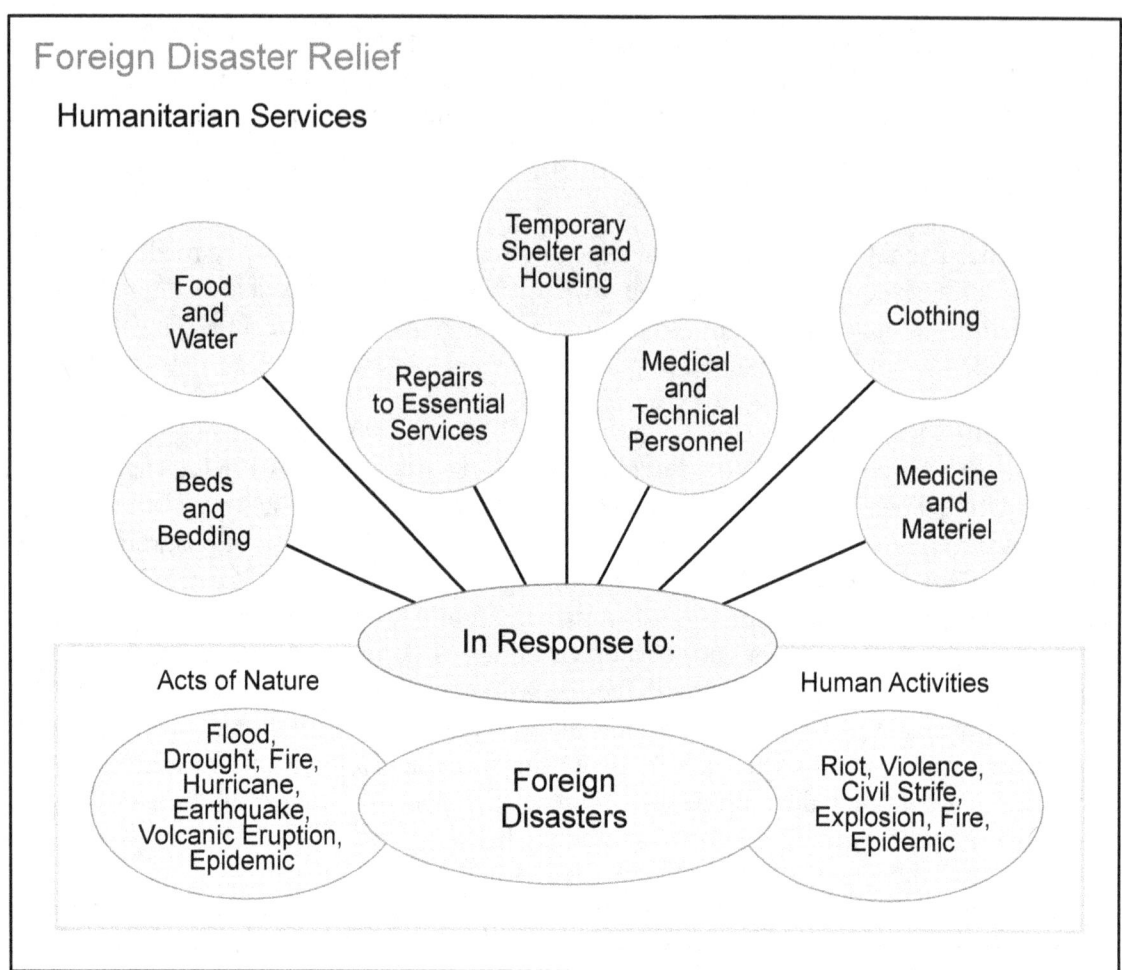

Figure I-1. Foreign Disaster Relief

3. Operational Environment

The operational environment (OE) is the composite of the conditions, circumstances, and influences that affect the employment of capabilities and bear on the commander's decisions. It encompasses **physical areas and factors** (the air, land, maritime, and space domains) **and the information environment** (which includes cyberspace). Included within these are the adversary, friendly, and neutral systems which are relevant to a specific joint operation. **Understanding this environment requires a broad perspective** during any operation; however, this holistic view is particularly important during FHA operations, where there are normally no overt adversary military forces, but forces of nature, nonmilitary personnel, organizations, and systems, and possibly covert adversary forces, that combine to complicate joint force operations and influence the application of force choices.

For further details on the OE, refer to JP 3-0, Joint Operations.

4. Types of Foreign Humanitarian Assistance and Supported Missions and Activities

FHA activities conducted by US Armed Forces range from steady-state program activities supporting GCC security cooperation and related programs to conducting limited contingency operations in support of another USG department or agency. FHA activities include FDR and other activities that directly address a humanitarian need. FHA operations can be supported by other activities conducted by US military forces or they may be conducted concurrently with other types of related operations and activities.

a. **FDR Missions.** FDR is assistance to alleviate the suffering of foreign disaster victims, including victims of natural disasters and conflicts, internally displaced persons (IDPs), refugees, stateless persons, and vulnerable migrants. Normally, it includes the provision of basic services and commodities such as food, water, sanitation, health care, non-food items (clothing, bedding, etc.), emergency shelter, as well as support to critical infrastructure and logistics necessary for the delivery of these essential services and commodities. The US military normally will only be asked to provide FDR when it brings a unique capability or when the civilian response community is overwhelmed.

b. **Dislocated Civilian Support Missions.** DOD may be requested to provide HA to dislocated civilians either to support the GCC's TCP or objectives or when the USG LFA requests DOD support due to its unique capabilities (e.g., specific engineering skills). A dislocated civilian is a broad term primarily used by DOD that includes a displaced person, an evacuee, an IDP, a migrant, a refugee, or a stateless person. These persons may be victims of conflicts or disasters. It should be noted that humanitarian organizations make a distinction between people displaced internally (IDPs) and people who flee across international borders to escape persecution (refugees). Humanitarian organizations do not use the term dislocated civilians. Typically, the UN or other IGOs and NGOs will provide basic assistance and services to the population; in special circumstances this may include building and administering camps. However, when the US military is requested to provide support, dislocated civilian support missions may include **camp construction; provision of care** (food/water, supplies, medical attention, and security); and **transportation.** An important priority for the management of dislocated civilians should be to utilize the services and facilities of non-DOD agencies when coordination can be accomplished as **dislocated civilian operations are often long-term and require extensive resourcing** normally not immediately available through DOD sources.

c. **Security Missions.** These missions may **establish and maintain conditions for the provision of FHA** by organizations of the world relief community. The delivery of humanitarian relief supplies often depends on the affected country having secure serviceable ports, air terminals, roads, and railways. In some cases, however, the affected country will not be able to meet this condition and may request assistance from the USG. Once the movement of supplies commences, **secure areas will be needed for storage of relief material** until it can be distributed to the affected population. Other tasks may involve providing routine clearance, security, and armed escorts for convoys and personnel delivering emergency aid, protection of shelters for dislocated civilians, and security for multinational forces, NGOs, and IGOs.

d. **Technical Assistance and Support Functions.** An FHA force may, for a short term, support tasks such as communications restoration, relief supply distribution management and delivery, transportation, port operations, base operating support, emergency medical care, search and rescue (SAR), and humanitarian demining or counter-improvised explosive device (IED) assistance. This technical assistance may take the form of advice and selected training, assessments, manpower, and equipment. Based upon SecDef and GCC guidance, **the FHA force commander should establish operational procedures regarding technical advice and assistance** to the COM, USAID, the affected country, NGOs, and IGOs as soon as possible. In order to deconflict activities and reduce redundancies, such procedures should recognize the role of USAID as the LFA for coordinating USG FDR. The technical assistance procedures should clarify what assistance may be provided as well as the source of authority for assistance. Humanitarian demining assistance includes activities related to the furnishing of education, training, and technical assistance with respect to the detection and clearance of land mines and other explosive remnants of war (ERW). No member of the Armed Forces of the US, while providing humanitarian demining assistance, will engage in the physical detection, lifting, or destroying of land mines or other ERW (unless the member does so for the concurrent purpose of supporting a US military operation); or provide such assistance as part of a military operation that does not involve the Armed Forces of the US.

For further information regarding humanitarian demining assistance, see Appendix B, "Department of Defense Humanitarian Assistance Tasking, Funding Procedures, and Humanitarian Assistance Programs," and CJCSI 3207.01, Military Support to Humanitarian Mine Operations.

5. Related Operations

a. Although FHA operations may be executed simultaneously with other types of operations, **each type has unique characteristics.** For example, FHA operations may be simultaneously conducted with peace operations (PO), but each has its own strategic end state. **Military commanders must be cautious not to commit their forces to projects and tasks that go beyond the FHA mission.** Military commanders conducting FHA simultaneously with other operations must develop end state, transition, and termination objectives as well as measures of effectiveness (MOEs) and measures of performance (MOPs) complementary to simultaneous military operations.

b. **Stability Operations.** These missions, tasks, and activities seek to maintain or reestablish a safe and secure environment and provide essential governmental services, emergency infrastructure reconstruction, or humanitarian relief. Many of these missions and tasks are the essence of civil-military operations (CMO). Joint operations must feature an appropriate balance between offensive, defensive, and stability operations in all phases. Although offensive and defensive operations may be required during an FHA operation, the preponderance of missions, tasks, and activities will be stability operations. Likewise, FHA may be executed to provide humanitarian relief following combat (whether or not US forces were involved in the combat), for example, in conjunction with a PO or during the stabilize phase of a major campaign or operation. FHA may be conducted separately, concurrently with, or as part of, stability operations. However, in either case, FHA activities may provide a catalyst for promoting stability either in the HN or regionally.

For further guidance on stability operations, refer to Department of Defense Instruction (DODI) 3000.05, Stability Operations, *JP 3-07,* Stability Operations, *and JP 3-0,* Joint Operations.

c. **Nation assistance (NA)** is often connected with FHA operations, but there are very distinct differences. NA is assistance rendered to a nation by foreign forces within that nation's territory based on agreements mutually concluded between nations. NA programs include, but are not limited to, security assistance, foreign internal defense (FID), other Title 10, USC, programs, and activities performed on a reimbursable basis by federal agencies or IGOs. NA generally refers to a long-term commitment to promote sustainable development and growth of responsive institutions. Most often, NA will be an important part of rebuilding after the completion of a disaster relief mission.

(1) **Humanitarian and Civic Assistance (HCA).** HCA is assistance to the local populace, specifically authorized by Title 10, USC, Section 401, and funded under separate authorities, provided by predominantly US forces in conjunction with authorized military operations. In accordance with DODI 2205.02, *Humanitarian and Civic Assistance (HCA) Activities,* HCA activities may be conducted as a part of deployments for training.

(a) Assistance provided under these provisions must promote the security interests of both the US and the HN and the specific operational readiness skills of the members of the armed forces who participate in the activities. Assistance is limited to:

1. Medical, surgical, dental, and veterinary care provided in areas of a country that are rural or are underserved by medical, surgical, dental, and veterinary professionals, respectively, including education, training, and technical assistance related to the care provided.

2. Construction of rudimentary surface transportation systems.

3. Well drilling and construction of basic sanitation facilities.

4. Rudimentary construction and repair of public facilities.

(b) HCA activities carried out under this section shall complement, and may not duplicate, any other form of social or economic assistance which may be provided to the country concerned by any other department or agency of the US. Such activities shall serve the basic economic and social needs of the people of the country concerned. HCA may not be provided under Title 10, USC, Section 401 (directly or indirectly) to any individual, group, or organization engaged in military or paramilitary activity. HCA may not be provided under this section to any foreign country unless the Secretary of State specifically approves the provision of such assistance.

(c) It is important to understand the difference between HCA and FHA. HCA activities are typically preplanned and designed to provide assistance to the HN populace while also meeting the requirements to promote operational readiness skills of the US Armed Forces who participate in the activities, and promote security interests of both the HN and US.

(d) To avoid possible overlap or duplication and ensure sustainability, HCA projects must be coordinated with the COM, the USAID mission director or designee, and appropriate HN officials. For example, school construction should not be undertaken if there is not a sustainable HN plan to provide teachers and administration, salaries, equipment, and books. DOD policy for HCA requires that a statement of the ability of the HN to sustain it be included for every project nomination.

(2) **Security assistance** refers to a group of programs by which the US provides defense articles, military training, and other defense-related services to foreign nations by grant, loan, credit, or cash sales in furtherance of US national policies and objectives (e.g., foreign military sales). Security assistance is an element of security cooperation funded and authorized by DOS and administered by DOD.

(3) **FID** involves participation by civilian and military agencies of a government in any of the action programs taken by another government or other designated organization to free and protect its society from subversion, lawlessness, or insurgency.

For further details on FID, refer to JP 3-22, Foreign Internal Defense.

d. **PO** encompass multiagency and multinational crisis response and limited contingency operations involving all instruments of national power with military missions to contain conflict, redress the peace, and shape the environment to support reconciliation and rebuilding and facilitate the transition to legitimate governance. PO include peacekeeping, peace enforcement, peacemaking, peacebuilding, and conflict prevention efforts.

For further information on PO, refer to JP 3-07.3, Peace Operations.

e. **Noncombatant evacuation operations (NEOs)** as used by DOS are an ordered departure from a threatened area abroad that is carried out with the assistance of DOD. Evacuation will generally correspond to protection and evacuation plans established by DOS. DOS may also declare a NEO based on the nature of the threat or the lack of availability of alternative forms of transportation. It is important to note that diplomatic or other considerations may make the use of certain terms, such as NEO, inadvisable and require the use of other terms instead. Although normally considered in connection with hostile action, evacuation may also be conducted in anticipation of, or in response to, a natural or man-made disaster.

For further information on NEOs, refer to JP 3-68, Noncombatant Evacuation Operations.

f. **CMO.** CMO consist of the activities of a commander performed by designated civil affairs (CA) or other military forces that establish, maintain, influence, or exploit relations between military forces, indigenous populations, and institutions, by directly supporting the attainment of objectives relating to the reestablishment or maintenance of stability within a region or HN. CMO may include performance by military forces of activities and functions normally the responsibility of the local, regional, or national government. These activities may occur prior to, during, or subsequent to other military actions. They may also occur, if directed, in the absence of other military operations.

Further information on CMO can be found in JP 3-57, Civil-Military Operations.

g. **Mass Atrocity Response Operations (MARO).** Commanders should be prepared to monitor, prevent, and, if necessary, respond to mass atrocity situations. Mass atrocities can erupt at any time during operations in response to man-made disasters (e.g., riots, violence, civil strife). Evidence of previously committed mass atrocities can also become known during the course of an FHA operation, potentially raising diplomatic, political, and social turmoil, the consequences of which can directly impact the mission.

For further information on MARO, see JP 3-07.3, Peace Operations.

h. **FCM.** FCM is a USG activity that assists friends and allies in responding to the effects from an intentional or accidental CBRN incident on foreign territory in order to maximize preservation of life. Primary responsibility for responding to the incident rests with the HN, unless stipulated under relevant international agreements or arrangements. Unless otherwise directed by the President, DOS is the LFA for USG FCM operations and coordinates the overall USG FCM response. When requested by the LFA and directed by SecDef, DOD will support USG FCM operations to the extent allowed by law and subject to the availability of forces. The ability of the USG to assist an HN government and its affected population is determined by the nature of the CBRN event, the forces available to provide assistance, and the time required to deploy to the vicinity of the incident. DOD's CBRN response includes efforts to protect its citizens and its Armed Forces abroad in order to mitigate human casualties and to provide temporary associated essential services. FCM may be conducted simultaneously with FHA operations. FCM plans should include support related to essential services and activities required to manage and mitigate problems resulting from disasters and catastrophes. Such services may include transportation, communications, CBRN reconnaissance, public works, fire-fighting, information planning, care of mass casualties, resources support, initial essential stabilizing medical care and forward resuscitative/surgical care, urban SAR, hazardous materials mitigation, food preparation and distribution, and energy generation and distribution.

For more detailed information on FCM, see CJCSI 3214.01, Defense Support for Chemical, Biological, Radiological, and Nuclear Incidents on Foreign Territory, JP 3-41, Chemical, Biological, Radiological, and Nuclear Consequence Management, and DTRA, Foreign Consequence Management Legal Deskbook.
http://www.dtra.mil/documents/business/current/FCMLegalDeskbook.pdf.

OPERATION TOMODACHI

On March 11, 2011, Japan suffered a 9.0-magnitude earthquake, one of the worst in recorded history. The earthquake triggered a destructive tsunami that struck the coastal areas of Northeast Japan, in some cases traveling up to 10 kilometers inland and damaged the Fukushima nuclear power plant.

In conjunction with the rest of the US Government, the US military quickly initiated crisis response actions in support of the Japanese government in an operation named "Tomodachi," the Japanese word for "friend." The military sent some 20,000 troops, 140 aircraft and at least 20 ships in support of Operation TOMODACHI.

During the operation, US military forces conducted search and rescue operations; transported emergency response teams, equipment, and relief supplies to hundreds of thousands of displaced people in affected remote Japanese communities; and provided emergency medical care.

Providing humanitarian assistance in the wake of a disaster is not an uncommon mission for the US military. However, the magnitude and the destruction caused by the earthquake and tsunami joined with the radiological threat from the damaged nuclear plant caused an unparalleled foreign disaster.

Commander, United States Pacific Command (USPACOM) established the command and control to execute Operation TOMODACHI. Commander, US Forces Japan initially served as the commander of Operation

TOMODACHI, until command was handed off to the activated joint task force (JTF). Seventh Fleet, Fifth Air Force, US Army Forces Japan, and Marine Forces Japan were assigned as supporting commands. USPACOM activated elements of JTF 519 to command the operation and operationally augment the staff of US Forces, Japan to form a joint support force. The mission of this joint support force was to support the Government of Japan with disaster response in the wake of the earthquake and subsequent tsunami.

During Operation TOMODACHI, US forces followed three lines of operation:

• Foreign humanitarian assistance and disaster relief.

• Chemical, biological, radiological, and nuclear response.

• Noncombatant evacuation (voluntary departure of Department of Defense [DOD] personnel and their dependents).

Operation TOMODACHI was successfully conducted to deal with a complex foreign disaster. US military forces provided critical humanitarian assistance, as well as assistance to Japanese chemical, biological, radiological, and nuclear consequence management efforts and a noncombatant evacuation of US DOD personnel. Not only were countless lives saved, but the US-Japan alliance was strengthened. Japanese Prime Minister Naoto Kan on April 20, 2011 acknowledged the support of the United States: "Immediately after the earthquake, the United States, our most important friend and ally, provided swift cooperation.... From an early stage in the response efforts, US forces have diligently performed relief activities on multiple fronts as part of Operation TOMODACHI. The attitude that Americans have demonstrated during this operation has deeply touched the hearts and minds of the Japanese."

Various Sources

6. Operational Context

a. US military forces participate in **unilateral** or **multinational** coordinated responses. Multinational responses may or may not involve the UN. FHA operations can occur in permissive, uncertain, and hostile environments and as either a unilateral or multinational operation. The security environment of a mission is a significant factor in how these missions respond.

b. **Unilateral.** In this type of operation, **the USG provides FHA without direct involvement by nations other than the HN.** A unilateral response would normally occur when expediency is essential, such as when a humanitarian crisis or disaster demands an immediate response. A unilateral effort may transition to a multinational operation.

c. **Multinational.** Multinational operations are usually undertaken within the structure of a coalition or alliance. Other possible arrangements include supervision by an IGO such as the UN or the Organization for Security and Cooperation in Europe (OSCE). An alliance is a relationship that results from a formal agreement (e.g., treaty) between two or more nations for broad, long-term objectives that further the common interests of the members. A coalition is an ad hoc arrangement between two or more nations for common action. Coalitions are formed by different nations, often with different objectives, usually for a single occasion or for longer cooperation in a narrow sector of common interest. Operations conducted with units from two or more coalition members are referred to as coalition operations.

For further information on multinational operations, refer to JP 3-16, Multinational Operations.

7. Crisis Response and Limited Contingency Operations

Crisis response and limited contingency operations are typically limited in scope and scale and conducted to achieve a very specific objective in an operational area. They may be conducted as stand-alone operations in response to a crisis or executed as an element of a larger, more complex joint campaign or operation. A limited contingency operation in response to a crisis includes all of those operations for which the joint operation planning process (JOPP) is required and a contingency or crisis action plan is developed. The level of complexity, duration, and resources depends on the circumstances. Included are operations to maintain and improve US ability to operate with multinational partners to deter the hostile ambitions of potential aggressors (e.g., Joint Task Force [JTF] SHINING HOPE in the spring of 1999 to support refugee humanitarian relief for hundreds of thousands of ethnic Albanians fleeing their homes in Kosovo). Many such operations involve a combination of military forces and capabilities in close cooperation with other USG departments and agencies, IGOs, and NGOs. The ability of the US to respond rapidly with appropriate options to potential or actual crises contributes to regional stability. Thus, joint operations often may be planned and executed as a crisis response or limited contingency. As soon as practical after it is determined that a crisis may develop or a contingency is declared, JFCs and their staffs begin a systematic analysis and determine the intelligence requirements needed to support the anticipated operation and fill the commander's information gaps. The CCDR or combatant command (CCMD) standing collection requirements can be a useful baseline for intelligence requirements. Intelligence derived from the various intelligence disciplines may confirm or support current estimates. The JFC should understand intelligence changes along with the dynamics of the OE, especially in humanitarian or disaster situations. Utilizing various and updated information sources provides better situational awareness and intelligence.

For further information on the range of military operations, refer to JP 3-0, Joint Operations.

8. Mission Transition or Termination

a. Based on the supported GCC's intent, the JFC determines the best arrangement of simultaneous and sequential actions and activities to create desired effects to support achievement of objectives to accomplish the assigned mission. This arrangement is broken into phases. A phase can be characterized by the focus that is placed on it. Phases are distinct in time, space, and/or purpose from one another, but must be planned in support of each other and should represent a natural progression and subdivision of the campaign or operation.

b. Transitions between operational phases are designed to be distinct shifts in focus by the joint force, often accompanied by changes in command relationships. The need to move into another phase normally is identified by assessing that a set of objectives are achieved or that the situation has evolved in a manner that requires a major change in focus for the joint force and is, therefore, usually event-driven, not time-driven. Changing the focus of the operation takes time and may require changing priorities, command relationships, force allocation, or even the operational area. This challenge demands an agile shift in joint force skill sets, actions, organizational behaviors, and mental outlooks; and coordination and collaboration with a wider range of other organizations—USG departments and agencies, multinational partners, IGOs, and NGOs—to provide those capabilities necessary to address the mission-specific factors.

c. Termination of operations must be considered from the outset of planning and should be a coordinated effort. Properly conceived termination criteria are key to ensuring that achieved military objectives endure. Further, development of a military end state is complementary to and supports attaining the specified termination criteria and national strategic end state. Commanders are cautioned that the end state conditions could change during the operations and that the end state envisioned by other participating organizations may differ.

d. Any use of military assets should be, at its onset, limited in time and scale and present criteria for transition that defines clearly how the function it undertakes could, in the future, be undertaken by civilian personnel. Normally, military forces operate in the initial stages of disaster relief to fill immediate gaps in assistance; military objectives will be to enable civilian control of disaster relief efforts (HN, international, or other USG departments or agencies).

e. The transition of humanitarian efforts to HN authorities will not occur by default. Planning of FHA must involve extensive international and interagency coordination from the very beginning in order to ensure a successful transition. FHA efforts by the joint force should focus on using unique military capacities to fill gaps in the humanitarian response provided by USAID, the HN, other USG departments and agencies, and IGOs. The goal for termination of operations is to coordinate the conclusion or transition of efforts with USAID, the HN, USG departments and agencies, IGOs, and NGOs to permit an orderly reduction of the joint force's involvement and presence.

9. Funding

The JFC should consider the financial impacts of FHA operations. Planning for FHA operations must take into account the legal authority, authority limits, and mechanisms that allow US forces to dispense supplies and services. It is important that the JFC **coordinate expenditures with the appropriate agency** prior to funds being expended, or reimbursement may be denied. Detailed records of expenditures are critical to the reimbursement process.

Appendix B, "Department of Defense Foreign Humanitarian Assistance Tasking, Funding Procedures and Humanitarian Assistance Programs," provides more information regarding DOD FHA tasking and funding procedures, and record-keeping requirements.

Intentionally Blank

CHAPTER II
ORGANIZATION AND INTERAGENCY COORDINATION

> *"The necessary first step in shaping effective interagency groups is making known what skills and resources one brings to the table."*
>
> **Admiral P.D. Miller, US Navy**
> **Commander in Chief, US Atlantic Command**
> **1 October 1993-31 October 1994**

1. Introduction

US military forces plan, coordinate, and execute FHA activities at the strategic, operational, and tactical levels to support national security interests as they pertain to GCCs' missions. FHA activities typically depend on a whole-of-government approach for success, whether or not DOD is the LFA. The President and/or SecDef provide guidance and objectives, task the GCC to respond to contingencies or engage in military engagement, security cooperation, and deterrence activities or operations. The GCC is identified as the supported commander for DOD actions at the strategic level; provides strategic direction and operational focus to subordinates at the operational level; and synchronizes and integrates the military instrument of national power in time, space, and purpose with the actions of interagency and multinational partners, NGOs, and IGOs toward theater strategic objectives. **This chapter provides information regarding interagency coordination, roles and responsibilities, and principal organizations.** This information will assist JFCs and their staffs in understanding these organizations and their responsibilities and relationships in FHA operations.

2. Overview

Because of the number of civilian and non-USG actors involved in FHA activities, command relationships outside DOD command structures may not be clearly defined, and unity of effort will be achieved with effective, timely coordination and cooperation. The challenge for CCDRs and their staffs is not only to understand and comply with various existing DOD policies and program guidance for FHA, but also to determine the right place and time to access interagency and other coordination networks as required to achieve GCC objectives and common goals of all the interorganizational stakeholders. Difficulties arise from the fact that many USG departments and agencies, civil and military authorities, foreign governments, the NGOs, and IGOs may be conducting assistance activities within the same operational area prior to, during, and after departure of the joint force. US military planners must remain cognizant that these various agencies fall outside the military C2 system. **Coordination and collaboration are essential in dealing with these organizations.** The strategic goals or operating procedures of all concerned may not be identical, or even compatible; however, with thorough collaboration and planning with concerned entities everyone can contribute to successful operations. (For an example of HA stakeholders, see Figure II-1). **Presidential and interagency policy and guidance impact mission statements, implied tasks, and plans.** The JFC develops a mission statement with clearly identified and achievable objectives. Key considerations in developing the mission

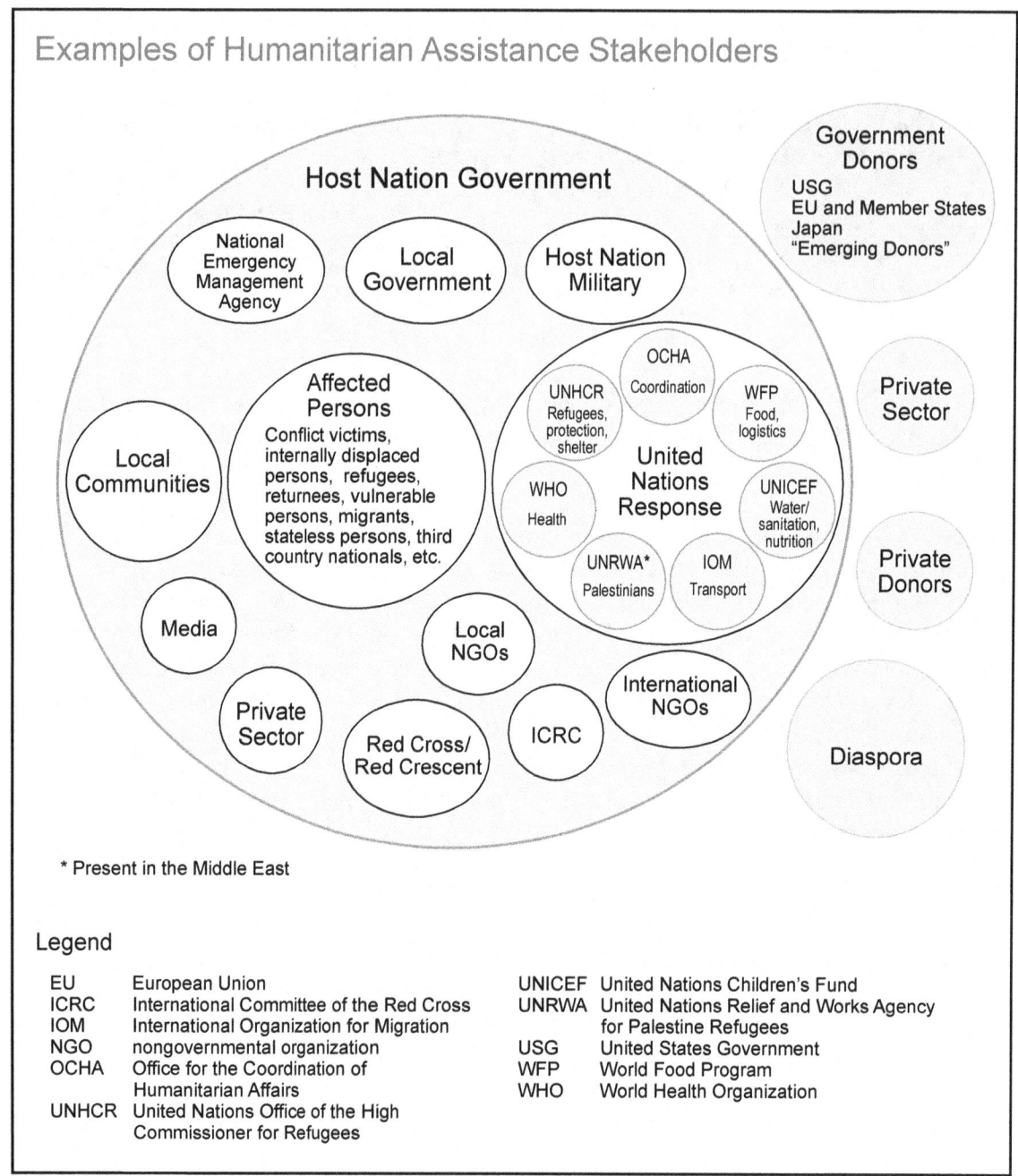

Figure II-1. Examples of Humanitarian Assistance Stakeholders

statement include the military role in the specific FHA mission and how DOD is to assist other USG departments and agencies, multinational partners, NGOs, and IGOs.

3. United States Government Civilian Departments and Agencies

a. **DOS.** DOS is the lead US foreign affairs agency. DOS advances US objectives and interests in the world through its primary role in developing and implementing the President's foreign policy. DOS also supports the foreign affairs activities of other USG departments and agencies (e.g., USAID, DOD, and Department of Commerce);

simultaneously, the foreign affairs activities of other executive agencies support the DOS foreign affairs strategies. DOS protects and assists US citizens living or traveling abroad; promotes US foreign policy objectives to other nations and the US public; oversees US foreign assistance; assists US businesses in the international marketplace; and coordinates and provides support for international activities of other USG departments and agencies. DOS is organized into functional and regional bureaus. The Under Secretary for Civilian Security, Democracy, and Human Rights oversees two functional bureaus involved in HA: the PRM and the Bureau of Conflict and Stabilization Operations (CSO). Regional bureaus include the following: Western Hemisphere, sub-Sahara Africa, Near East (North Africa and Middle East), South and Central Asia, East Asia and the Pacific, and Europe and Eurasia.

(1) The Bureau of Political-Military Affairs (PM) is the principal link between DOD and DOS. Among other coordinating functions, the bureau manages humanitarian mine action (HMA) programs around the world, and promotes public-private mine action partnerships.

(2) PRM has primary responsibility for formulating humanitarian policies and providing HA in conflict situations and complex emergencies. PRM's mission is to provide protection, ease suffering, and resolve the plight of persecuted and uprooted people around the world on behalf of the American people by providing life-sustaining assistance, working through multilateral systems to build global partnerships, promoting best practices in humanitarian response, and ensuring that humanitarian principles are thoroughly integrated into US foreign and national security policy. PRM has a lead policy and programmatic role in refugee and migration crises and manages refugee admissions to the US. PRM provides funding through the Migration and Refugee Assistance account and the President's Emergency Refugee and Migration Assistance Fund. PRM has officers overseas in Geneva and Brussels, and regional refugee coordinators in multiple locations. The PRM staff are key interlocutors for other USG officials and international humanitarian partners in a humanitarian crisis. These regional refugee coordinators monitor and evaluate humanitarian programs and provide reporting on humanitarian issues that informs the USG response to conflict and displacement.

(3) The Bureau of Conflict and Stabilization Operations (CSO). The CSO advances US national security by breaking cycles of violent conflict and mitigating crises in priority countries. The CSO engages in conflict prevention, crisis response, and stabilization, aiming to address the underlying causes of destabilizing violence.

(4) Within the Bureau of Intelligence and Research is the Humanitarian Information Unit (HIU) office. The mission of the HIU is to serve as a USG interagency center to identify, collect, analyze, and disseminate all-source information critical to USG decision makers and partners in preparation for and response to humanitarian emergencies worldwide, and to promote innovative technologies and best practices for humanitarian information management.

(5) The Office of the Coordinator of Assistance to Europe, Eurasia, and Central Asia is mandated by statute to coordinate all US assistance to Europe, Eurasia, and Central Asia, including HA, security assistance, and development assistance. Located with the

European and Eurasian Affairs Bureau, it also straddles the South Central Asia Bureau, covering assistance to the Central Asian Republics.

b. **USAID.** USAID is an independent agency that provides economic, development, HA, and disaster relief around the world in support of the foreign policy goals of the US. Although a separate agency from DOS, it shares certain administrative functions with DOS, and reports to and receives overall foreign policy guidance from the Secretary of State. USAID plays a major role in US foreign assistance policy and a principal role in interagency coordination. This agency administers and directs the US foreign economic assistance program and acts as the LFA for USG FDR. USAID's Bureau for Democracy, Conflict, and Humanitarian Assistance (DCHA) coordinates USAID's democracy programs, international disaster assistance, emergency and developmental food aid, aid to manage and mitigate conflict, civil-military coordination, security sector assistance, and volunteer programs. Within DCHA, the Office of US Foreign Disaster Assistance (OFDA) and the Office of Civilian Military Cooperation (CMC) are key offices that interact with DOD during FHA operations.

(1) **OFDA.** OFDA is delegated the responsibility to provide international disaster and HA and coordinate the USG response to declared disasters in foreign countries. USAID/OFDA's mandate is to save lives, alleviate human suffering, and reduce the economic and social impact of disasters. OFDA formulates US foreign disaster assistance policy in coordination with other USG departments and agencies. It coordinates with USAID offices and others to provide relief supplies (e.g., blankets, plastic sheeting, sanitation, and hygiene kits), funds implementing partners (e.g., UN agencies, NGOs, Red Cross) to provide direct support and HA, and develops and manages logistical, operational, and technical support for disaster responses. Besides its coordination activities within the USG, USAID/OFDA carries out these response options in coordination with the HN, donor countries, UN, NGOs, and IGOs. OFDA has assigned HA advisors/military to each geographic CCMD to coordinate responses involving DOD assistance, provide training, and advise planning.

(2) **CMC.** CMC serves as USAID's primary point of contact with DOD for developmental matters and provides liaison to major military commands, trains USAID and US military personnel, and plans and coordinates assistance in support of all programs of interest to both USAID and the military. It addresses areas of common interests between defense and development, with a focus on improving civilian-military field readiness, programs, and coordination. CMC has assigned senior development officers to each GCC and has received LNOs in return.

4. Department of Defense

a. **SecDef.** SecDef, either at the direction of the President or with the concurrence of the Secretary of State, directs DOD support to USG humanitarian operations or establishes appropriate command relationships. Within DOD, the **Office of the Secretary of Defense coordinates FHA policy and funding.** The **Under Secretary of Defense for Policy** (USD[P]) develops military policy for FHA operations. Within USD(P), the Assistant Secretary of Defense (Special Operations and Low-Intensity Conflict) (ASD[SO/LIC]) is responsible for FHA policy and statutory programs within DOD; policy oversight is executed by the **Deputy Assistant Secretary of Defense for Partnership Strategy and Stability Operations;** program management and funding of these programs is the responsibility of the Defense Security Cooperation Agency (DSCA).

b **The Joint Staff. The Chairman of the Joint Chiefs of Staff (CJCS)** is responsible for recommending military capabilities and appropriate relationships for FHA operations to **SecDef.** Once these relationships have been established, the **Joint Staff coordinates detailed staff planning under the cognizance of the CJCS.** The **Joint Staff J-5 (Strategic Plans and Policy Directorate)** has the primary responsibility for the concept review of operation plans (OPLANs) in support of FHA. It also coordinates policy and represents CJCS in interagency forums related to FHA. The Joint Staff Partnership Strategy Deputy Directorate also provides oversight for the GCCs' HCA programs. Through the Joint Logistics Operations Center (JLOC), the **Joint Staff J-4 (Logistics Directorate)** oversees joint logistic support for FHA operations. The **Joint Staff J-3 (Operations Directorate)** will also be involved when a military force is deployed to a foreign country as part of a US FHA operation.

c. **GCC.** GCCs direct military operations, including FHA, within their areas of responsibility (AORs). FHA should be done with the concurrence of the COM. GCCs develop and maintain commanders' estimates, base plans, concept plans (CONPLANs), or OPLANs for FHA, including FDR operations. In response to a disaster, the supported GCC structures the force necessary to conduct and sustain the FHA operation, typically forming a JTF. Advisors on the GCC's staff will be in close communications with various advisors and counterparts on the JTF staff. Notable examples are the GCC's DOS foreign policy advisor (POLAD) and USAID's senior development officer and HA advisors, who provide subject matter expertise and nonmilitary insights, enhancing direct communications and coordination with the affected embassy, country team, and responding LFA. Various functions on the GCC's staff, including policy, plans, security cooperation, training and exercises, and managers of key programs conduct military-to-military relations with other nations' defense ministries. Staff personnel in these functions can provide valuable coordination assistance for military operations during FHA. Additionally, supporting CCDRs may provide necessary support, including transportation, forces, and communications capabilities, as required.

(1) **Joint Interagency Coordination Group (JIACG).** The JIACG is an interagency staff group that establishes regular, timely, and collaborative working relationships between civilian and military operational planners. Composed of USG civilian and military experts apportioned to the GCC and tailored in staff location and/or title to meet the requirements of a supported GCC, the JIACG provides the GCC with the capability to collaborate at the operational level with other USG departments and agencies. The primary role of the JIACG is to enhance interagency coordination. The JIACG complements the interagency coordination that takes place at the national level through DOD and the NSC. JIACG members participate in contingency, crisis action, security cooperation, and other operational planning. They provide a conduit back to their parent organizations to help synchronize joint operations with the efforts of USG departments and agencies. The JIACG may play an important role in contingency planning for FHA and in initial interagency

coordination prior to establishment of a humanitarian assistance coordination center (HACC) or other coordination body.

For more information on the JIACG, see JP 3-08, Interorganizational Coordination During Joint Operations.

(2) **JLOC.** The JLOC is a current operations directorate within the Joint Staff J-4. The JLOC monitors crises, exercises, and interagency actions. It also works acquisition and cross-servicing agreements as well as international logistics. The JLOC receives reports from supporting commands, Service components, and external sources, distills information for decision and briefings, and responds to questions. The JLOC coordinates and synchronizes the planning and execution of ongoing CCMD operations and interagency support requirements, reviews deployments orders for logistics issues, and ensures correct airlift priority is assigned.

For further details on the JLOC, refer to JP 4-0, Joint Logistics.

(3) **Deployment and Distribution Operations Center (DDOC).** The DDOC located in the Fusion Center of United States Transportation Command (USTRANSCOM) directs the global air, land, and sea transportation capabilities of the Defense Transportation System to meet national security objectives provided by DOD. The DDOC fuses capabilities of multimodal deployment and distribution operations, intelligence, force protection, capacity acquisition, resource management, and other staff functions to collaboratively provide distribution options to the warfighter. C2 of the majority of intertheater lift forces and logistic infrastructure is accomplished through the DDOC, which tracks the movement requirement from lift allocation and initial execution through closure at final destination.

For additional information on the DDOC, refer to JP 3-35, Deployment and Redeployment Operations.

(4) **Joint Deployment and Distribution Operations Center (JDDOC).** USTRANSCOM, as the Distribution Process Owner, through its DDOC, collaborates with JDDOCs to link strategic deployment and distribution processes to operational and tactical functions in support of the warfighter. The GCCs are responsible for implementing their JDDOC core structure. The JDDOC is an integral organization of the GCC's staff, normally under the direction of the logistics directorate of a joint staff (J-4) at the CCMD level and collocated with the JLOC (if established) during operations. However, the GCC can place the JDDOC at any location required or under the operational control (OPCON) of other command or staff organizations. The JDDOC can reach back to the national partners to address and solve deployment and distribution issues for the GCC and can have the capability to develop deployment and distribution plans, integrate multinational and/or interagency deployment and distribution, and coordinate and synchronize the movement of sustainment in support of the GCC's priorities.

(5) **Joint Enabling Capabilities Command (JECC).** A USTRANSCOM subordinate command, the JECC provides mission-tailored, joint capability packages to

CCDRs in order to facilitate rapid establishment of joint force headquarters (HQ) and bridge joint operational requirements. JECC forces comprise the following elements:

(a) The **Joint Planning Support Element** provides rapidly deployable personnel from five functional planning groups: planning, operations, logisticians, information management, and intelligence support in order to accelerate the formation and increase the effectiveness of newly formed joint force HQ. These personnel are experienced in planning and collaborating with US and multinational partners during FHA operations and are trained to assist in establishing, organizing, and operating the HQ elements that provide the necessary joint C2 capability throughout the operations.

(b) The **Joint Public Affairs Support Element (JPASE)** provides ready, rapidly deployable joint public affairs (PA) capability to CCDRs in order to facilitate rapid establishment of joint force HQ, bridge joint PA requirements, and conduct PA training to meet theater information challenges. The criticality of PA during FHA places considerable strain on existing PA staffs, which JPASE can augment during the planning and execution of an FHA mission.

(c) The **Joint Communications Support Element** provides rapidly deployable, en route, early entry, and scalable communications services capability to CCDRs or USG departments or agencies, as directed, in order to facilitate rapid establishment of joint force HQ and bridge joint communications requirements.

For further details on the JECC, refer to JP 3-33, Joint Task Force Headquarters.

d. **DSCA.** DSCA is the central agency that synchronizes global security cooperation programs, funding and efforts across the Office of the Secretary of Defense, Joint Staff, DOS, CCMDs, the Services, and US industry. DSCA is responsible for the effective policy, processes, training, and financial management necessary to execute security cooperation within DOD.

(1) **Office of Humanitarian Assistance, Disaster Relief, and Mine Action (OHDM).** OHDM provides program management for DOD HA programs funded with the Overseas Humanitarian, Disaster, and Civic Aid (OHDACA) appropriation across all regional CCDRs. This includes HA projects, transportation of DOD and privately donated humanitarian material, HMA train-the-trainer programs, and FDR. OHDM works closely with its counterparts in the Office of the Under Secretary of Defense (Policy), as well as congressional staffs, to ensure the CCDRs are appropriately resourced, and that they execute in accordance with policy, fiscal, and legal guidelines.

(2) **DOD Humanitarian Demining Training Center (HDTC).** The HDTC prepares US military forces for humanitarian missions in mine-affected countries throughout the world. The HDTC directly supports US policy in humanitarian demining assistance through a "train-the-trainer" methodology of engagement. It serves as the USG training and information center for humanitarian demining assistance; researches current worldwide tactics on land mine use and demining techniques employed by both military

and civilian organizations; and provides innovative and realistic training tailored to meet DOD and DOS requirements.

e. **National Geospatial-Intelligence Agency (NGA).** The NGA provides direct analytical support for FHA through the LFAs and CCMDs primarily through the deployment of team specialists in response to natural disasters, to include earthquakes, floods, hurricanes, and wildfires. The standard production includes initial damage or recovery mitigation assessment derived from imagery and analytical imagery assessments, analytical reporting through NGA intelligence briefs, and geospatial situational awareness products.

f. **Defense Threat Reduction Agency (DTRA).** During a crisis involving CBRN materials, at the request of a CCDR, and in coordination with the Joint Staff, the Director DTRA may direct the immediate deployment of a consequence management advisory team (CMAT). The CMAT provides task-organized, deployable, doctrinal, and technical chemical, biological, radiological, and nuclear consequence management (CBRN CM) expertise, support, advice, and hazard prediction modeling assistance for DOD and other federal agencies during all phases of CBRN accidents or incidents. The CMAT may be augmented with specialists in PA, legal counsel, radiobiology, and other fields pertinent to the mission or hazards. The CMAT will provide a conduit to leverage DTRA's technical CBRN reachback capability across DOD, the federal government, and academia to provide mission critical information to the supported organization. DTRA has the ability through its Consequence Management Assistance Program to provide mobile training teams for custom CBRN CM instruction for the development of a nation's indigenous CM planning and response capability.

For additional information on the role of the CMAT, refer to JP 3-41, Chemical, Biological, Radiological, and Nuclear Consequence Management.

g. **The Center for Excellence in Disaster Management and Humanitarian Assistance (COEDMHA)** established by congressional legislation in 1994, operates under the authority of SecDef and fulfills a worldwide mission to enhance civil-military coordination through collaborative partnerships, education and training, and applied research. The Deputy Assistant Secretary of Defense for Partnership Strategy and Stability Operations provides guidance through the Commander, United States Pacific Command (USPACOM), who exercises direct control of COEDMHA. As such, USPACOM and its Service components are primary customers. COEDMHA efforts focus on the operational level, supporting the CCDR's TCP and preparing JTF commanders and staffs for disaster response and HA operations. Education, training, and applied research activities are designed to improve civil-military performance across the spectrum of humanitarian response from natural disasters to complex contingencies.

h. **The Center for Disaster and Humanitarian Assistance Medicine (CDHAM)** is a DOD organization within the Department of Military and Emergency Medicine at the Uniformed Services University of Health Sciences. CDHAM is a university-based venture whose mission is to advance the understanding and delivery of disaster medical care and HA worldwide. The uniquely positioned academic center is actively developing relationships between governmental agencies, NGOs, and IGOs as a means of improving relief efforts. It is the focal point for medical aspects of disaster relief and HA.

i. **Defense Institute for Medical Operations** strengthens global medical capabilities in disaster response and healthcare management through education and training with HNs.

j. **The Pacific Disaster Center (PDC)** is an applied science, information, and technology center, working to reduce disaster risks and impacts to people's lives and property. Established by the USG in 1996, the PDC is congressionally mandated and funded (sponsored through the office of the USD[P]), and is currently managed by the University of Hawaii. PDC also augments its congressional budget by undertaking paid risk-reduction projects and consultancies in the Asia Pacific region and around the world. PDC's mission is to provide applied information research and analysis to support the development of more effective policies, institutions, programs, and information products for the disaster management and HA communities. PDC creates new information products, and supports and facilitates the innovative use of information, technology, and applied research to increase efficiency of operational organizations by introducing novel and appropriately scaled information resources, tools, and analyses. Central to achieving these objectives is providing unique and valuable geospatial and disaster-related information through web-based data systems for international, regional, national, and local information access and dissemination. Through the use of PDC-developed and PDC-hosted web-based information systems, disaster managers can develop both situational awareness and appropriate responses before, during, and after disaster events. PDC information technology and communications products and systems support the full range of disaster management needs from the assessment of hazards and risk, to managing risk through mitigation, preparedness, response, recovery, and reconstruction.

5. Key Non-United States Government Participants and Organizations

a. **HN.** The HN is the nation receiving the assistance, in whose territory the forces and/or supplies of PNs, and/or NATO organizations transit or operate. The HN will coordinate all relief efforts within its territory. US forces conducting FHA do so with the permission of the HN under the guidance of formal and informal agreements. JFCs should become knowledgeable of all bilateral agreements for mutual support, and exercise these agreements to the maximum extent possible. If the necessary agreements are not in place, GCCs must obtain authority to negotiate (through the Joint Staff) and then actively seek bilateral agreements to support the joint reception, staging, onward movement, and integration (JRSOI) of forces, equipment, and supplies. The country team will be critical to this effort. The US embassy is the primary liaison with the HN government.

b. **UN.** The UN is an international organization, composed of member nations, chartered to facilitate cooperation in international law, international security, economic development, social progress, human rights, and achievement of world peace. The UN has the lead role in the international community to respond to natural and man-made disasters that are beyond the capacity of national authorities alone. The UN is a major provider of emergency relief and long-term assistance, a catalyst for action by governments and relief agencies, and an advocate on behalf of populations affected by disasters. A description of key UN personnel, elements, and agencies follows.

(1) **UN Emergency Resident Coordinator/Humanitarian Coordinator.** The UN resident coordinator/humanitarian coordinator has a leading role in coordinating international relief with an affected state, functioning as the chair of the humanitarian country team, and assisting international UN humanitarian efforts in the affected state.

(2) **UN Country Team.** A UN country team consists of UN agencies, funds, and programs that primarily do development work, but are mobilized for disaster response missions. The UN country team should not be confused with a US embassy country team, which consists of the ambassador/COM and personnel assigned to a US embassy.

(3) **Inter-Agency Standing Committee (IASC).** Under the leadership of the UN, Under Secretary General/Emergency Relief Coordinator (ERC), the IASC develops humanitarian policies, agrees on a clear division of responsibility for the various aspects of HA, identifies and addresses gaps in response, and advocates for effective application of humanitarian principles. The IASC is a unique interagency standing committee that provides a strategic forum for coordination, policy development, and decision making involving key UN and non-UN HA partners.

(4) **UN Disaster Management Team (DMT).** In consultation with the affected state and the UN country team, the UN resident coordinator/humanitarian coordinator is expected to form a UN DMT, which will prepare a disaster management plan. The UN resident coordinator/humanitarian coordinator acts as the focal point to ensure the effective dovetailing of relief assistance into rehabilitation and reconstruction programs. The purpose of a UN DMT is to ensure a prompt, effective, and concerted country-level response by the UN system. The team coordinates all disaster-related activities, technical advice, and material assistance provided by UN agencies, and takes steps to avoid wasteful duplication or competition for resources by UN agencies. It is vital that the policies of the UN DMT mirror those approved by the affected state.

(5) **United Nations Office for the Coordination of Humanitarian Affairs (UNOCHA).** UNOCHA is the arm of the UN Secretariat that is responsible for bringing together humanitarian response participants to ensure a coherent response to disasters. UNOCHA is also responsible for operating the ReliefWeb and One Response web sites, and manages the following resources:

(a) **United Nations Disaster Assessment and Coordination (UNDAC) Team.** A team assigned to support the humanitarian country team with initial assessment and coordination of UN and other humanitarian efforts in response to a disaster. UNDAC team normally arrives very early in a response.

(b) **On-Site Operations Coordination Center (OSOCC).** The OSOCC is established by the UN in the affected state to coordinate incoming international disaster assistance.

(c) **United Nations Humanitarian Air Service (UNHAS).** UNHAS is operated by the World Food Programme to provide UN and other humanitarian organizations with safe and reliable air transport during disasters.

(6) **UN Cluster Approach.** The UN cluster approach is the principle construct utilized by the international humanitarian community to facilitate a coordinated humanitarian response to an affected state. The cluster approach ensures predictability and accountability in international responses to humanitarian emergencies, by clarifying the division of labor among organizations, and better defining their roles and responsibilities within the different sectors of response.

c. **Other IGOs.** An IGO is an organization created by a formal agreement (e.g., a treaty) between two or more governments. It may be established on a global, regional, or functional basis for wide-ranging or narrowly defined purposes. It is formed to protect and promote national interests shared by member states. Examples include NATO, OSCE, the Organization of American States (OAS), and the African Union. NATO and OSCE are regional security organizations, while the African Union and the OAS are general regional organizations. A new trend toward subregional organizations is also evident, particularly in Africa where, for example, the Economic Community of West African States has taken on some security functions. These organizations have defined structures, roles, and responsibilities, and may be equipped with the resources and expertise to participate in complex interagency, IGO, and NGO coordination and collaboration. The US maintains formal or informal ties with some of the largest of these IGOs.

d. **NGOs.** An NGO is a private, self-governing, not-for-profit organization dedicated to alleviating human suffering; and/or promoting education, health care, economic development, environmental protection, human rights, and conflict resolution; and/or encouraging the establishment of democratic institutions and civil society. Where long-term problems precede a deepening crisis, NGOs are frequently on scene before the US military and are willing to operate in high-risk areas. They may have a long-term established presence in the crisis area. They will most likely remain long after military forces have departed. Because of their capability to respond quickly and effectively to crises, they can lessen the civil-military resources that a commander would otherwise have to devote to an operation. Working independently, with other NGOs, with US and UN agencies, or alongside the military, NGOs assist in all the world's trouble spots where humanitarian or other assistance is needed. NGOs may range in size and experience from those with multimillion dollar budgets, substantial funding from USG and other institutional sources, and decades of global experience in developmental and humanitarian relief to newly created small organizations dedicated to a particular emergency or disaster. Whereas governments and militaries might have various objectives in FHA, NGOs place priority on addressing humanitarian needs first. In areas of conflict, NGOs' security may be derived solely from their absolute neutrality and humanitarian focus. The extent to which specific NGOs are willing to cooperate with the military can vary considerably.

e. **Multinational Units.** Other nations may deploy military forces to support the FHA effort or existing UN/multinational forces may be present. These forces may provide LNOs to the CCMD, the JTF, and the civil-military operations center (CMOC).

f. **Private Sector.** Increasingly, the resources of the international business community are being utilized to mitigate human suffering associated with disasters. Businesses donate talent or in-kind goods and services to disaster relief and recovery operations in developing countries and wish to ensure that their help is delivered in a coordinated and effective manner. The same is true for foreign disaster response. Many large private-sector companies maintain disaster/crisis response teams that can respond and add value to USG operations by providing infrastructure and other supporting services. DOD mechanisms that plan for, train, and implement emergency responses to disasters should consider the private sector. This should be done through USAID OFDA, which maintains communication with UN agencies and other international organizations and private sector donors to ensure the USG complements rather than duplicates existing assistance programs. In addition to large transnational corporations, the private sector also includes the local, national, and other companies and organizations which should be considered and engaged through the country team, USAID, or other existing USG channels. While US military contractors are addressed in other sections, commanders should be aware that private contractors are employed by a wide range of actors, inside and outside the USG. They are often employed to provide security, training, technical expertise, and logistical support. Commanders should be cognizant that contractors are often viewed by the local population as USG representatives and any negative behavior or interaction with the local population on the part of contractors can have an adverse impact on US efforts. Commanders should consider developing guidance for the contractors in support of FHA operations and should consider the need to develop PA guidance which takes into account potential issues with private contractors, should they arise.

6. Nongovernmental Organizations, Intergovernmental Organizations, and Private Sector Partners

a. **Relationships with NGOs and IGOs are based on multiple factors some of which include a mutual understanding** of each other's goals and objectives, planned lines of operations, and concept of operations (CONOPS), support requirements, coordination procedures, information sharing, capabilities and, most importantly, missions. **Several organizations can facilitate coordination.** Although not field-based, the **American Council for Voluntary International Action (InterAction)** is the largest coalition of US based NGOs. UNOCHA (commonly referred to as OCHA) is another valuable resource for coordination of efforts. Due to their regular interaction with NGOs and IGOs, and its role as the LFA for FDR, OFDA, and PRM will be critical sources of help in establishing relationships with these organizations. The following may assist in building unity of effort among these various organizations and the JFCs. OFDA's primary implementing partners are a wide range of UN agencies, IGOs, and NGOs. Per its authorizing legislation, PRM's primary international organizational partners are the Office of the United Nations Office of the High Commissioner for Refugees (UNHCR), the International Committee of the Red Cross (ICRC), the International Organization for Migration (IOM), and the UN Relief and Works Agency for Palestine Refugees in the Near East.

(1) **Increase awareness** and **encourage contact** between the military and NGOs and IGOs through symposia, meetings, briefings, and joint planning sessions.

LEVERAGING OTHER SUPPORT

Of particular note, Google stands up 24/7 crisis support centers following major disasters and provided considerable and immediate technical support following the 2011 Tohoku earthquake, tsunami, and Fukushima nuclear power plant crisis in Japan. Google engineers worked immediately, regularly, and directly with Operation TOMODACHI operational planners to provide free training, analysis, crowd sourcing, and overhead imagery support that was critical to advancing the foreign humanitarian assistance mission in Japan. It is highly recommended to establish contact with Google in future crisis situations to leverage the free and considerable assistance offered by Google.

Various Sources

(2) **Incorporate selected NGO and IGO training** into Service and joint training and exercise programs.

(3) **Review lessons learned** as recorded in both the joint and Services' lessons learned databases.

(4) **Clearly articulate the role of the military to the NGOs and IGOs.** It is imperative that these organizations understand the military mission, the level of support it can provide, and the process to receive support. Explain what service and/or supplies NGOs and IGOs may receive from DOD forces (e.g., medical care, force protection, transportation). Explain who determines priority for movement of NGO personnel and equipment (in most cases this will be determined by USAID/OFDA.) NGOs desire transparency, which implies openness, communication, and accountability when dealing with the military. The crisis action team, humanitarian operations center (HOC), HACC, CMOC, and LNOs can provide such information.

b. Ensure the joint force understands its support role. While UN and NGO guidelines stipulate that requesting assistance from the military is a last resort, **some NGOs and IGOs may assume the military has an inexhaustible resource reservoir** and inundate the FHA force with requests for various types of support. Members of the joint force must have a clear understanding of the nature and amount of support they will be authorized to provide. When the JFC has been delegated the authority to fill certain types of requests from these organizations, the granting of that authority, and guidance on its use, are reflected in appropriate orders. Normally, FDR requests from non-USG organizations will come to the JFC through OFDA via the mission tasking matrix (MITAM) process or via PRM for refugees. Keep in mind that **equivocal responses,** such as "we will try," **can be misinterpreted as an affirmative response** and establish unrealistic expectations. Failure to meet expectations (real or not) can adversely affect relationships in both current and future operations.

c. **Not all NGOs and IGOs appreciate military assistance involvement** in HA operations. Some NGO and IGO charters do not allow them to collaborate with armed forces based on political mandate, neutrality, religious, or impartiality concerns. Commanders need to honor this fact, while still striving for unity of effort.

(1) Most NGOs follow humanitarian principles (i.e., impartiality, independence, humanitarianism, and neutrality) when giving aid; and therefore base aid on need alone. Some NGOs perceive military aid as politically motivated and conditional.

(2) The USG departments and agencies, NGOs, and IGOs may not share common objectives.

(3) Commanders may find it beneficial to use a third party to establish liaison with NGOs and IGOs reluctant to establish direct contact with military organizations. USAID and/or DOS/PRM are critical to this effort.

d. Be cognizant of **legal requirements and regulations** that apply to relationships between the military, NGOs, and IGOs.

e. Ensure that agreements and memoranda of understanding fully **address funding considerations, delineate authority, and define negotiation channels.** Agreements may include air and surface transportation, petroleum products, telecommunications, labor, security, facilities, contracting, engineer support, supplies, services, and medical support.

f. **Exchange** NGO, IGO, and military unit **operating procedures and capabilities**.

g. Exercise due diligence in dealing with NGOs that do not adhere to accepted professional standards. Most NGOs follow the UN Principles of HA and the *Code of Conduct for the International Red Cross and Red Crescent Movement and NGOs in Disaster Relief.* Disaster-affected communities have a right to expect those who seek to assist them to measure up to these standards. In maintaining these standards, CMOC officers and all other members of the joint force should not be perceived as favoring a particular relief organization, particularly at the expense of other organizations.

h. In a permissive environment, seek the assistance of an individual from the NGO or IGO community to locate with the US force staff and function as an LNO to the NGO/IGO community. This LNO can perform duties such as initial collaboration activities with the humanitarian relief community prior to deployment, representation of the humanitarian relief perspective during planning, and advice to the joint force through membership in the CMOC or other coordinating mechanisms during operations. This LNO should be willing and able to interact with all IGOs and NGOs so as not to be perceived as favoring some organizations over others.

i. Provide information for posting on the UN's ReliefWeb Internet site and other applicable sites. ReliefWeb is a global hub for humanitarian information on complex emergencies and natural disasters. ReliefWeb is widely used by NGOs, IGOs, and other participants in HA operations to share and coordinate information. If established, the humanitarian information center (HIC) is also a site for information as are the bulletin boards at the OSOCC location and the NGO websites themselves.

j. Share information with NGOs and IGOs to the greatest extent possible, especially regarding the security environment. Using information and communications technology will allow IGOs and NGOs to plan their response with up-to-date and accurate information and to integrate into the overall response more efficiently.

k. When working with NGOs in an uncertain or hostile OE, the guidelines found in the United States Institute of Peace *Guidelines for Relations Between US Armed Forces and Non-Governmental Humanitarian Organizations in Hostile or Potentially Hostile Environments* will help mitigate friction between military and NGO personnel.

For more information on the guidelines, see JP 3-08, Interorganizational Coordination During Joint Operations.

l. Identify and collaborate with the first responders to a disaster—done through USAID/OFDA, or the LFA. While the US military may be the largest organization on the ground in a disaster area, it is critical to understand that the US military may not be the first one on the ground. The NGOs and IGOs that normally operate in the disaster region or those that can respond quickly to a disaster may be there prior to the US military arrival on the ground.

For further details on coordination and relationships with NGOs and IGOs, refer to JP 3-08, Interorganizational Coordination During Joint Operations.

7. Interagency Process for Foreign Disaster Relief

a. **Strategic Level Interagency Coordination.** While most USG disaster responses are coordinated by USAID through the OFDA director, for certain unique or large-scale disasters, the USAID Administrator may work with the NSC to convene interagency meetings when a humanitarian crisis occurs, e.g., an interagency policy committee (IPC). The International Development and HA NSC policy coordination committee (PCC) participation will generally include:

    (1) Senior DOS and DOD representatives.

    (2) COM.

    (3) USAID representative.

    (4) Heads of other concerned agencies.

b. The IPC concurrently develops a comprehensive strategy for emergency response and develops tasks for each key participant. Consideration of other elements or organizations that may be involved in the crisis is crucial to the development of sound recommendations. For example, the IPC should consider the involvement of UN organizations, other responding nations, NGOs, and IGOs that may already be operating in the crisis area. Interagency coordination for FDR (Figure II-2) continues throughout the mission. Successful interagency coordination requires effective interaction among all organizational and functional elements.

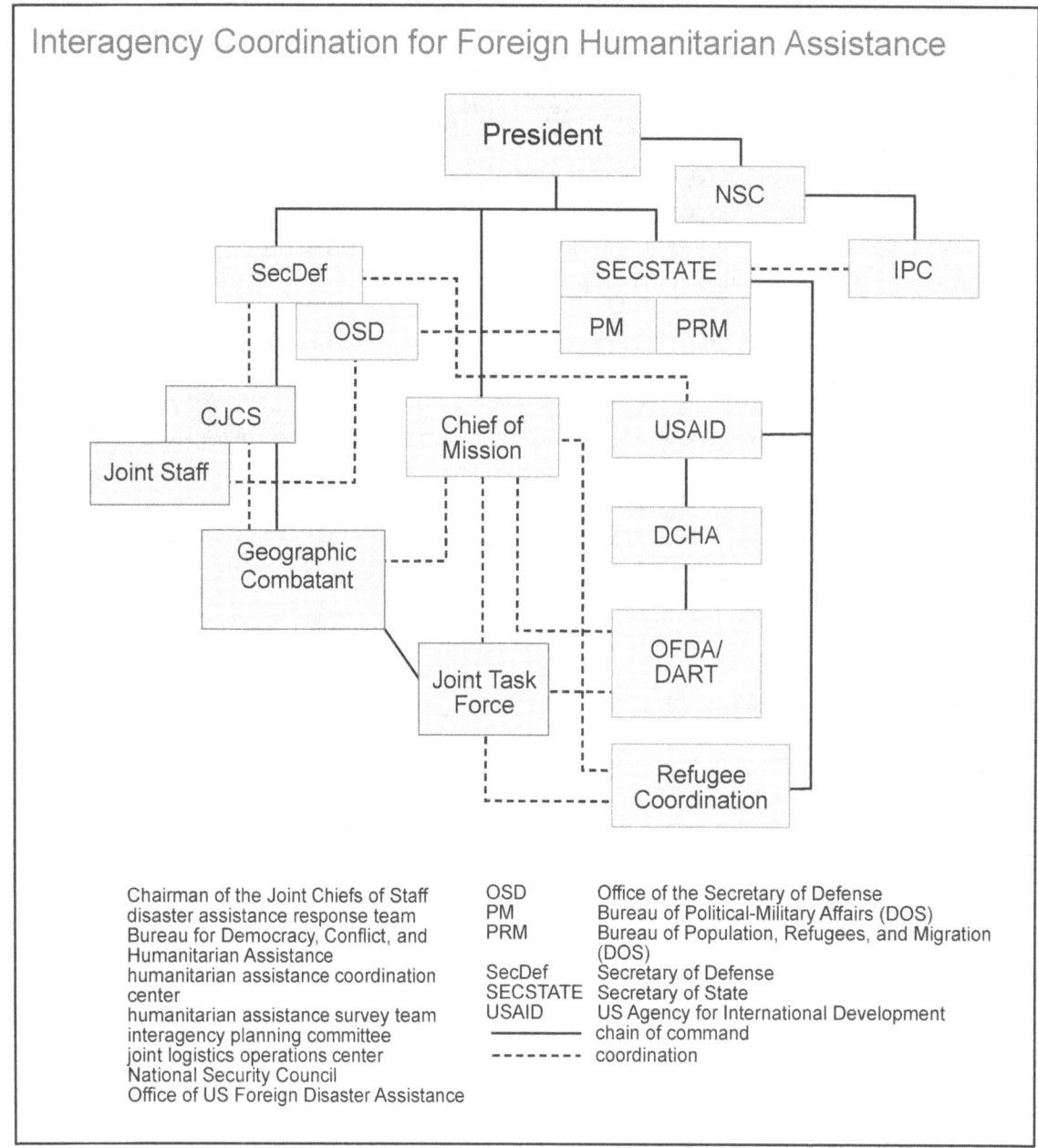

Interagency Coordination for Foreign Humanitarian Assistance

Chairman of the Joint Chiefs of Staff	OSD Office of the Secretary of Defense
disaster assistance response team	PM Bureau of Political-Military Affairs (DOS)
Bureau for Democracy, Conflict, and	PRM Bureau of Population, Refugees, and Migration
Humanitarian Assistance	(DOS)
humanitarian assistance coordination	SecDef Secretary of Defense
center	SECSTATE Secretary of State
humanitarian assistance survey team	USAID US Agency for International Development
interagency planning committee	———— chain of command
joint logistics operations center	- - - - - - - coordination
National Security Council	
Office of US Foreign Disaster Assistance	

Figure II-2. Interagency Coordination for Foreign Humanitarian Assistance

The NSC may recommend another USG agency other than USAID to lead FHA or FDR based on multiple sets of conditions and security issues.

The interagency coordination process often is described as "more art than science," while military operations tend to depend more on structure and doctrine. However, some of the techniques, procedures, and systems of military C2 can facilitate unity of effort if they are adjusted to the dynamic world of interagency coordination and different organizational cultures. The USAID Administrator is the Special Coordinator for International Disaster Assistance. The coordinator is responsible for promoting maximum effectiveness and coordination in responses to foreign disasters by USG departments and agencies and between the US and other donors. While most USG disaster responses are coordinated by USAID, through the OFDA Director, for certain unique or large-scale disasters, the USAID Administrator may work with the NSC to convene interagency meetings. When a disaster is declared, the DOS geographic bureau of the affected area becomes the key participating bureau. The functional bureaus of PRM; International Organization Affairs; PM; Democracy, Human Rights, and Labor; PA; Intelligence and Research; International Narcotics and Law Enforcement Affairs and the Bureau of CSO may also be involved. PRM has specific FHA responsibilities in refugee crises and other complex emergencies or situations of displacement. While other functional bureaus do not have specific FHA responsibilities, if they are already active in a post-conflict area that suffers a disaster they may be able to assist during the FHA effort.

For more information on the NSC, see JP 3-08, Interorganizational Coordination During Joint Operations.

d. **Operational and Tactical Level Interagency Coordination.** Immediately after a disaster strikes, the COM may send a disaster declaration cable. The disaster declaration is required for USAID to have the legal authority to expend funds for FDR. IGOs and NGOs may respond to a disaster regardless of whether the USG has declared one. PRM does not require a disaster declaration by the COM in order to respond to appeals for assistance from IGOs or proposals from NGOs. With input from USAID and others at post, the disaster declaration cable outlines the extent of the damage, possible needs, and may recommend assistance in the form of funding, material, or technical assistance. The process to request DOD support for HA, whether for a disaster (via a disaster declaration) or for a conflict situation (via an executive secretary request), is outlined in Figure II-3. The COM, or assistant secretary of state responsible for the particular area, can declare a disaster, providing the event meets three criteria: the disaster exceeds the HN's ability to respond; the affected country's government either requests or is willing to receive US assistance; and a response to the disaster is in the US national interest. This declaration is transmitted to OFDA and DOS to begin possible USG assistance. Each embassy or USAID mission has a mission disaster response officer (MDRO), normally a collateral duty officer responsible for disaster planning and management as well as maintenance of the mission disaster response plan. The MDRO educates, trains, and exercises mission personnel on the disaster response plan; liaises with government disaster authorities on an ongoing basis to ensure familiarity with disaster risks and organizational response arrangements; serves as the chief operating officer for the embassy's emergency action committee during all phases of the disaster; and acts as the COM's initial coordinator of USG disaster relief operations in country. The MDRO coordinates closely with relevant USAID/OFDA HQ and field staff and often drafts the disaster declaration cable. In countries with a USAID mission, the MDRO will usually be a USAID representative. Many embassies also have regional refugee coordinators. These are foreign service officers employed by PRM to monitor humanitarian programs, liaise with humanitarian partners, and advise humanitarian policies. Refugee coordinators report to the COM and typically have a regional portfolio covering humanitarian issues in several countries in their region. For example, PRM's refugee coordinators in Bangkok cover refugee and migration issues in Thailand, Burma, Bangladesh, Malaysia, Laos, and other countries in Southeast Asia. Refugee coordinators travel frequently to monitor humanitarian conditions in the field. The composition of a country team varies widely, depending on the

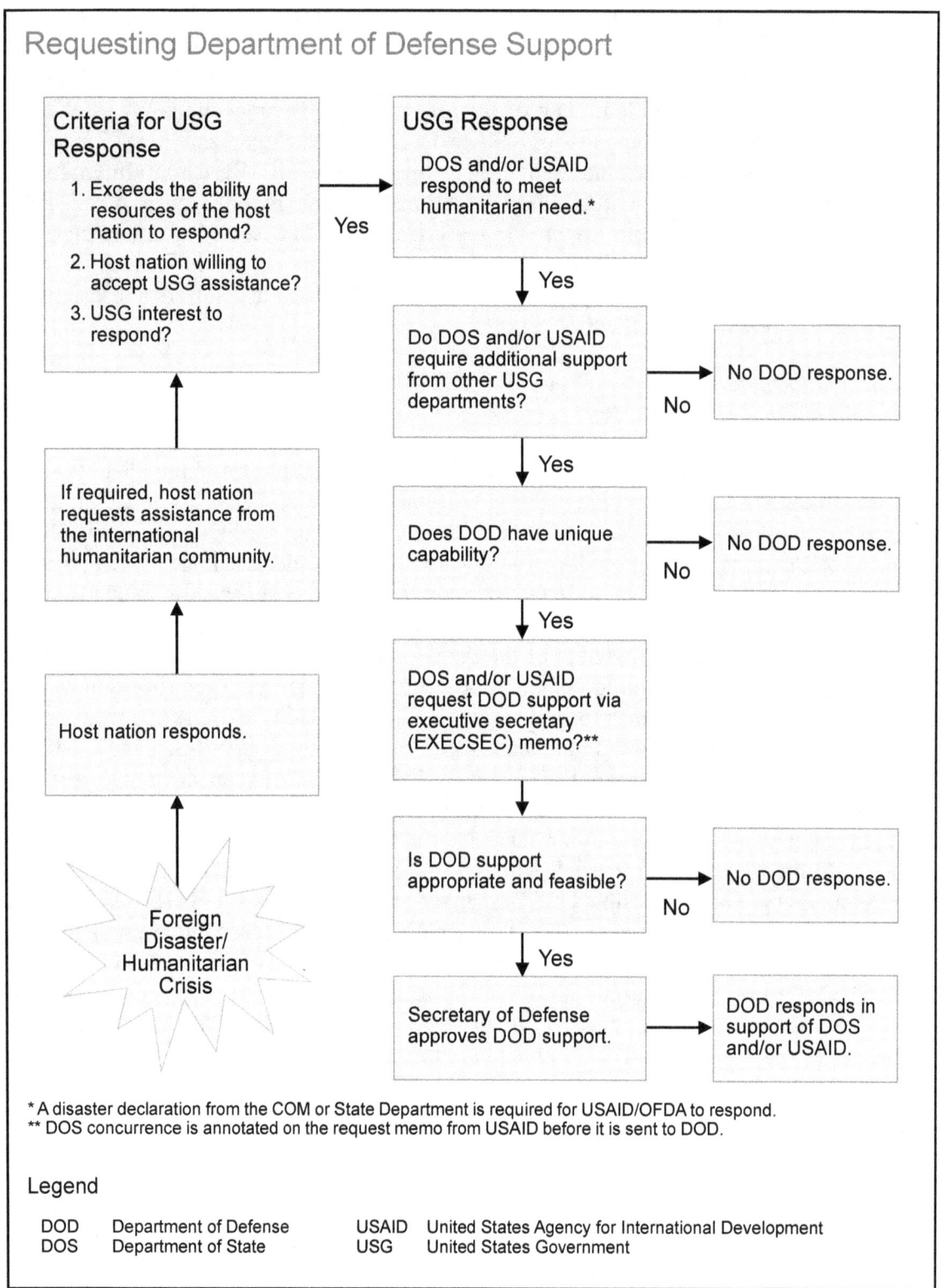

Figure II-3. Requesting Department of Defense Support

desires of the COM, the in-country situation, and the number and levels of USG departments and agencies present. The COM is the head of the country team. Other members may include a defense attaché, security assistance officer, political counselor, PA counselor, economic counselor, representatives from USAID, and the Peace Corps. The COM has responsibility for all USG personnel in country, except for those assigned to a CCMD, and may limit the number and mix of people entering based on current or anticipated conditions. At the initiation of an FDR operation, the GCC should coordinate directly with the country team and offer to send an LNO for coordination purposes.

For more detailed information on the operations with a US country team, see JP 3-22, Foreign Internal Defense.

(1) With the concurrence of the US ambassador, OFDA may deploy a disaster assistance response team (DART) into the crisis area to assist coordination of the FDR effort and activate an on-call Washington-based response management team (RMT). A DART provides specialists, trained in a variety of disaster relief skills, to assist US embassies and USAID missions with the management of the USG response to a foreign disaster. The DART will also work closely with the US military when it is participating in FDR operations. DARTs assess and report on the disaster situation and recommend follow-up actions. They also process, validate, and coordinate external requests for USG assistance. Figure II-4 provides a visualization of the coordination flow between DCHA/OFDA and DOD when both respond to a disaster relief event.

For more discussion on DART, see Appendix C, "Department of State and United States Agency for International Development Organizations," paragraph 9, "Disaster Assistance Response Team."

(2) OFDA's *Field Operations Guide for Disaster Assessment and Response* is an important reference tool for personnel who may be involved in FDR operations. It explains the roles and responsibilities of individuals sent to disaster sites to undertake initial assessments or to participate as members of an OFDA DART. The *Field Operations Guide for Disaster Assessment and Response* contains information on general responsibilities for disaster responders, formats and reference material for assessing and reporting on populations at risk, DART position descriptions and duty checklists, descriptions of OFDA stockpile commodities, general information related to disaster activities, information on working with the military in the field, and a glossary of acronyms and terms used by OFDA and other organizations with which OFDA works.

8. Department of Defense Entities That May Support Contingency Operations

a. **Crisis Action Team.** GCCs may have an organization within their HQ or at the component level designed to respond to immediate requirements, often called a crisis action or rapid deployment team, which serves as an immediate responder and assessor for the GCC. The exact composition of this team and the subsequent follow-on assets will vary depending on the type and severity of the incident and in some cases, restrictions placed on the COM by the HN (through status-of-forces agreements [SOFAs], treaties, or informal agreements) in limiting the number of foreign military permitted in country. In all cases, the team must coordinate with the COM and country team prior to deploying. When an FHA operation has been or will likely be directed, the crisis action team can recommend to the

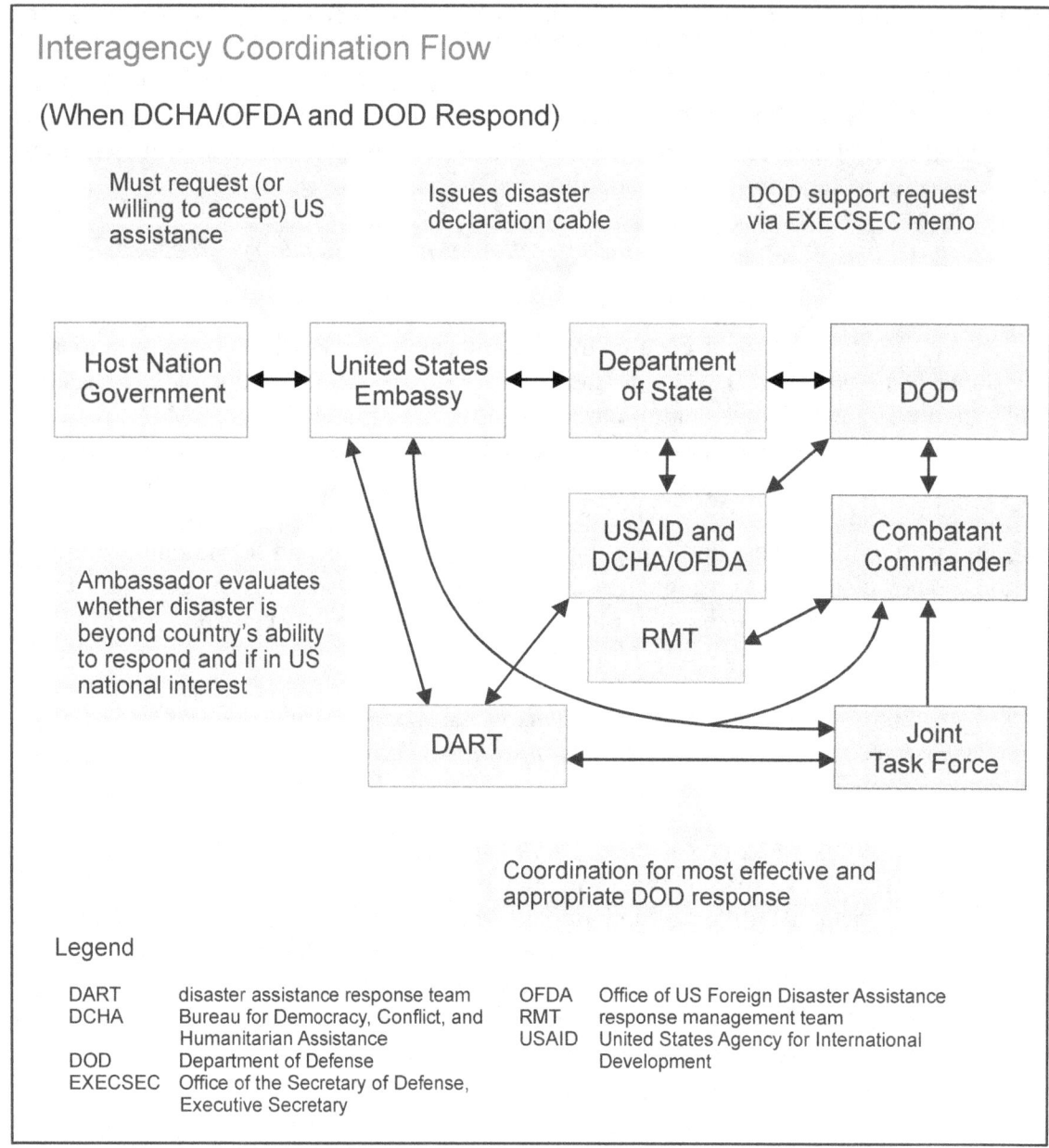

Figure II-4. Interagency Coordination Flow

GCC priority issues (medical support, water, food, equipment, etc.) as well as how to organize for the most effective response. The crisis action team may form the nucleus of the FHA force HQ or the JTF command element or may function as the staff entity at the CCMD HQ that coordinates with deploying/deployed teams.

b. **Humanitarian Assistance Survey Team (HAST).** The supported GCC may, if requested by USAID organize and deploy a HAST to acquire information required for planning. Before deploying, the HAST should be provided the current threat assessment and relevant intelligence; geospatial information and services support; and embassy, DOS, and USAID points of contact. Once deployed, the HAST, working with the country team and

USAID, may be asked to assess the ability of the HN government to respond to the disaster; identify primary points of contact for coordination and collaboration; determine the threat environment for force protection purposes; survey facilities and infrastructure that may be used to support FDR operations including aerial port of debarkation, seaport of debarkation, and forward operating base; conduct health and medical assessments, and coordinate specific logistical support to assist with the relief effort. The DART is the USG on scene FDR coordinator, and the HAST must ensure early and continuous coordination with the DART to facilitate USG unity of effort and prevent duplication of effort. Suggested team composition should include medical personnel qualified to conduct health and medical assessments (including environmental vulnerability assessments); engineers (structural, mechanical, etc.); logisticians; communications experts; transportation management specialists; and force protection experts. The HAST can assist with the following tasks:

(1) Assess the nature and extent of:

(a) Available food, water, sanitation, and shelter.

(b) Casualties and loss of life.

(c) Injury, illness, outbreak of disease, and access to health and medical services.

(d) Dislocated civilian population and location (to include security requirements of the population).

(e) HN capabilities and capacities to include medical facilities.

(f) Degree of destruction to property and infrastructure.

(g) Available logistic facilities for air- and sealift, roads, rail, and bridges.

(h) Significant actors; the span and depth of their control over territory, resources, and individuals; and their objectives.

(i) Overall telecommunications infrastructure (ability/capability of the HN and global leadership to receive information from the populace).

(j) Overall public information infrastructure (ability/capability of the HN and global leadership to transmit HA information to the populace and global responders).

(2) Formulate recommendations for provision of DOD funding, equipment, supplies, and personnel.

(3) Establish liaison, identify information-sharing procedures, and coordinate assessment with agencies of the affected country; supported commanders or their representatives; US diplomatic personnel and USAID, especially the DART; and other relief agencies operating within the crisis area.

(4) In conjunction with USTRANSCOM, arrange for the reception of US personnel, supplies, and equipment.

(5) Be prepared to begin coordinating FHA to relieve suffering and avoid further loss of life, as directed by the GCC.

(6) Assess the threat environment; determine force protection and personnel recovery (PR) requirements; and survey facilities that may be required for self-defense of forces.

(7) Determine the COM's desires and capacity to support the media in FDR operations and the JFC's role in media support.

c. **HACC.** The supported GCC may establish a HACC to assist with interagency coordination and planning. The HACC provides one possible mechanism for coordination between the GCC and other USG departments and agencies, IGOs, and NGOs that may participate in the FHA operation at the theater strategic level. Normally, the HACC is a temporary organization that operates during the early planning and coordination stages of the operation. Once a CMOC or HOC has been established, the role of the HACC diminishes, and its functions are accomplished through the normal organization of the GCC's staff and crisis action organization for establishing authority. Staffing for the HACC should include a director appointed by the supported GCC, a CMO planner, PR planner, an OFDA advisor or liaison if available, a public affairs officer (PAO), an NGO advisor, and other augmentation (e.g., legal advisor, preventive medicine physician) when required. Liaisons from USG departments and agencies, US Army Corps of Engineers, key NGOs, IGOs, and HN agencies also may be members of the HACC in large-scale FHA operations.

9. Joint Task Force Organization

a. A JTF is a joint force that is constituted and so designated by SecDef, a CCDR, a subordinate unified commander, or an existing commander, joint task force (CJTF). **The authority establishing the JTF determines the command relationships for the JTF and assigns the missions and forces.** The adaptive nature of the C2 structure, the unique component capabilities, and their ability to deploy quickly to execute a variety of FHA missions make a JTF ideally suited to perform FHA. A JTF is normally assigned a joint operations area (JOA) in the GCC's AOR. The JTF normally operates at the operational level; however, there may be instances requiring the CJTF to focus at the tactical level. **While the JTF is the most common type of organizational structure used for FHA, a JFC may also opt to create a joint special operations task force (JSOTF), joint civil-military operations task force (JCMOTF), or a joint military information support task force (JMISTF) to assist in operations.**

b. The **JTF organization for FHA is similar to traditional military organizations** with a commander, command element, and mission-tailored forces. However, the nature of FHA usually results in combat support and combat service support forces (e.g., engineers, military police/security forces, logistics, transportation, legal, chaplain, CA, PA, and medical) serving more prominent roles than combat elements. The unique aspects of interagency, IGO, and NGO coordination and collaboration require the JFC to be especially flexible, responsive, and cognizant of the capabilities of USG departments and agencies, IGOs, NGOs, affected en route and participating HNs, and multinational partners. The JFC establishes organizational structures, processes, and procedures to consider interagency, IGO, and NGO perspectives and positions into its planning, execution, and assessment process. Depending on the type of contingency operation, the extent of military operations, and degree of interagency involvement, the focal point for operational and tactical level coordination with civilian agencies may occur at the embassy, the JTF HQ, the CMOC, or the HOC. Depending upon the diplomatic sensitivities of the HN and international partners, the FHA JTF title may be replaced with a more appropriate title such as joint support force or combined support force.

For further details on JTF organization, refer to JP 3-33, Joint Task Force Headquarters.

c. **JTF Staff Organization. The JFC organizes the JTF staff to provide the appropriate expertise required to carry out the specific FHA mission.** Some staff functions that may require increased support and manning include legal services, security, engineers, PA, health services, military information support operations (MISO), CA, financial management, and logistics. Additional staff sections may also be established to complement and emphasize critical functions (such as linguist, protocol, and LNO support). JTFs conducting FDR operations will include an OFDA advisor(s). JTFs conducting FDR operations may be designated by unique titles. For example, during Operation UNIFIED ASSISTANCE 2005 (Indian Ocean Tsunami), the JTF was designated Combined Support Force 536; and for the Pakistan earthquake response in 2005, the JTF was referred to as the Disaster Assistance Center Pakistan. The name differentiation for the JTF was to emphasize the supporting role of the JTF in the FHA environment.

d. **Assessment Team.** A valuable tool in the mission analysis process is the deployment of a JTF assessment team to the projected JOA. When the JTF is in support of another agency, such as USAID/OFDA, the assessment team should first and foremost establish liaison with the ambassador or COM and with the supported agency in order to reduce duplication of effort and avoid confliction. The JTF assessment team is similar in composition to the HAST and, if provided early warning of pending operations, may be able to conduct assessment in association with the HAST. The CJTF determines the composition of the assessment team and includes staff members who are subject matter experts and representatives from Service and functional components expected to participate in the actual operation. When the JTF is in support of another federal agency, the JTF assessment teams will focus primarily on determining information that will enable the JTF to fulfill its supporting role. For example, if requested to provide transportation support to USAID, assessment teams will survey airfields, fuel capabilities, and other areas necessary to support transportation and logistics operations. JTF assessment teams should coordinate with USAID/OFDA and the DART (if deployed) to avoid duplicating ongoing assessments of the humanitarian impacts of disasters that are conducted by the lead agency. USG department and agency representation should include the DART representatives for purposes of coordination and synchronization of FDR operations. Special operations force personnel who possess necessary cultural, language, and technical skills may be included. The assessment team may also assist in clarifying the mission and determining force requirements and force deployment sequences for the JTF.

For further details on JTF assessment teams, refer to JP 3-08, Interorganizational Coordination During Joint Operations.

e. **Cross-Functional Collaboration.** Effective joint operations require close coordination, synchronization, and information sharing across the staff directorates. The most common technique for promoting this cross-functional collaboration is the formation of centers, groups, bureaus, cells, offices, elements, boards, working groups, and planning teams and other enduring or temporary organizations that manage specific processes and accomplish tasks in support of mission accomplishment. They facilitate planning by the staff, decision making by the commander, and execution by the HQ. They mostly fall under the principal oversight of the staff directorates. This arrangement strengthens the staff effort in ways that benefit the JTF and its commander in mission execution. The following are typical organizations formed by JTFs, during FHA operations, and some of their unique considerations:

(1) **Joint Facilities Utilization Board (JFUB).** The JFUB is formed under JTF engineer supervision. When large numbers of US and multinational forces operate within the same geographic area, facility allocation to accommodate requirements is necessary. The JFUB deconflicts issues arising from multiple-user demands on limited facilities and recommended courses of action (COAs) to resolve issues. The JFUB addresses multinational force accommodation, ammunition storage points, joint visitors' bureau, postal facilities, transit facilities, and other related areas. JFCs can establish a joint civil-military engineer board to execute JFUB decisions and collaborations as required.

For further details on the JFUB, refer to JP 3-34, Joint Engineer Operations.

(2) **Coalition Forces Support Team (CFST).** The CFST is organized to coordinate activities between participating multinational forces. The CFST focuses on controlling all support and coordination tasks. CFST duties include:

(a) Welcome and orient newly arrived FHA forces.

(b) Designate initial staging areas, provide water, rations, and other support.

(c) Identify sensitivities (historic animosity or religious differences) among multinational forces and the affected populace.

(d) Receive, process, and provide situation updates to arriving multinational forces, including a briefing on the legal limits of US support.

(e) Brief rules of engagement (ROE)/rules for the use of force to arriving multinational forces.

(f) Brief PR procedures to arriving multinational forces.

(g) Brief C2 and relief agency relationships.

(3) **Joint Network Operations Control Center (JNCC).** The JTF communications directorate may establish a JNCC to plan, manage, and operate all JTF communications systems. The JNCC exercises technical management over communications control centers belonging to deployed components and subordinate commands. It serves as the single control agency for management and operational direction of the joint communications networks and infrastructure. It plans, executes, and performs technical and management functions. The JNCC develops and/or disseminates standards and/or procedures and collects and/or presents communications system management statistical data. The JNCC must be prepared to integrate the communications systems of foreign militaries, IGOs, and NGOs as appropriate, to facilitate collaboration and cooperation.

For further details on the JNCC, refer to JP 6-0, Joint Communications System.

(4) **Joint Intelligence Support Element (JISE).** The JTF will usually be augmented with theater intelligence production resources, which are organized into a JISE or joint intelligence operations center (JIOC) under the supervision of the JTF intelligence directorate. The structure and functions of a JISE or JIOC may differ in an FHA from those of another type of operation.

For further details on the JISE and JIOC, refer to JP 2-01, Joint and National Intelligence Support to Military Operations, and JP 3-33, Joint Task Force Headquarters.

(5) **Media Operations Center (MOC).** The MOC is the focal point for the interface between the JTF and the media covering the operation. The MOC provides the news media with timely and accurate information about military support to FHA and facilitates media coverage of operations. When operated in support of multinational operations, a MOC may be called a "combined information bureau" or an "allied press information center." For longer-term FHA operations, the MOC may also conduct a command information program.

For further details on the MOC, refer to JP 3-61, Public Affairs.

(6) **Joint Movement Center (JMC).** The JMC coordinates the employment of all means of transportation (including that provided by allies or HNs, when requested) to support the CONOPS. This coordination is accomplished through establishment of transportation policies within the assigned operational areas, consistent with relative urgency of need, port and terminal capabilities, transportation asset availability, and priorities set by the CJTF. When required, the JMC coordinates with the logistics cluster, which is the logistic hub for the UN and many NGOs and IGOs, and with the JDDOC. Coordination at the JTF level is illustrated in Figure II-5.

For detailed information on movement control, see JP 4-09, Distribution Operations.

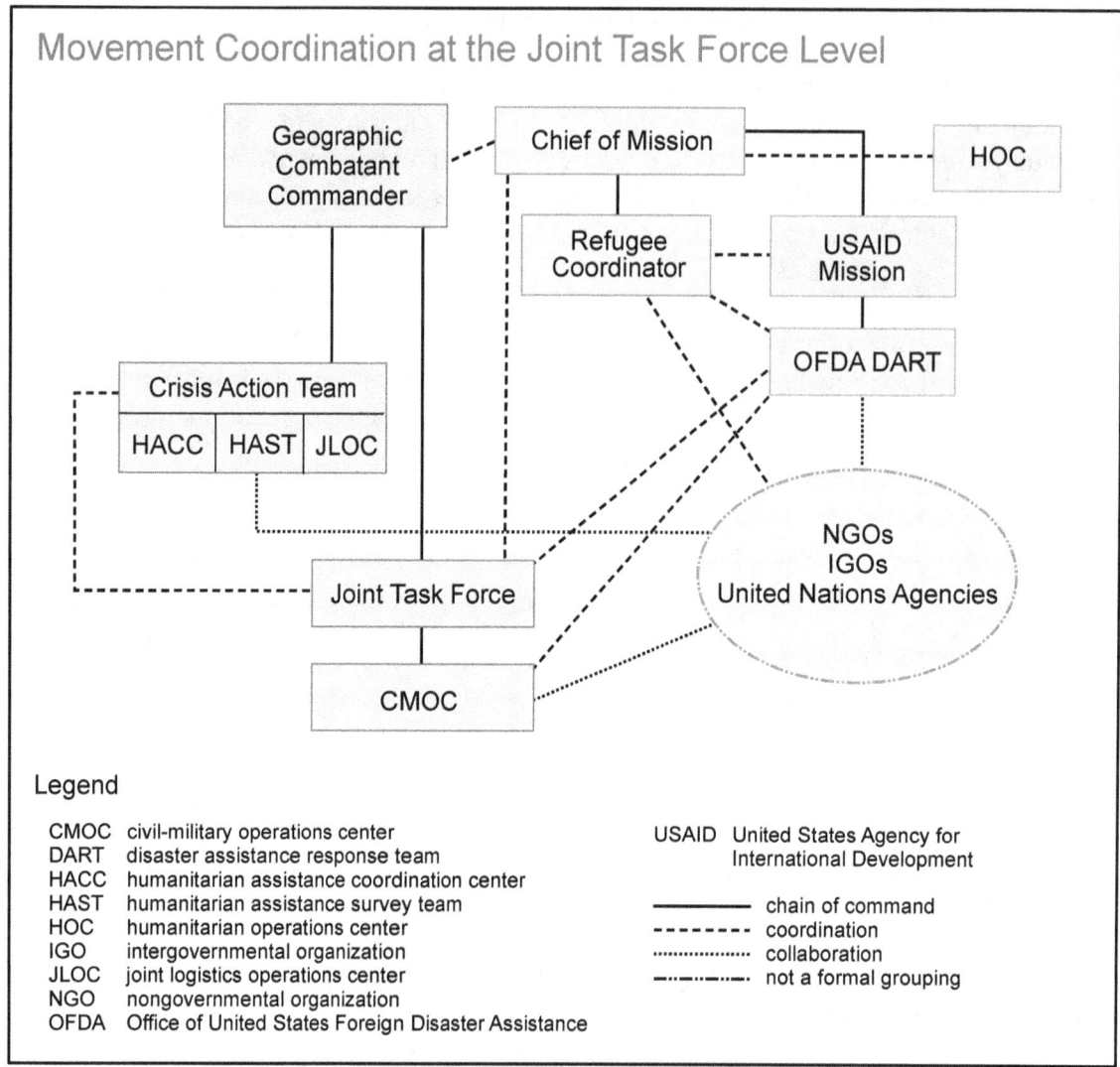

Figure II-5. Movement Coordination at the Joint Task Force Level

10. Civil-Military Operations Center

The CMOC is an organization formed by the JFC, normally comprised of CA, established to plan and facilitate coordination of activities of the Armed Forces of the US with indigenous populations and institutions (IPI), the private sector, IGOs, NGOs, multinational forces, and other USG departments and agencies. The JFC may establish a CMOC to coordinate and facilitate US and multinational forces' humanitarian operations with those of international and local relief agencies and HN agencies and authorities. **If established, the CMOC,** coordinating closely with the OFDA DART, should **serve as the primary collaboration interface for the joint force among IPI, IGOs, NGOs, multinational military forces, the private sector, and USG departments and agencies.** Despite its name, the CMOC generally does not set policy or direct operations. Generally, the CMOC is the meeting place of stakeholders. In reality, the CMOC may be physical or virtual. The organization of the CMOC is theater- and mission-dependent—flexible in size and composition. A commander at any echelon may establish a CMOC. In fact, more than one CMOC may be established in an operational area, and each is task-organized based on the mission. If the UNOCHA has already established a HIC or similar center, most UN organizations and many NGOs will prefer to use that as the preferred platform for coordination and information sharing. Care should be taken not to duplicate these efforts, but, ideally, to add value to existing coordination efforts.

For further details on CMOCs, refer to JP 3-57, Civil-Military Operations.

11. International Humanitarian Coordination Options

a. HOC is a senior-level international and interagency coordinating body that may be stood up to coordinate the overall relief strategy and unity of effort among all participants in a large FHA operation. HOC is a generic term and may have a different title based on the situation. It normally is established under the direction of the government of the HN or the UN. Because the HOC operates at the national level, it will normally consist of senior representatives from the affected country, assisting countries, the UN, NGOs, IGOs, and other major organizations in the operation. US participation may include the COM (including the USG representation), DOS and/or USAID representatives, and commanders, or their representatives, of the senior FHA operations force. The HOC is horizontally structured with no C2 authority and all members are ultimately responsible to their own organizations or countries. There is a significant difference between the HOC and CMOC. The CMOC is established by and works for the JFC. However, a commander at any level can establish a CMOC to synchronize and build unity of effort for the FHA mission. The HOC is normally established under the direction of the HN government or the UN, or possibly OFDA during a US unilateral operation. In the absence of a HOC, the CMOC can be established and used for the coordination of all stakeholders assisting in the FHA mission.

b. Close JTF collaboration with the affected country, UN, and other key members of the humanitarian relief community forms the core of FHA operations. The HOC coordinates the overall relief strategy; identifies logistic requirements for NGOs, UN, and IGOs; and identifies, prioritizes, and submits requests for military support to the JTF, through the LFA.

(1) The HN will normally have a ministry designated as the senior point of coordination for all HA activities. In more developed countries, there may be an organization similar to the US Federal Emergency Management Agency. **Ministries involved could include the ministry of health, ministry of transportation, ministry of defense, or an emergency management office within a ministry.** These ministries will establish the priority needs for their country and solicit international assistance from donor countries and relief organizations, either bilaterally or through the UN.

(2) In a failed state situation where no HN government is capable of coordinating the HA effort, the UN will normally establish overall coordination of the HA effort. **A greater representation of the various relief agencies and donor countries at the HOC results in more coordinated HA efforts.** The structure of a HOC can be formal or informal. HOCs may have political significance and authority when directed by the affected country, or may be less formal if established by the UN. The HOC is normally collocated with the appropriate lead or UN HQ conducting the operation.

c. **HOCs may establish working groups and committees.** These groups and committees discuss and resolve issues including relief material prioritization, medical, sanitation, health, and other related areas.

d. The CMOC, HACC, and HOC are distinct but interrelated organizations. The relationship among these organizations and interagency, international, and HN structures can be complex and challenging. Normally, the CMOC will not be the main coordinating center for the entire response operation. For example, during 2005 in East Timor the UN ran the coordination center and the CMOC representative was a participant in the larger center. Figure II-6 shows the comparison between the HOC, HACC, and the CMOC.

Comparison Between Humanitarian Operations Center, Humanitarian Assistance Coordination Center, and Civil-Military Operations Center

	Establishing Authority	Function	Composition	Authority
Humanitarian Operations Center (HOC)	Designated individual of affected country, United Nations, or US Government agency	Coordinates overall relief strategy at the national (country) level.	Representatives from: • Affected country • United Nations • US embassy or consulate • Joint task force • Other nonmilitary agencies • Concerned parties (private sector)	Coordination
Humanitarian Assistance Coordination Center	Combatant commander	Assists with interagency coordination and planning at the strategic level. Normally is disestablished once a HOC or CMOC is established.	Representatives from: • Combatant command • Nongovernmental organizations • Intergovernmental organizations • Regional organizations • Concerned parties (private sector)	Coordination
Civil-Military Operations Center (CMOC)	Joint task force or component commander	Assists in collaboration at the operational level with military forces, US Government agencies, nongovernmental and intergovernmental organizations, and regional organizations.	Representatives from: • Joint task force • Nongovernmental organizations • Intergovernmental organizations • Regional organizations • US Government agencies • Local government (host country) • Multinational forces • Other concerned parties (private sector)	Coordination

Figure II-6. Comparison Between Humanitarian Operations Center, Humanitarian Assistance Coordination Center, and Civil-Military Operations Center

e. **UN Country Team.** Like the country team in most US embassies, the UN country team ensures UN coordination and decision making at the country level and encompasses all the entities of the UN system that carry out operational activities for development, emergency, recovery, and transition programs. The UN country team is led by the UN resident coordinator, who is the designated representative of the UN Secretary General. The UN country team is composed of representatives of the UN funds program, specialized agencies, other UN entities accredited to a given country, and may also include representatives of the Bretton Woods institutions (e.g., the World Bank and International Monetary Fund). All UN country team members have direct line accountability to their own organizations, as well as accountability to the UN resident coordinator and the rest of the UN country team.

f. During HA operations in which the UN is involved, the Under Secretary General for Humanitarian Affairs also functions as the UN's ERC and reports to the UN Secretary General. The ERC may designate a humanitarian coordinator at the country level, or in some cases at the regional level. The humanitarian coordinator oversees the UN's humanitarian country team, and determines whether to activate the cluster approach. The UN may deploy a UNDAC team. That group will accomplish UN coordination and liaison in-country at the national and ambassadorial level. At the site of a natural disaster, the UN will establish an OSOCC. The OSOCC normally reports to the humanitarian coordinator who establishes and convenes an HCT, which includes representation from non-UN operational agencies. The humanitarian coordinator renders a field situation report with worldwide distribution. This position is generally held by the United Nations Development Programme (UNDP) resident representative or until another coordinator is designated. The CMOC and the OSOCC should be closely located to synchronize US contributions to the overall international effort. Care should be taken, however, to respect the space of humanitarian actors. The humanitarian coordinator can be designated in one of four ways:

(1) Normally, the functions of the humanitarian coordinator are assigned to the resident coordinator for that country, who, therefore, becomes the resident and humanitarian coordinator.

(2) Appoint a separate humanitarian coordinator.

(3) Designate a lead agency for the provision of HA, with the in-country agency head also serving as humanitarian coordinator.

(4) Appoint a regional humanitarian coordinator when an emergency occurs that involves more than one country at the same time.

(5) In especially large-scale emergencies (e.g., the 2010 Haiti earthquake), the Interagency Standing Committee has agreed to consider within 72 hours the possibility of deploying a senior humanitarian leader with special authority to oversee the humanitarian response. Depending on the capabilities of the UN's in-country leadership, this individual may replace or oversee the existing resident coordinator.

g. The humanitarian coordinator facilitates humanitarian accountability through the promotion and monitoring of implementation of relevant policies and guidelines, and establishes and maintains comprehensive coordination mechanisms to support the work of the humanitarian agencies and organizations in the country. Additionally, the humanitarian coordinator develops a comprehensive strategic plan for responding to the assistance and protection needs of dislocated civilians and facilitates the provision of common services.

h. The humanitarian coordinator retains overall responsibility for ensuring the effectiveness of the humanitarian response. The cluster system is activated at the discretion of the UN humanitarian country team or at the direction of the UN ERC. Because UNHCR is the lead UN agency in all refugee crises, the cluster approach does not apply in refugee crises. The UN cluster approach is the principle construct utilized by the international humanitarian community, to facilitate a coordinated humanitarian response to internal displacement. The cluster approach ensures predictability and accountability in international responses to humanitarian emergencies by clarifying the division of labor among organizations and better defining their roles and responsibilities within the different sectors of response. The UN cluster approach designates lead entities to coordinate response efforts for specific mission areas. To the extent possible, cluster leads are accountable to the humanitarian coordinator for ensuring the establishment of adequate coordination mechanisms for the sector or area of activity concerned, adequate preparedness, as well as adequate strategic planning for an effective operational response. Requirements are identified by participating organizations, in collaboration with the affected state, and UN member organizations volunteer to fulfill them. Cluster leads have no authority to assign missions; they must meet requirements using coordination, collaboration, cooperation, and communication. The cluster sector activities and respective leads are reflected in Figure II-7. The humanitarian coordinator ensures:

(1) Cluster leads, together with other leaders of the UN humanitarian agencies in the country, are consulted closely in developing the overall strategic direction of the humanitarian operation, and the work of the different clusters is integrated into a coherent, overall response.

(2) Unnecessary duplication and overlap among sectors is avoided.

(3) Cross-cutting issues are effectively addressed in all sectors.

(4) Strategic planning is coherent throughout the country.

(5) Clusters are provided with the necessary common services and tools for effective cross-cluster collaboration.

(6) Cluster meetings are streamlined and supplement, rather than replace, general interagency coordination meetings to prevent a fragmentation of the humanitarian response.

(7) Support is provided to clusters in advocacy and resource-mobilization efforts to ensure a balanced, comprehensive, and well-prioritized humanitarian response.

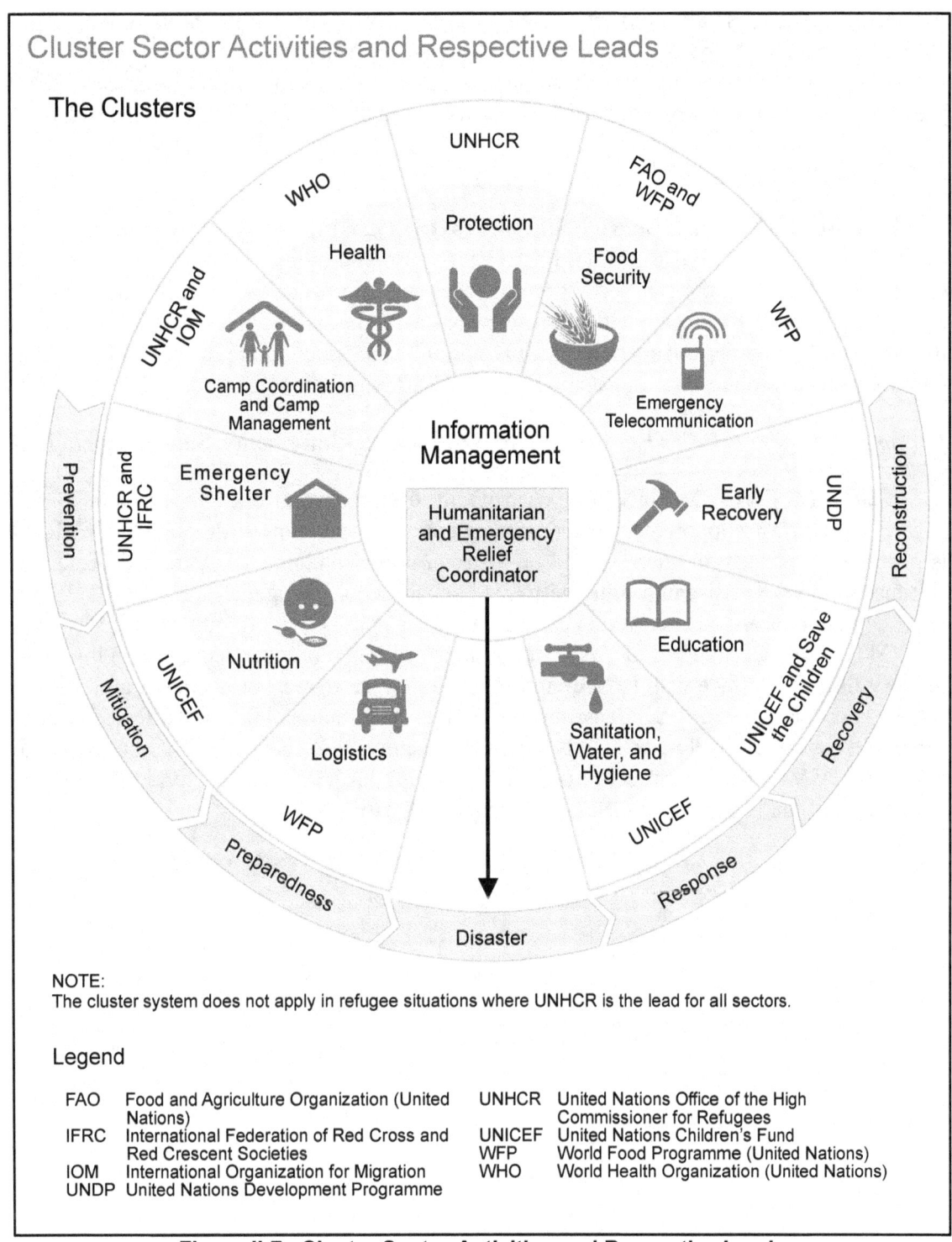

Figure II-7. Cluster Sector Activities and Respective Leads

12. Other Joint Task Forces

a. **JSOTF.** Special operations forces (SOF) may be able to make a significant contribution to the FHA operations based on their language proficiency, cultural awareness, familiarity with the operational area, small footprint, and an ability to work in an austere environment. Their ability to liaise with the local populace and assistance organizations and provide timely assessments of conditions in remote locations via their long-range communications capabilities provide the JFC with timely information for decision making and additional, viable COAs.

For further details refer to JP 3-05, Special Operations.

   b. **Joint Military Information Support (MIS) Task Force.** MIS forces, organized as a JMISTF, normally serve as a subordinate joint command of a joint force. The JMISTF's capabilities and products can be tailored to meet specific needs of the joint forces' FHA efforts. For example, working with the country team, the JMISTF can develop and broadcast the USG's departments and agencies, NGOs, and IGOs messages and produce and distribute pamphlets that provide information on how the local population can obtain aid.

For further details on JMISTFs, refer to JP 3-13.2, Military Information Support Operations.

   c. **JCMOTF.** A JCMOTF is composed of units from more than one Service, and is formed to carry out CMO in support of a theater campaign or other operations. Although the JCMOTF is not a CA organization, there should be a strong representation of CA trained personnel. Because of their expertise in dealing with USG departments and agencies, NGOs, IGOs, and USG departments and agencies, they will greatly enhance the opportunity for success. The JCMOTF may be established to carry out missions of limited or extended duration involving military forces' interface with local civilian populations, resources, or agencies; and military forces' coordination with USG departments and agencies, multinational and affected country forces, UN agencies, NGOs, and IGOs. JFCs are responsible to conduct CMO but they may establish a JCMOTF when the scope of CMO requires coordination and activities beyond the capabilities of the JTF's or assigned unit's organic CA capabilities.

For further details on JCMOTFs, refer to JP 3-57, Civil-Military Operations.

CHAPTER III
PLANNING

"We are in fact minimizing the loss of life and mitigating the incredible human suffering that we see across the region. This has been a unique military operation from that perspective, in that we have been planning, assessing, deploying, and executing concurrently. It would be like, I guess, if you were taking a family vacation and you were trying to pack the car and decide where you were going while you were driving down the road. But we are being successful in doing just that."

Lieutenant General Robert R. Blackman, US Marine Corps
Commander, Combined Support Force 536
Operation UNIFIED ASSISTANCE
Utapao, Thailand
January 7, 2005

1. Introduction

a. This chapter highlights aspects of joint operation planning specific to FHA operations. Joint operation planning encompasses the full range of activities required to conduct joint operations. These activities include planning for the mobilization, deployment, employment, sustainment, redeployment, and demobilization of forces. Joint operation planning occurs within the Adaptive Planning and Execution (APEX) system.

b. Crisis action planning (CAP) refers to the time-sensitive development of joint operation orders (OPORDs) for the deployment, employment, and sustainment of assigned, attached, and allocated forces and capabilities in response to a crisis. CAP is based on the actual circumstances that exist at the time planning occurs. The time available to plan responses to real-time events is short, particularly in the case of disasters requiring an FDR response. **In as little as a few days, the supported GCC and the JFCs and their staffs must develop and approve a feasible COA, publish the OPORD, prepare forces, ensure sufficient support, and arrange sustainment for the employment of US military forces.** Accordingly, considerations for CAP are emphasized throughout this chapter, although much of the information is also applicable during deliberate planning.

c. Joint operation planning begins when an appropriate authority recognizes potential for military capability to be employed in response to a potential or actual crisis. In areas where natural disasters are prevalent or FDR exercises are a key part of the GCC's security cooperation portion of TCP, GCCs should have a commander's estimate, base plan, CONPLAN, or OPLAN for the affected area for an FDR mission. Multinational planning or exercise results may also be available. Although an existing contingency plan almost never completely aligns with an emerging crisis, it can be used to facilitate rapid COA development. Planning factors found in Appendix F, "Planning Factors for Foreign Humanitarian Assistance and Foreign Disaster Relief Operations," incorporate and elaborate many of the topics discussed in this chapter.

d. The commander should understand the relief process used by the HN and IGOs, as depicted in Figure III-1. This model captures the continuous, cyclic nature of the overarching relief process. Critical to this process is information sharing among all the parties. The relief cycle is repeated as needs assessments are updated, requirements refined, additional requests for assistance (RFAs) made, and operations continue. While this model conveys the impression of an orderly process, in reality the process is complex and sometimes fragmented due to the large number of different organizations with their own missions and sometimes competing agendas.

(1) **Needs Assessments.** HN, USAID, IGOs, NGOs, and USG departments and agencies conduct needs assessments on the extent of the disaster/emergency and the needs/requirements. Needs assessments also include determining the capabilities and resources of various relief organizations, including military, if they are part of the effort.

(2) **Needs Analysis.** Analysis is an essential component of the relief process.

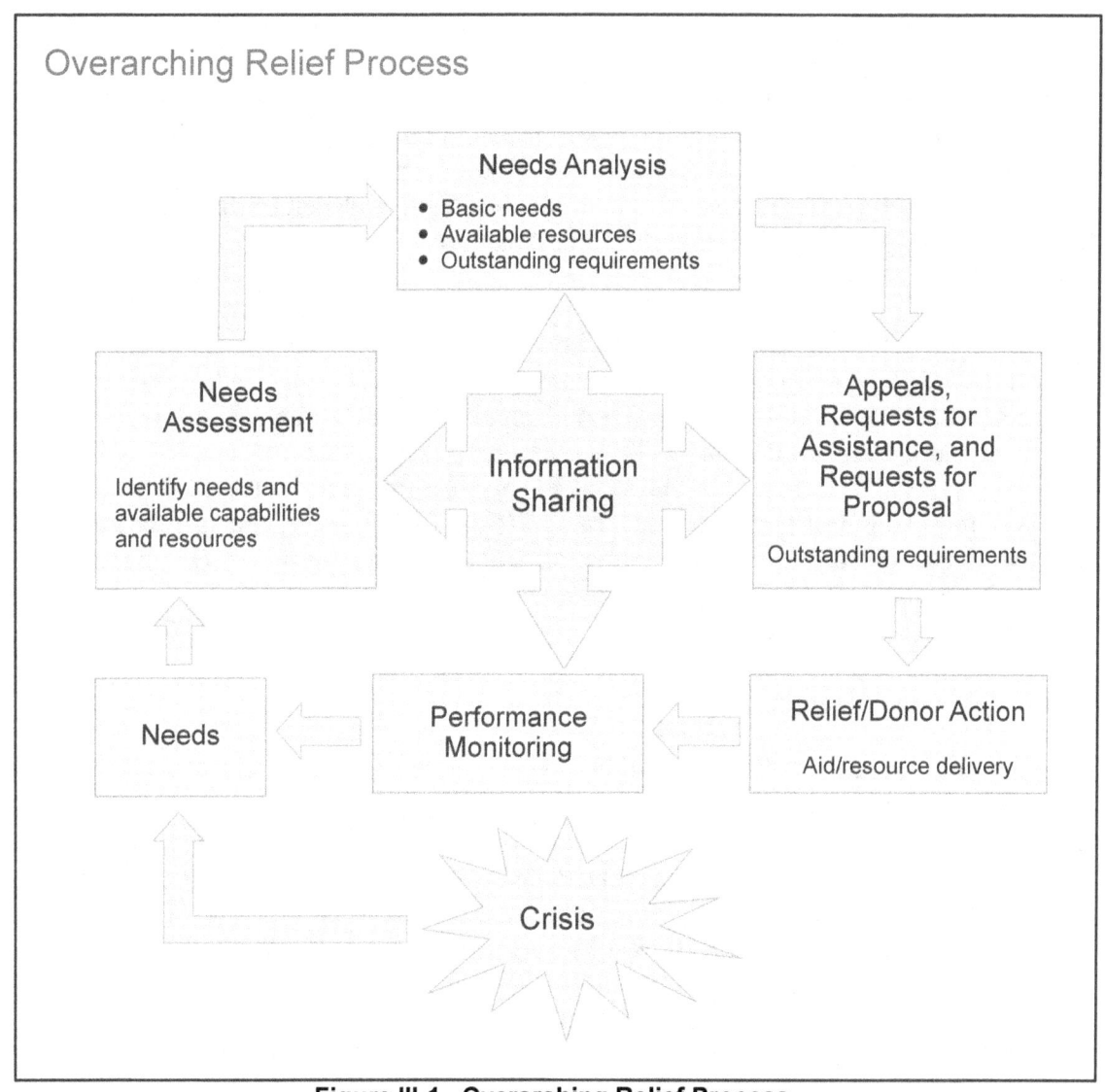

Figure III-1. Overarching Relief Process

Needs assessments and capabilities are analyzed to update and resolve differences, determine outstanding needs/requirements, and reasonably anticipated future needs.

(3) Based upon outstanding needs/requirements, the HN may request international assistance. NGOs and IGOs may also appeal to the international community and donors for funding and assistance. The military may receive, normally through OFDA, RFAs to provide HA support, subject to the policies of the USG.

(4) **Relief/Donor Action.** Humanitarian agencies, donors, and foreign military commands provide relief based on their ability to respond to appeals and RFAs. Foreign government, regional organizations, and the UN may make available immediate funds and other resources very early in the relief cycle. UNOCHA administers a Central Emergency Revolving Fund to provide immediate assistance.

(5) **Performance Monitoring.** Donors and humanitarian agencies monitor the performance of their programs in the field to measure results and identify gaps or problems. Performance monitoring informs humanitarian policy decisions and the design of future humanitarian programs, while ensuring accountability to taxpayers and beneficiaries.

Procedures for both deliberate planning and CAP are described in Chairman of the Joint Chiefs of Staff Manual (CJCSM) 3122, Joint Operation Planning and Execution System (JOPES) Series, *CJCSM 3130,* Adaptive Planning and Execution (APEX) Series, and *JP 5-0,* Joint Operation Planning.

2. Understanding the Operational Environment

a. The nature of the OE obviously impacts the conduct of FHA operations. Important elements of the OE considered during planning and executing FDR operations include the type of disaster involved (including underlying causes), the prevailing security environment, and the system of international relief at work. The process of joint intelligence preparation of the operational environment (JIPOE) will assist in developing this understanding and applying it to planning and execution.

b. **Types of Disasters.** Most disasters have underlying causes that may demand changes in human systems and processes (e.g., tsunami alert systems, better food management, weak or failing HN infrastructure or processes, or even civil war). Normally, forces conducting FHA following a disaster are tasked to focus on the event at hand rather than the underlying causes. However, understanding these causes can enhance mission accomplishment and force protection. Disasters and consequent emergencies may occur suddenly or develop over a period of time. Speed of onset has important consequences for action that can be taken. Prevention, preparedness, and early warning measures are much less developed for rapid onset disasters.

(1) **Slow Onset.** Slow onset emergencies include those resulting from crop failure due to drought, the spread of an agricultural pest or disease, or a gradually deteriorating situation leading to conflict.

(2) **Rapid Onset.** Rapid onset emergencies are usually the result of sudden, natural events such as wind storms, hurricanes, typhoons, floods, tsunamis, wildfires, landslides, avalanches, earthquakes, and volcanic eruptions. They also may be caused by accidental or human-caused catastrophes such as civil conflict, acts of terrorism, sabotage, or industrial accidents.

(3) **Complex.** An increasing number of emergencies are related to conflict and have come to be known as "complex emergencies." The UN defines a "complex emergency" as "a humanitarian crisis in a country, region, or society where there is a total or considerable breakdown of authority resulting from internal or external conflict and which requires an international response that goes beyond the mandate or capacity of any single agency and/or the ongoing UN country program." USAID defines it as "natural or man-made disaster with economic, social, and political dimensions. The result is a profound social crisis in which a large number of people die and suffer from war, disease, hunger, and displacement owing to man-made and natural disasters, while some others may benefit from it. Four factors can be measured: the fatalities from violence; the mortality of children under five years of age; the percentage of underweight children under five; and the number of external refugees and IDPs." Common characteristics include:

(a) Many civilian casualties and populations besieged or displaced.

(b) Serious political or conflict-related impediments to delivery of assistance.

(c) Inability of people to pursue normal social, political, or economic activities.

(d) High security risks for relief workers.

(e) International and cross-border operations affected by diplomatic or political differences.

c. The OE can be characterized by the degree of control HN forces have to support and assist in the operation. As shown in Figure III-2, there are three types of OEs when providing FHA: permissive, uncertain, and hostile. The type of OE will have direct impact on the decision to conduct the FHA operation, as well as many planning aspects. Regardless of the OE, force protection will remain of paramount concern to the JFC.

d. **Relief System.** An assessment of the situation should include a **description of the relief organizations** (NGOs, IGOs, HN, and private sector), **foreign governments and military forces**, **UN agencies**, or **any other pertinent element** already involved in the FHA effort, what relationship exists among them, and the effectiveness of the organizations in place. Depending on the type of operation, DOS or USAID will be critical in mapping this system and identifying key players in multiple organizations. The range of civilian actors and programs is often determined by security factors, i.e., whether it is a permissive, uncertain, or hostile OE. For example, the International Federation of Red Cross and Red Crescent Societies (IFRC) typically work in permissive natural disasters, while the ICRC can operate in uncertain or hostile OEs.

```
┌─────────────────────────────────────────────────────────────┐
│  Foreign Humanitarian Assistance Operational Environments     │
│                                                               │
│  Permissive                                                   │
│                                                               │
│    Host country military and law enforcement agencies have    │
│    control and the intent and capability to assist foreign    │
│    humanitarian assistance (FHA) operations.                  │
│                                                               │
│  Uncertain                                                    │
│                                                               │
│    Host government forces, whether opposed to or receptive to │
│    FHA operations, do not have totally effective control of   │
│    the territory and population within the intended           │
│    operational area.                                          │
│                                                               │
│  Hostile                                                     │
│                                                               │
│    Hostile forces have control and the intent and capability  │
│    to effectively oppose or react to FHA operations.          │
│                                                               │
└─────────────────────────────────────────────────────────────┘
```

Figure III-2. Foreign Humanitarian Assistance Operational Environments

For more information on the IFRC and ICRC, refer to Appendix D, "Humanitarian Intergovernmental and Nongovernmental Organizations."

e. **JIPOE.** During the JIPOE process, the JFC's intelligence staff element manages the analysis and development of products that provide a systemic understanding of the OE in which the joint force must operate. JIPOE follows a multistep process to define the OE, describe the effects of the environment, evaluate the enemy, and determine enemy courses of action. JIPOE support during FHA requires a different mindset and techniques than a JIPOE effort to defeat an adversary. The mindset will likely be more collaborative and open to correct false data and improve analysis. This analysis identifies a number of nodes (specific physical, functional, or cultural entities within each system.) Nodes can include people; transportation infrastructure; sociological and political structure; economic systems; potential friendly, neutral, and adversary elements; the information environment; and other components of the OE. JIPOE analysts also identify links (the cultural, physical, or functional relationship between nodes.) As with many aspects of CAP, JIPOE will be continuous throughout the planning and execution process. Due to the complexity of the JIPOE process during FHA, the intelligence directorate of a joint staff (J-2) within a JTF may or may not have the requisite support on hand to perform a detailed JIPOE analysis. Therefore, the JTF J-2 should consider requesting support from the theater JIOC.

For further details on JIPOE, refer to JP 2-01.3, Joint Intelligence Preparation of the Operational Environment.

---

f. **Assessment Factors.** Assessment factors that may assist in the JIPOE process are found in USAID's *Field Operations Guide for Disaster Assessment and Response*, the Sphere Project *Humanitarian Charter and Minimum Standards in Disaster Response*, UNHCR *Handbook for Emergencies*, and the DOS *Post-Conflict Reconstruction Essential Tasks.* **The following are examples of factors that can aid in assessing the situation:**

(1) What is the status and intent of military or paramilitary forces?

(2) Who are the relevant governmental and nongovernmental actors in the operational area? What are their objectives? Are their objectives at odds or compatible with the JFC's objectives?

(3) What resources exist locally (e.g., government, private sector, and resources that can be procured or rehabilitated)?

(4) Who are the key communicators (persons who hold the ear of the populace, e.g., mayors, village elders, teachers) within the operational area?

(5) What is the status of essential public services (water, electricity, communication, sanitation, and transportation, including road, rail, bridge, and seaport and airport conditions and capabilities)? How does the current status compare to predisaster status?

(6) What is the status of health care providers, firefighters, police, and court systems? Include availability, level of expertise (skilled laborers), equipment, and supplies.

(7) What relief agencies are in place, what are their roles and capabilities, and what resources do they have?

(8) What is the physical condition of the civilian populace?

(9) Where are the locations of medical facilities; what are their capabilities (e.g., diagnostic, ancillary, surgery, obstetrics, neonatal); are they operational, and to what level?

(10) What humanitarian needs are established (human suffering, disease, hunger, privation)? What activities are needed to directly address them? What supporting activities and functions are required?

(11) What facilities and support are available to forces from the affected country?

(12) What unique social, ethnic, or religious concerns affect the conduct of the operation?

(13) What are the legal limitations and funding restrictions to US assistance in this case?

(14) What is the local population's attitude toward who or what is causing their plight?

(15) What is the local population's attitude toward the presence of US forces?

(16) What are the force requirements to protect the force?

(17) What is the PR plan if a US individual becomes isolated?

(18) What is the status of the host strategic transportation infrastructure? Are available seaports and airfields in usable condition? What is the status of materials handling equipment? Are connecting roads and railroads usable?

g. **Sources of Information. Intelligence estimates, area assessments, and surveys** provide information on the situation in the crisis area, providing political, cultural, economic, military, geographic and topographic, climatic, infrastructure and engineering, health, and other essential information. Other sources for an initial assessment include the US country team, CCDR country books, recent OFDA situation reports, UN Secretariat assessments, the UN's ReliefWeb Internet site, PDC's Asia Pacific Natural Hazards and Vulnerabilities Atlas (http://atlas.pdc.org) and other PDC resources, relief organizations already operating in the area, and SOF personnel (see Figure III-3). A GCC may also choose to deploy a HAST to assess the situation.

3. Mission Analysis

a. The joint force's mission is the task or set of tasks, together with the purpose, that clearly indicate the action to be taken and the reason for doing so. The primary purpose of mission analysis is to understand the problem and purpose of the operation and issue appropriate guidance to drive the rest of the planning process. Although some steps occur before others, mission analysis typically involves substantial parallel processing of information by the commander and staff, particularly in a CAP situation.

For further details on mission analysis, refer to JP 5-0, Joint Operation Planning.

b. **The Military Role.** The aim of the *Guidelines on the Use of Foreign Military and Civil Defence Assets in Disaster Relief—Oslo Guidelines—*is to establish the basic framework for formalizing and improving the effectiveness and efficiency of the use of foreign military and civil defense assets in international disaster relief operations.

(1) The USG participated in the development of the guidelines and endorsed their use. However, they are not binding. The USG recognizes that the *Oslo Guidelines* outline the process for making military or civil-military requests through UNOCHA. NATO military forces may be requested to assist in disaster relief in accordance with the *Oslo Guidelines*.

(2) The *Oslo Guidelines* provide that foreign military assets should be requested only where there is no comparable civilian alternative and only when the use of military assets can meet a critical humanitarian need. The military asset, therefore, must be unique in capability and availability. Military assets should be seen as a tool complementing existing relief mechanisms to provide specific support to specific requirements, in response to the acknowledged "humanitarian gap" between the disaster needs that the relief community is

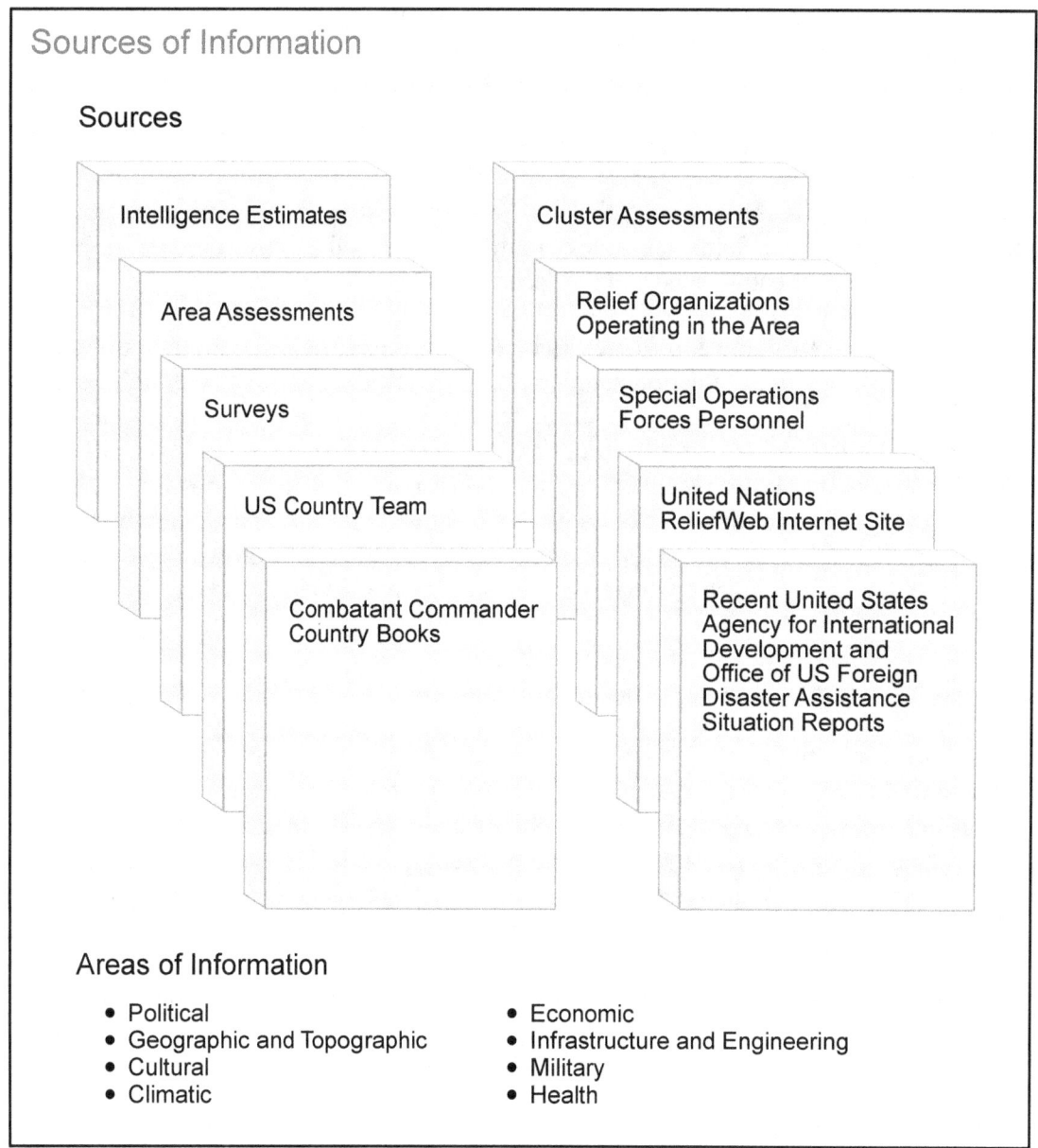

Figure III-3. Sources of Information

being asked to satisfy and the resources available to meet them. At the onset, any use of military assets should be limited in time and scale and present an exit strategy that defines clearly how the function it undertakes could, in the future, be undertaken by civilian personnel. For the purposes of the *Oslo Guidelines,* HA can be divided into three categories based on the degree of contact with the affected population. These categories are important because they help define which types of humanitarian activities might be appropriate to support with international military resources under different conditions, given that ample consultation has been conducted with all concerned parties to explain the nature and necessity of the assistance. The three categories are:

(a) **Direct Assistance.** The face-to-face distribution of goods and services.

(b) **Indirect Assistance.** This involves such activities as transporting relief goods or relief personnel and other activities that are at least one step removed from the population.

(c) **Infrastructure Support.** This involves providing general services, such as road repair, airspace management, and power generation that facilitate relief, but are not necessarily visible to or solely for the benefit of the affected population.

(3) Where practicable, the military role should focus on providing indirect assistance and infrastructure support while minimizing direct assistance.

c. **National Strategic End State and the Military End State.** For specific situations that require the employment of military capabilities, the President, Secretary of State, and SecDef typically will establish a set of national strategic objectives. Achievement of these objectives should result in attainment of the national strategic end state—the broadly expressed conditions that should exist after the conclusion of an operation. Based on the strategic guidance, the CCDR will determine the military end state and strategic military objectives, which define the role of military forces. Due to the crisis nature of FHA operations, initial planning may proceed without a formal set of national or theater strategic objectives specific to the operation, using assumed objectives based on existing strategic plans. These objectives are the basis for operational design.

For further details on end state and strategic objectives, refer to JP 1, Doctrine for the Armed Forces of the United States.

d. **Risk Assessment.** Commanders must identify the specific hazards that the joint force may encounter during the mission, and determine the probability and severity of loss, to include personnel being captured or detained, linked to those hazards. After assessing these hazards, the staff must develop risk mitigation measures. To assist in risk management, commanders and their staffs may develop or institute a risk management process tailored to their particular mission or operational area.

e. **Mission Statement Development.** A critical task for the GCC is developing the FHA military mission statement. The mission statement must provide specific direction for attaining the desired end state via clear and attainable military objectives. The GCC normally coordinates the mission statement with the LFA. GCCs consider several factors in developing the mission statement, to include the military force's role in assisting relief agencies, the OE, and security considerations. The mission statement for the USPACOM Operation UNIFIED ASSISTANCE (2004-2005) is an example: "USPACOM provides assistance to the governments of Indonesia, Sri Lanka, Thailand, and other affected nations to mitigate the effects of the recent earthquake and tsunami in the Indian Ocean. Conduct of operation is in support of USG lead agency, and in coordination with IGOs, NGOs, and PN."

4. **Concept of Operations**

a. The CONOPS is a verbal or graphic statement that clearly and concisely expresses what the JFC intends to accomplish and how it will be done using available resources. It describes how the actions of the joint force components and supporting organizations will be integrated, synchronized, and phased to accomplish the mission, including potential branches and sequels.

For further details on CONOPS development, refer to JP 5-0, Joint Operation Planning.

b. **Phasing of the Operation.** Phasing assists JFCs and staffs to visualize and think through the entire operation and to define requirements in terms of forces, resources, time, space, and purpose. The actual phases used will vary (compressed, expanded, or omitted entirely) with the joint operation, as determined by the JFC. Plan phases should not be "locked into concrete," and phase timing may be shifted as the situation dictates.

(1) While FHA operations may occur during any phase of a larger joint operation,

---

OPERATION SUPPORT HOPE PHASES

Phase I, Stabilize the Situation in Goma. "Stop The Dying." Support life-saving efforts (primarily water production, distribution, and sanitation) in the Goma, Zaire refugee camps. Phase I was to be declared complete when the death rate and refugee deprivation reached predesignated levels and when distribution began to function at an acceptable rate.

Phase II, Move Refugees Back Toward Rwanda. Assist in establishing a way station network from the major refugee centers toward the Rwandan interior. The objective was to assist relief agencies to develop a sustainment infrastructure and distribution system to help refugees return voluntarily to their homes. Phase II completion criteria required establishment of the way station support infrastructure and distribution network.

Phase III, Stabilize the Refugee Situation and Begin Reconstruction in Rwanda. This phase supported ongoing relief efforts and established preconditions for operational transition to the United Nations High Commissioner for Refugees (UNHCR). Phase III was to be declared complete upon initial operational capability of a viable transportation, distribution, and storage infrastructure capable of meeting basic Rwandan needs.

Phase IV, Turnover Operations to the UNHCR. This phase begins as UNHCR, third country forces, and various relief agencies developed adequate water production as well as food and medical distribution to sustain recovery. During this phase, joint force operations begin transition to a US liaison element to work closely with the UNHCR. Phase completion involved seamless transfer of ongoing relief operations to UNHCR and other agencies capable of sustained operations.

Phase V, Redeploy the Force. The redeployment phase consists of relief operations control transfer to the UNHCR or redeployment of nonessential personnel and equipment.

Various Sources

---

they will most often occur in the shape phase of the GCC's strategic engagement operations, or during the stabilize and enable civil authority phase of a major operation.

(2) Within the context of a larger operation, JFCs and component commanders may establish additional phases that fit their CONOPS. These sub-phases, designed to focus relief assets and emphasis, should generally follow the six-phase model and include transitions from one phase to the next. Another useful example is the phases used during Operation SUPPORT HOPE 1994.

For further details on phasing, refer to JP 3-0, Joint Operations, and JP 5-0, Joint Operation Planning.

5. **Force Planning**

a. The primary purposes of force planning are to influence COA development and selection based on force allocations, availability, and readiness; identify all forces needed to accomplish the supported CCDR's CONOPS with some rigor; and effectively phase the forces into the operational area. JFCs may have plans and/or predesignated joint forces for the conduct of FHA missions. The JFC has a number of available options, including use of a predesignated joint force or an ad hoc joint force, organized and tailored specifically to conduct FHA missions. In FHA operations, **the joint force structure must provide for the means to coordinate and communicate with the numerous military/civilian US/foreign organizations that are involved in the overall FHA effort.** Effective liaison among these organizations will help reduce organizational conflicts and redundant relief efforts. Personnel trained in **political-military skills** are valuable in establishing necessary liaison with policymakers and the diplomatic community. Additionally, personnel skilled in **multifunctional logistics** and **security assistance operations** should be part of the joint force organization, since FHA operations tend to be logistics intensive. **There is a high probability that the joint force will be a multinational force,** and that some of the multinational forces may require and have received USG approval to be supported with US equipment and sustained by US forces throughout the duration of the operation. This support may include the activation and deployment of Reserve Component (RC) personnel or units to support specific mission requirements, such as CA.

b. **Defining capabilities requirements.** The supported commander identifies force requirements as operational capabilities in the form of force packages to facilitate sourcing by the Services, United States Special Operations Command (USSOCOM), USTRANSCOM, and other force providers' supporting commands. A force package is a list (group of force capabilities) of the various forces (force requirements) that the supported commander requires to conduct the operation described in the CONOPS. The supported commander typically describes force requirements in the form of broad capability descriptions or unit type codes (UTCs), depending on the circumstances.

c. **Force Sourcing**

(1) **Request for Forces and Capabilities.** The supported commander submits the required force packages through the Joint Staff to the force providers for sourcing. Force

providers review the readiness and deployability posture of their available units before deciding which units to allocate to the supported commander's force requirements. Services and their component commands also determine mobilization requirements and plan for the provision of non-unit sustainment.

(2) **Global Force Management (GFM).** The supported commander will review the sourcing recommendations through the GFM process to ensure compatibility with capability requirements and CONOPS. GFM identifies full-range support capabilities and forces, identifies the right mix, and brings that mix into a streamlined and integrated process designed to support CCMD requirements. GFM allows a global view of the requirements and a global view of the availability of the forces to meet those requirements using a collaborative and open environment. The process allows planners to shift their focus of preparation to the most important areas.

d. **Service Capabilities for FHA**

(1) **Conventional forces,** though not organized, trained, and equipped specifically for FHA, have inherent and unique capabilities that allow these forces to conduct FHA activities, including FHA and FDR operations.

(a) **Maritime Forces.** Maritime forces can provide operational maneuver and assured access while significantly reducing the footprint ashore and minimizing the permissions required to operate from the HN.

<u>1</u>. Forward deployed amphibious forces can provide immediate national response in support of humanitarian and natural disaster relief operations. The Marine expeditionary unit (MEU) is the Marine Corps' lightest and most expeditionary version of the Marine air-ground task force (MAGTF). Embarked aboard a Navy amphibious ready group (ARG), the ARG/MEU provides a GCC or other operational commander a quick, sea-based reaction force for a wide variety of missions, to include FHA. In response to HA, the ARG/MEU provides capabilities to conduct the following: FHA; populace and resources control (PRC); civil information management (CIM); NA; support to civil administration; dislocated civilian operations; and NEOs.

<u>2</u>. Other forward deployed maritime units, including carrier strike groups, individual ships or cutters, and deployed Navy Expeditionary Combat Command units, may provide more limited immediate relief support, including airlift support, PR, engineering services, such as bridging and debris removal, and a secure platform for staging or rest and recuperation until a larger force arrives.

<u>3</u>. US Navy ships can provide a safe and accessible location for the JFC HQ, provide seabasing support to the joint force, and have a limited ability to produce and distribute electrical power and clean water. Large deck amphibious ships are particularity useful for FHA operations, as they can support both helicopters and small vessels that can move supplies and equipment to shore. These vessels also have organic medical support, command, control, communications, computers and intelligence capabilities, and berthing and messing facilities that may be available to a limited number of responders. Coastal

riverine forces, expeditionary training teams, hospital ships, expeditionary medical facilities (EMFs), and forward-deployable preventive medicine units (FDPMUs) are other US Navy assets that can be tailored to support FHA missions. Navy Expeditionary Logistics Support Group (NAVELSG) forces have supported numerous FHA operations in the past. NAVELSG forces can be utilized to offload cargo from maritime pre-positioning force (MPF) vessels or support air cargo operations at airfields.

4. Military Sealift Command is a strategic power-projection capability that combines the lift capacity, flexibility, and responsiveness of surface ships with the speed of strategic airlift. Pre-positioned strategically around the world, these ships move to a crisis when needed and offload either in port or underway. Offloaded equipment and supplies are then linked up with Marines and Navy Seabees arriving at nearby airfields. MPF is especially responsive to regional crises that involve HA and disaster relief. These ships also have the capability to purify water and transfer it ashore. Bulk petroleum, oils, and lubricants transfer capability is also available. The Army's afloat pre-positioning ships provide a similar capability to the MPF, but these ships require port facilities.

5. Reopening ports and resuming operations can be critical for sustained relief operations. Natural disasters—especially heavy weather events and earthquakes—can hamper safe navigation into both sea and aerial ports. Each Service has expertise in conducting emergency port opening surveys and assessments. USTRANSCOM also has a JTF-port opening capability that consists of both aerial port and seaport capability. These capabilities enable USTRANSCOM to rapidly establish and operate a port of debarkation and distribution node and facilitate port throughput in support of the CCDR.

For detailed information on the JTF-port opening and joint terminal operations, refer to JP 4-01.5, Joint Terminal Operations.

(b) **Air Forces**

1. Airlift is an important method of moving relief supplies and rapidly moving personnel and equipment such as hospitals and water purification units to support FHA operations.

2. Airfields can quickly be overwhelmed with aircraft transporting relief supplies. Aviation C2 elements, air traffic control elements, and aerial port units can facilitate the effective movement of supplies transported by aircraft. Civil engineer units have the capability to repair damaged airfields rapidly.

3. Airfields are a center of gravity for the relief effort and require a permissive localized environment to operate. Therefore, airfields must be provided security by task organized defense forces as outlined in JP 3-10, *Joint Security Operations in Theater.* The Services' military police assets are adept at this role.

4. In addition to the major functions of airlift and airfield development, air forces may also support FHA through PR, airspace control, and intelligence, surveillance, and reconnaissance.

5. Helicopters have become a critical asset during FHA operations. When roads, bridges, and railroads have been damaged by a disaster, helicopters may be the only method to deliver relief supplies and transport relief workers to the operational area.

6. Air forces can provide engineering capabilities, supply, distribution, base camp support, material handling, water purification, inspection of facilities, and PR to fill critical gaps in the humanitarian response.

(c) **Ground Forces**

1. Ground forces can provide surface transportation, engineering capabilities, supply, distribution, base camp support, material handling, water purification, inspection of facilities, and PR to fill critical gaps in the humanitarian response.

2. Ground forces will also be instrumental for providing protection for the joint force and security for civilians, both victims and relief workers, as well as for USG departments and agencies, IGOs, and NGOs.

3. Ground forces may be able to provide health services.

See Appendix E, "Health and Medical Support in Foreign Humanitarian Assistance Operations," and JP 4-02, Health Services, *for a detailed discussion.*

(2) **CA.** CA assets are capable of supporting FHA operations in a variety of functional areas through planned civil affairs operations (CAO) or support to CMO. Commanders and their staffs assess the type and nature of CMO and CA support required by the CONOPS. This support includes six broad categories of CA functional specialty areas: rule of law, economic stability, governance, public health and welfare, infrastructure, and public education and information. CA core tasks include support to civil administration, PRC, FHA, NA, and CIM. CA assets can prove extremely valuable as the JFC's advisor on the impact of military activities on the civilian sector. CA assets assess infrastructure damage, assist in developing and managing temporary shelters, and are trained to operate within and coordinate activities with the CMOC. In the CMOC, CA personnel serve as liaison between military, diplomatic, and NGO participants in FHA operations.

(a) **Selection of CA Forces.** The functional composition of CA varies with mission, availability, and qualifications of CA. The Active Component (AC) of the Army provides two CA brigades: one designed to support SOF operations and another designed to support conventional forces. The majority of the Army's CA organizations are US Army Reserve and consist of commands, brigades, battalions, and companies capable of supporting SOF and conventional forces at the tactical, operational, and strategic levels. RC Army, Marine Corps (both AC and RC), and US Navy (RC) CA forces are considered conventional forces and are provided by the Services. C2 for CA forces should be clearly established in the deployment order and/or execute order.

(b) The early deployment of CA in the operational area can be a force multiplier, setting the stage for the introduction of follow-on forces into an environment that has benefited from detailed assessments and specialized interaction with the local population.

(c) CA should be assigned as a JTF staff element. Additionally, CA should be assigned to support the CMOC, the operations directorate of a joint staff (J-3), or JTF subordinate units, including a JCMOTF, if established.

(d) Following the rapid deployment of active duty CA and initial CA assessments that either validate or invalidate the original CMO estimate, a plan is developed that articulates the specific functional skills required to support the mission. The results of this assessment and recommended task organization flow from the supported CCDR to the Joint Staff for validation, feasibility assessment, and eventual resourcing. Resourcing will generally be provided by the regionally aligned CA commands found in the US Army Reserve, if available and the mission so dictates. Concurrently, requests for the Presidential Reserve Call-up (if required) or other authorities for mobilization are initiated through the Joint Staff and DOD. When authorized, reserve CA elements are mobilized and deployed.

(e) As with all aspects of an FHA operation, JFCs should make every effort to transition operations to civil control through the interagency community, the HN, and NGOs and IGOs. Early transition will support the possible reduction of the US forces committed to the FHA operation and allow those forces to be employed, if necessary, in support of other emerging contingencies.

(f) CIM is the process whereby civil information is collected, entered into a central database, and fused with the supported JFC, higher HQ, DOD and joint intelligence organizations, other DOD agencies, interagency partners, IGOs, NGOs, and the private sector to ensure the timely availability of information for analysis and the widest possible dissemination of the raw and analyzed civil information to military and nonmilitary partners.

(g) Civil reconnaissance is a targeted, planned, and coordinated observation and evaluation of those specific civil aspects of the environment. CA or other assets (e.g., engineer, medical, military police/security forces, HN or multinational organizations, unmanned aircraft systems, interagency partners, or intelligence systems) can conduct civil reconnaissance. The focus of collection in the JFC's operational area is the daily interaction between civilians and US forces. This results in capturing contacts and data points. In coordination with the CMOC, CAO and CMO planners integrate civil reconnaissance into the overall supported commander's plans and orders.

See JP 3-57, Civil-Military Operations, for specific guidance on planning and executing CAO.

(3) **MISO.** MISO are planned operations to convey selected information and indicators to foreign audiences to influence their emotions, motives, objective reasoning, and ultimately the behavior of foreign governments, organizations, groups, and individuals in a manner favorable to the originator's objectives. **MIS units can provide analysis of perceptions and attitudes of the civilian population and effectiveness of ongoing information and FHA operations.** MIS units provide language capability and equipment (radio broadcasting, print, audio, and audio visual) essential to disseminate necessary information to the populace. For example, during Operation PROVIDE COMFORT (April-July 1991 multinational relief effort in Eastern Turkey and Northern Iraq), MIS units disseminated information on relief camp procedures, organization, and food preparation.

Tactical MIS teams were considered the best force to control crowds and disseminate information. Videos informed distant population groups of camp existence and assistance resource locations.

(a) **During FHA operations, MIS units** assist in managing dislocated civilians. MIS units can provide health and safety messages, disseminate locations of shelter and food distribution points, warn of restricted or danger areas, and disseminate security information. For example, MIS units were employed successfully during Operation SAFE HAVEN (September 1994-March 1995 migrant camp operation in Panama). MIS units provided a critical capability in disseminating information throughout the migrant camps established during that operation.

(b) **The following considerations are provided for MIS in FHA operations:**

1. MISO must be coordinated with information-related capabilities to ensure that their complementary capabilities are integrated into synergistic plans that are fully coordinated and executed, and that consistent themes and messages are communicated. MIS and PA staffs should coordinate and deconflict activities to preclude any possible negative impact of one operation on the other, including information being disseminated by civilian HA organizations. The PA and CMO staffs must work in close coordination with the information operations (IO) planning staff, typically through IO cell meetings, to ensure a consistent message while maintaining operations security (OPSEC). MISO messages and other products are coordinated with other information activities to avoid conflicting messages. MISO information delivery capabilities can be used to disseminate public information products produced by PA in addition to messages developed by the MIS staff. Similarly, PA can highlight MISO efforts, when appropriate through PA efforts such as facilitating media coverage of successful MIS programs and actions (preventive medicine programs, reconciliation programs, show of force, rebuilding of symbolic infrastructure, public address by spokesperson, etc). As open sources to foreign countries and the US, PA channels can be used to disseminate timely, truthful, and accurate international information and counter propaganda directed against the operation and the US.

2. MIS units should either deploy with **organic transportation** or be provided adequate, dedicated vehicles for necessary mobility.

3. **MIS staff positions should be integrated into the JTF joint manning document to insure integration into JTF planning from its onset.** MIS staff ensure the entire staff understands the importance of integrating MISO into the overall plan to achieve the mission. An important aspect in early MISO planning is establishing the proper priority for **MIS** capability to flow into the operational area.

4. DOD humanitarian daily rations (HDRs) are printed with "A Food Gift from the People of the United States of America" on the packaging. There is intrinsic value in distributing goods unilaterally or with multinational partners. Cultural expectations, inferences, and taboos are considered prior to deciding on whether or not to include written **MISO** messages on relief products. **MIS** planners balance any written message against the value of distributing useful or essential goods with implicit rather than

explicit messages. The marking of aid packages should be consistent with USAID branding and marking guidelines.

JP 3-13.2, Military Information Support Operations, *provides specific guidance on planning and executing MISO.*

(4) **SOF.** SOF are agile and adaptable, can deploy rapidly, have excellent long-range communications equipment and unique capabilities, and operate effectively in the austere environments typical of FHA efforts. Perhaps the most important capabilities for SOF supporting FHA are their geographic orientation, cultural knowledge, language capabilities, and the ability to work with the local authorities and civilian population to provide initial and ongoing assessments.

For further details on SOF employment, refer to JP 3-05, Special Operations.

6. **Predeployment and Deployment**

a. GCCs coordinate with US embassies within their AORs to ensure that necessary overflight and transit en route agreements are negotiated to permit transit to operational areas to conduct and sustain FHA operations. DOS coordinates overflight and landing rights, diplomatic clearances, and visa and passport requirements for all deployment operations. Supporting GCCs should have overflight, transit, and staging agreements in place to support operations in other AORs, when appropriate.

For more information on current overflight/transit requirements, see the electronic DOD Foreign Clearance Guide (https://www.fcg.pentagon.mil); and for guidance on negotiating agreements, see DODD 5530.3, International Agreements.

b. **Deployment.** Deployment planning and execution considerations for FHA missions and other military operations are fundamentally the same. Joint force deployment is predicated on the severity of the humanitarian situation and the perception of US interests. It is important to remember that political factors drive military decisions and planning at every level. Mission analysis may validate the need for further assessments or the establishment of a lodgment, and in consultation with the component commanders, the JFC determines the deployment priority for all elements of the joint force. Force protection is an important part of this process.

(1) **Movement.** The joint force will obtain **strategic lift allocations and constraints** from USTRANSCOM via the CCDR. The **time-phased force and deployment data** for the operations must be developed to remain within these guidelines. USTRANSCOM provides **movement schedules** for deployment requirements in the sequence, or as near as possible to that requested by the joint force. The joint force staff should continually update all subordinate commands on deployment scheduling, situation, or mission changes. Such changes may require significant shifts in force deployment. Consideration should also be given to any deployment support requested by OFDA DART and USG departments and agencies, the UN, NGOs, and IGOs. FHA related movement of non-DOD people and relief supplies aboard DOD air and maritime assets usually requires specific lift authorizations from the CCDR and the Office of the Secretary of Defense.

(2) **Priority of Deployment.** Initial deployment for an FHA operation generally requires only critical **C2, communications systems; security; CMOC(s); PA, and logistic capabilities** (e.g., initial theater opening capability). Follow-on forces deploy as capabilities expand and requirements are better defined. However, US forces often conduct FHA operations in austere locations where airport and seaport facilities may be limited or inadequate. If the affected country has insufficient port offloading facilities, US personnel and equipment needed to establish or augment this capability should arrive prior to the primary force packages. In some cases, it may be necessary to expand existing facilities or construct new facilities to accommodate essential transshipment or the flow of forces into the country.

For more information, see JP 3-35, Deployment and Redeployment Operations.

7. **Other Planning Considerations**

a. **Simultaneous Operations.** The US military often will be engaged in several types of joint operations with different end states simultaneously across the range of military operations. Some military operations may be conducted for one purpose, such as disaster relief. However, others will have multiple purposes and will be influenced by a fluid and changing situation. Branch and sequel events may require additional tasks by the joint force (e.g., Operations PROVIDE RELIEF and RESTORE HOPE, 1992-1993, peace enforcement operations evolved from FHA efforts, which challenged the command with multiple missions). Furthermore, a crisis response or limited contingency operation may be initiated separately or as part of a campaign or major operation (e.g., the 1991 NEO in Somalia during Operation DESERT SHIELD). Foreign CBRN incidents may require the GCC or JFC to plan for multiple, concurrent operations including FHA, FCM, NEO, and forensics that will require coordination with different elements of the foreign emergency support team (FEST), US embassy, and HN. Joint forces must strive to meet such challenges with clearly defined objectives addressing diverse purposes.

b. **Interagency Planning.** Integrating the interagency community effectively can be vital to successful military operations, especially when JFCs operate in support of USG departments and agencies. JFCs and their staffs must consider how the capabilities of the joint force can be leveraged to accomplish the broader national strategic objectives by assisting the LFA. During planning, JFCs should coordinate directly with USG representatives within their operational areas to ensure appropriate agreements exist that support their plans (such as working with US embassies to secure overflight rights with other nations).

For more information on interagency planning, see JP 5-0, Joint Operation Planning.

c. **Multinational Planning.** Joint forces should be prepared for operations with forces from other nations within the framework of an alliance or coalition under US or multinational leadership. Planning for multinational operations is accomplished in multinational and national channels. Coordination of these separate planning channels occurs at the national level by established multinational bodies or PNs and at the theater-strategic and operational levels by JFCs, who are responsible within both channels for operation planning matters. US doctrine and procedures for JOPP also are conceptually applicable to multinational problems. The fundamental issues are much the same for both situations. For more specific guidance on NATO planning and execution, see appropriate publications within the doctrine hierarchy.

d. **Canada-US Civil Assistance Plan.** The Canada-US Civil Assistance Plan is a five-phase plan enabling US military forces to support Canadian military forces engaged in civil support operations. It provides collaborative planning for the deployment of US forces to support Canadian military forces, establishes a C2 construct for placing US forces under tactical control (TACON) of Canada Command, and provides that operations will be conducted in accordance with the HN's civil support plans (i.e., Canada Command Direction for Domestic Operations).

e. **Global Area Reference System (GARS).** GARS is an area referencing system which reaches all areas of the globe and can be used as a tool in synchronizing operations across multiple applications. Establishing a common reference system early in planning will enhance operational execution by mitigating confusion in geographic coordination.

For further information, refer to JP 2-03, Geospatial Intelligence in Joint Operations.

Intentionally Blank

CHAPTER IV
EXECUTION AND ASSESSMENT

"SEA SIGNAL quickly became a chameleon-like operation whose character changed constantly. Political and international dynamics, US policy changes, and issues of local concern required a constant re-evaluation of the situation, often producing considerable change to the nature and scope of the mission."

Operation SEA SIGNAL
After Action Report
Joint Task Force 160
2 February 1996

1. Introduction

This chapter highlights aspects of joint force execution and assessment related to FHA operations.

2. Deployment

The capability to deploy forces to the operational area and rapidly integrate them into the joint force as directed by the JFC is essential. The joint deployment process consists of four phases: planning; predeployment activities; movement; and JRSOI. JRSOI can be the most challenging phase in FHA operations. Supported GCCs are responsible for JRSOI within their AORs. This includes all actions required to make arriving units operationally ready and integrated into the joint force. Challenges arise when the operational area has been severely impacted by the incident or disaster and US forces have had no presence or routine access to the operational area. HN, multinational, and contractor support may not be feasible during the initial stages of an FHA operation, but they normally are available to support JRSOI.

More detailed information may be found in JP 3-35, Deployment and Redeployment Operations.

3. Sustainment

a. Logistic planners estimate assistance requirements and assess organic, theater support, and affected country capabilities to meet the forecasted need. Inherent risks and logistic objectives should also be identified. **Emphasis must be placed upon locating logistic bases as close as possible to the relief recipients.** Should relief recipients be located within a major population center, all reasonable measures should be taken when establishing logistic bases that prevent migration of relief recipients from their economic and social areas. **All potential supply sources should be considered,** including affected country, commercial, multinational, and pre-positioned supplies. Lessons learned indicate that logistics and the associated support facilities and infrastructure necessary to sustain an FHA operation are frequently underestimated. FHA operations are logistic intensive and will most likely include significant engineering requirements. Therefore, **the overall logistic**

concept should be closely tied into the operational strategy and be mutually supporting.
This includes actions to:

(1) Identify time-phased materiel requirements, facilities, and other resources.
Remote and austere locations may require deployment of materials-handling equipment and
pre-positioned stocks.

(2) Identify support methods and procedures required to meet air, land, and
maritime lines of communications (LOCs).

(3) Establish procedures and means to coordinate and control materiel movements
to and within the operational area. Priorities may be established using apportionment
systems, providing the commander with the flexibility to reinforce priority efforts with
additional assets.

(4) Determine availability of sea-based operations as an effective means of
delivering aid ashore for FHA without requiring infrastructure or sustainment support from
the HN.

(5) Plan for the security of materials and supplies is imperative.

b. For the FHA operation to succeed, the commander must be able to fulfill priorities
through adequate resource control. Logisticians, in conjunction with operational planners,
must consider which equipment and supplies may be left behind at the completion of the
mission. Supplies and equipment cannot be arbitrarily left behind and donated to the HN.
Supplies and equipment left behind as a result of HA support operations must be in
accordance with all applicable Federal laws and statutes relating to the donation or transfer
of military articles and supplies. Consult legal counsel prior to any release of supplies and
equipment.

c. **Logistic Database Information.** Automated information systems used in FHA
include the following:

(1) **Disaster Assistance Logistics Information System (DALIS).** DALIS was
designed by the US Army to enhance the operations of one or more logistic coordination
centers supporting multiple worldwide FHA operations.

(2) **Commodity Tracking System (CTS).** CTS is a computer program developed
by the UNHCR as a warehouse and logistic management tool. CTS uses DALIS for its basic
design.

(3) **Integrated Data Environment/Global Transportation Network
Convergence (IGC).** IGC is a standardized DOD system that provides access to
transportation data inputs from a wide variety of in-transit visibility systems. Users can
query the IGC database to track cargo and passengers from origin to destination, anywhere in
the Defense Transportation System.

(4) **Logistics Support System (LSS).** A software program developed by several UN agencies, governments, and NGOs to improve the management of humanitarian aid, by strengthening the national capacity to manage effectively the humanitarian supplies. Not a tracking system, LSS provides coordinating bodies with an overall picture of what has been pledged and what has arrived for a specific emergency.

d. **Contracting Support.** Integrating contracting and contractor management functions into military planning and operations is a complex and very challenging process. Multiple joint and Service component organizations are involved in this process including commanders and the primary and special staffs at the CCMD through major tactical force levels. Additionally, numerous contracting organizations from inside and outside the operational area play a vital role in contracting and contractor management planning and contract execution. Finally, developing the contracting support plans and conducting the associated contractor integration planning crosses most joint force and Service component primary and special staff lanes; yet most of these staffs are unfamiliar with the contracting process and associated contractor integration challenges. Contracting support may be obtained from within or outside the affected country. Military forces should not compete for scarce civilian resources. To avoid competition for similar support and to promote economy of contracting effort, contracts for logistic support must be coordinated through the designated J-4 or lead agent for logistics joint contracting support board or center. Logisticians should be thoroughly familiar with contracting options available through the **Navy's global contingency construction and Services contracts,** the **Army's logistics civil augmentation program,** and the **Air Force contract augmentation program.** All three of these contracting options are designed to be flexible in order to address emergent requirements worldwide which can aid the economy of the affected country and facilitate the subsequent transfer of responsibility to the affected country, NGOs, or IGOs.

DODI 3020.41, Operational Contract Support (OCS), *provides comprehensive DOD policy on the subject of contractor personnel management in contingency operations and JP 4-10,* Operational Contract Support, *provides common contracting and contractor management doctrine principles.*

e. **Cluster Management and Support.** A cluster, activated by the UN humanitarian coordinator with the permission of the ERC, is a group of organizations and other stakeholders, with a designated lead, working in an area of humanitarian response in which gaps have been identified. These areas include some traditional relief and assistance sectors (i.e., water and sanitation, nutrition, health, emergency shelter); service provision (i.e., emergency telecommunications, logistics); and cross-cutting issues (i.e., camp coordination, early recovery, protection). The nature of the emergency determines which clusters become active. Clusters are organized at both field and global level. In more traditional terminology, clusters may be termed as "sectors," "sectoral groups," and "sector leads" (or in some cases, "working groups" or "thematic groups"). Clusters provide a framework for organizing the humanitarian response in a similar manner as lines of operation define the orientation of the joint force in time and space or purpose in relation to an objective.

Appendix D, "Humanitarian Intergovernmental and Nongovernmental Organizations," paragraph 9, "United Nations Cluster Approach," contains more information on the cluster approach.

4. Command and Control

a. **FHA operations must include responsibility for air, land, maritime, space, and SOF.** It is especially necessary to delegate authority to establish supply or transportation priorities. **Delegation speeds decision making** and reaction to changes in life-threatening situations faced in many FHA operations. Although there is no command relationship between military forces and other USG departments and agencies, UN agencies, NGOs, IGOs, affected country elements, and foreign governments, **clearly defined relationships may foster harmony and reduce friction** between participating organizations.

b. **Communications. Effective communications systems are vital to planning, conducting, and sustaining successful FHA operations.** Operations, logistic, and intelligence functions depend on responsive communications. **Communications are the central system that not only ties together all aspects of joint operations, but also allows C2 of forces.** Therefore, the FHA plan must include procedures to provide interoperable and compatible communications among participants. Commercial telephone networks, military satellite channels, and conventional military C2 systems will support communication of directions, orders, and information. Commercial communications systems can be used to coordinate with other USG departments and agencies, disseminate meeting schedules, deconflict resource movement, and track logistic flow. **Direct communications between commanders and nonmilitary organizations should be established** to facilitate effective collaboration and decision making. Peer to peer networks (desktop software designed to facilitate collaboration and communication among small groups) are also used by NGOs. Information protection for nonsecured communications must be implemented. Additionally, communications systems planning must consider the termination or transition of US involvement and the transfer of responsibility to other agencies such as the UN or NGOs. Frequency management will **help allocate finite frequency availability.** The HN government (if functioning) may control frequency management. FHA forces may not have exclusive use of frequencies. Some FHA related interagency communications can be greatly facilitated by utilizing a web-based approach to disseminate information. One example of such an unclassified web tool is the All Partners Access Network (APAN).

c. **Interoperability. Identify communications equipment interoperability among all participants.** It is likely that civilian USG departments and agencies, HN agencies, and multinational forces will have their own communications networks. These may include commercial leased circuits and satellite services as well as high-frequency radio equipment. CMOCs should be equipped with communication equipment that facilitates collaboration with all participants. The need for interoperability of communications equipment in FHA operations may also necessitate using unclassified communications. US military forces may face challenges in conducting operations via unclassified means in order to promote interorganizational coordination and synchronization. The use of classified and unclassified modes of communication are both necessary, as classified modes are routinely used to relay militarily significant information while unclassified modes are needed for communication with nonmilitary entities. Write for release techniques include portion marking, the use of tear lines, and sanitizing sensitive text.

d. **Reporting.** USG department and agency reports will be consolidated into normal country team reporting procedures and structures with increased frequency, as directed. In more complex situations, DOS will activate a "crisis action task force" which will establish reporting procedures that will likely be via a collaborative portal so that all USG reports are consolidated in one location. The JFC should expect to coordinate on reports on country activities with the country team; this is in addition to any DOD or GCC directed reporting requirements. The joint force staff will encounter numerous other USG departments and agencies, NGOs, and IGOs that produce reports on the OE and joint force actions. The COM's cable, the USAID representative's reports, and DART reports are reviewed by the DOS and other USG departments and agencies. Additionally, other elements of the country team produce reports on the same issues about which the joint force staff reports. **Despite efforts to maintain accuracy, the proliferation of reports may result in conflicting information.** One approach to deconflicting reports is to **develop a consolidated report between the joint force and the country team.** Posting consolidated reports to APAN will also serve to reduce administrative overhead while reducing opportunities for conflicting information to surface. As an additional consideration, information provided by NGOs and IGOs should not be identified by organization on reports that may be seen outside the USG. To do otherwise would jeopardize the organization's standing and possibly their staff's safety.

e. **Operational Areas.** Particularly when the JOA is large, the JFC may organize the JOA into areas of operations in consultation with NGOs, IGOs, other USG departments and agencies, and in consideration of the organization already established by the affected country. In establishing boundaries, planners should consider existing political subdivisions, ethnic or traditional tribal boundaries, political affiliations, relief agency areas, political and cultural acceptance of other nations' forces, and contiguous areas with forces assigned. If possible, a CMOC should be established within each operational area capable of working with agencies in the area as well as the OSOCC (through the joint force HQ). The JFC will also normally designate an area of influence and an area of interest (AOI).

More detailed information on operational areas may be found in JP 3-0, Joint Operations.

5. **Assessment**

a. The JFC should evaluate task performance and measure effects and determine the progress of operations toward achieving objectives. MOEs assess changes in system behavior, capability, or OE. MOEs in FHA operations should be based on impact indicators that measure the change in the lives of the people on the ground, rather than process indicators that calculate USG efforts and their immediate outputs. MOPs measure task performance. MOPs are generally quantitative, but also can apply qualitative attributes to task accomplishment. Well-devised measures can help the commanders and staffs understand the causal relationship between specific tasks and desired effects. MOEs assist the commander in determining when the situation has been returned to pre-disaster conditions.

b. **Developing MOEs.** During the JOPP for FHA operations, as with any operation, there is no singular established method for developing MOEs. MOEs will vary according to the mission and the effects desired by the JFC. However, commanders and staffs should keep certain factors in mind when developing and using MOEs in FHA operations. MOEs may be difficult to develop; the assessment process and related measures should be relevant, measurable, responsive, and resourced so there is no false impression of accomplishment. MOEs should also be based upon the US military objectives, lines of operation, and end states to ensure that the JFC is measuring those effects within the joint force's control. While the military objectives support the national objectives, tying military MOEs to tasks to be accomplished by others does not accurately reflect progress towards completion of the military mission. In nearly all FHA operations, the military will be working in support of or alongside other USG departments and agencies and international partners. Most of these nonmilitary actors conduct their own assessment. However, they generally use different terminologies and methods. Military assessment staff should become familiar with the terminology of the agencies and entities operating within the operational area.

For further information on assessment, see JP 5-0, Joint Operation Planning, *and the* Commander's Handbook for Assessment Planning and Execution, Joint Coalition Warfighting, *found at http://www.dtic.mil/doctrine/doctrine/jwfc_pam.htm.*

c. **Possible MOEs.** It is normally appropriate to base MOEs for FHA on the *Sphere Project Humanitarian Charter and Minimum Standards in Disaster Response.* The Sphere Project, developed by governments (including the USG), IGOs, and NGOs involved in HA, recommends key indicators for provision of water, sanitation, food, health, shelter, and non-food items in disasters, and establishes voluntary minimum standards for each sector. The *Sphere Project Humanitarian Charter and Minimum Standards in Disaster Response* are nonbinding. MOEs in FHA operations could include:

(1) Decrease in mortality rates in the affected population, below a specified level per day.

(2) Increase in water available to each disaster victim per day to various levels established for human consumption, sanitation measures, and for livestock consumption.

(3) Decrease in population of dislocated civilians to a level sustainable by the affected country or non-US military organizations. (Another aspect of this MOE is the increase in the number of persons per day returning to their homes.)

(4) Decrease in incidence of disease to an acceptable or manageable level.

(5) Increase in the presence and capabilities of NGOs and IGOs.

d. The impact of FHA cannot be measured only in terms of supplies shipped; the ultimate test comes from judging whether lives have been saved and communities revived. This is a complex and long-term process, and to find answers, USAID has developed the following four areas for assessing performance:

MEASURES OF EFFECTIVENESS IN OPERATION SUPPORT HOPE

During Operation SUPPORT HOPE, the joint force tracked several specific measures of effectiveness (MOEs) to ascertain when it had accomplished its assigned mission. These MOEs included:

• The refugee population in Goma, Zaire dropped from 1,200,000 on 26 July 1994 to 575,000 on 26 August 1994 (Numbers of refugees were estimates only);

• The estimated mortality rate in Goma camps, based on bodies buried per day, dropped from 6,500 per day on 27 July 1994 to less than 500 per day on 1 August 1994;

• Cargo capacity at Kigali, Rwanda airfield increased from virtually zero on 30 July 1994 to 300-600 tons per day on 26 August 1994; and

• The number of United Nations agencies and nongovernmental agencies represented in Kigali grew from 6 on 22 July 1994 to over 60 on 26 August 1994. This increase represented adequate nonmilitary capability to provide humanitarian assistance.

Various Sources

(1) **First, the structure for responding to disasters and to the needs of countries in crisis and transition must be in place.** Before crises occur, USAID—in close coordination with other agencies of the USG, multilateral agencies, and local authorities—will ascertain the following:

(a) Have supplies been stockpiled and service providers identified? Are supplies secure from loss and theft? When USAID moves to deliver goods and services, will they go to the right place in the right amount with the intended effect?

(b) Have the prevention, mitigation, and preparedness activities of USAID anticipated needs and are they effective? Have local communities and businesses been enlisted for planning, prevention, and response?

(c) Do proposed shipments of supplies match and maximize local skills and capacities? In view of past disasters locally and regionally, are preparations commensurate with likely needs?

(d) Are the partnerships and relations with the UN (including the World Food Programme [WFP]) understood by all? Are mechanisms in place to coordinate supplies, donations, and offers of skilled labor and ensure that they are delivered where and when they are needed?

(2) **Second, actual delivery of supplies and services must be timely and effective.** During crises, USAID and its partners will determine the following:

(a) Do disaster relief supplies and services reach their intended destination in time to make a difference? Are all forms of emergency relief supplies readily available and accessible to the intended beneficiaries, including women, children, the elderly, local people, refugees, and members of minorities?

(b) Do specific programs intended to save lives or reduce malnutrition, such as emergency feeding programs, have the intended impact?

(c) Are profiteering and misuse effectively controlled? Are food and other relief supplies distributed so as not to discourage local production or distort local prices and markets?

(d) Do programs of disease control and emergency medical services (including immunizations, child survival interventions, and maternal and reproductive health care) have access to necessary supplies, and are they coordinated with food and nutrition interventions?

(3) **Third, in transitional and crisis situations, assistance must target the institutions and needs critical to the resumption of sustained development, civil life, and democratic governance.** USAID and its partners will determine the following:

(a) Has the response to countries in crisis and transition been appropriate to their needs, political situation, and indigenous capacities?

(b) Have national and local political institutions been strengthened? Have key elements of the infrastructure, such as housing, communications, basic transportation, and financial services been reinforced? Are the specific needs of IDPs and refugees being addressed?

(c) Has food security increased throughout the country? Do farmers have greater access to seed, fertilizer, and appropriate technology? Has local food production increased significantly, and are more people able to acquire the income needed to purchase food?

(d) Has there been measurable progress toward national reconciliation and invigoration of the mechanisms of conflict resolution, as indicated by fair and open elections, constitutional conventions, new legal codes, reintegration of combatants, etc? Is there evidence of decreased disorder in cities and in the countryside? Is there increased respect for human rights?

(4) **Fourth, follow-on mechanisms, after relief and rehabilitation, must be in place to help prevent cycles of crisis and to permit countries to cope with their own natural disasters and political crises.** After the crisis stage has passed, USAID and its partners will determine the following:

(a) In conjunction with local authorities and communities and multilayer institutions, is USAID developing and implementing long-term development programs that measurably enhance the ability of countries to anticipate and manage disasters? Are the economic, political, environmental, social, and institutional causes of man-made disasters being addressed?

(b) Have countries in crisis and transition made measurable progress toward a political and economic transformation?

(5) Ultimately, HA activities must be measured by simple, yet profound standards. Do these activities prevent human misery that is avoidable? Do they provide relief for human misery that is not avoidable? Does this assistance help countries that have suffered natural or man-made disasters and crises return to the path of sustainable development?

For more detail, see Appendix F, "Planning Factors for Foreign Humanitarian Assistance and Foreign Disaster Relief Operations."

6. Intelligence

a. **Intelligence and information gathering in FHA operations should be broadly focused** and include collection concerning political, military, paramilitary, ethnic, religious, economic, medical, environmental, geospatial, and criminal indicators. The primary intelligence effort should answer the commander's **priority intelligence requirements (PIRs)** to accomplish the mission. While normally this involves assessing potential threats to the FHA mission (from forces external and internal to the affected population), the unique aspects of FHA operations may result in significant or even primary emphasis placed upon logistic or political intelligence and intelligence support to CA and MISO. Available means of intelligence sourcing should be fused into tailored data useful for deployment planning, mission requirements, and projected requirements. As soon as practical after it is determined that a crisis may develop or a contingency is declared, JFCs and their staffs begin analyzing to determine the intelligence requirements needed to support the anticipated operation. Human intelligence (HUMINT) and open-source intelligence are often the primary sources of information. However, crises may occur without warning and in regions with no HUMINT sources. When there are limited HUMINT assets, commanders must ensure that only appropriately trained and certified personnel are authorized to conduct HUMINT operations in accordance with DOD policy. Depending on CCDR needs, intelligence assets can provide persistent coverage for situational awareness or precise information to answer PIRs. These are considered as part of the collection strategy and are used to formulate a collection plan.

b. **Force protection is a priority for intelligence collection.** Collection plans are developed around various considerations and priorities, including force protection, PIR, information gaps, and the hostile penetration of a country's internal affairs. Counterintelligence (CI) support plays a crucial role in force protection. CI liaison activities with host country security institutions and PNs involved in FHA can provide a significant source of force protection-related intelligence. A comprehensive intelligence analysis can help commanders avoid hostilities during the conduct of FHA missions. Intelligence operations during FHA operations are generally conducted in the same manner as in any other military operation.

c. **An intelligence architecture for the operation is required** to enable the commander to fuse all-source intelligence in a timely manner, enhancing visualization of the OE. Provisions and systems should be established to collaborate with governments for which no previously established intelligence agreements exist. Consideration should be given to the growing dependency on **imagery assets** to enhance information gathering. **National, theater, and tactical collection systems** and related production agencies can be tasked to provide various intelligence-related products detailing the crisis area. Examples of how imagery can be used include determining the status of an area's transportation network following an earthquake or locating large groups of dislocated civilians.

d. NGOs and IGOs should not be perceived as providing intelligence to the military. Consideration should be given to answering the information requirements of adjacent task forces as well as theater- and national-level requirements. Classification and releasability standards for intelligence and sensitive information should be determined early in the planning process and reviewed as the operation proceeds.

(1) To share critical intelligence information with multinational partners efficiently, US intelligence information should be written for release at the lowest possible classification level and given the fewest possible dissemination restrictions within foreign disclosure guidelines. The J-2 must establish procedures and methods for separating intelligence from sources and methods. Intelligence production agencies often print highly classified reports in such a manner that compartmented information is separated from intelligence that can be widely disseminated by a "tear line" (the J-2 and component intelligence staff officers keep information above the tear line and disseminate the intelligence below). Having intelligence production agencies use such tear lines will greatly facilitate intelligence sharing.

(2) The joint force J-2, or delegated representative, obtains all the necessary foreign disclosure authorization from the Defense Intelligence Agency (DIA), national agencies, and other originators of controlled classified information as soon as possible to allow for the seamless transfer of information to foreign partners engaged in joint operations. The efficient flow of intelligence is enhanced by assigning trained and certified foreign disclosure personnel.

7. Information Sharing

a. Information sharing is critical to the efficient pursuit of a common humanitarian purpose. Although many different groups and authorities can (and should) work in parallel, a collaborative information environment (CIE) facilitates information sharing. Constructing a CIE is not primarily a technology issue—effective, low-cost, network equipment and data management systems exist today, and more are being developed. Rather, the challenges are largely social, institutional, cultural, and organizational. These impediments can limit and shape the willingness of civilian and military personnel and organizations to openly cooperate and share information and capabilities.

b. The components of civil-military coordination consist of information and task sharing and collaborative planning—all of which depend on communications and management of data and information. The following issues, however, often complicate effective civil-military coordination:

(1) Lack of understanding about the information culture of the affected nation.

(2) Suspicions regarding the balance between information sharing and intelligence gathering.

(3) Tensions between military needs for classification (secrecy) of data, versus the civilian need for transparency.

(4) Differences in C2 between military operations versus civilian activities.

(5) The compatibility and interoperability of planning tools, processes, and civil-military organization cultures.

c. The sharing of information is particularly critical because no single responding entity—whether it is an NGO, IGO, assisting country government or host government—can be the source of all of the required data and information. Making critical information widely available to multiple responding civilian and military elements not only reduces duplication of effort, but also enhances coordination and collaboration and provides a common knowledge base so that critical information can be pooled, analyzed, compared, contrasted, validated, and reconciled. Civil-military collaboration networks need to be designed to dismantle traditional institutional stovepipes and facilitate the sharing of information among civilian and military organizations. Web based tools such as APAN can facilitate this information sharing process.

d. Foreign disclosure procedures should be prescribed in annex O (Foreign Disclosure Guidance) to the OPLAN or OPORD and utilized to the maximum extent feasible. These procedures must account for the totality of the disclosure requirements necessary to support FHA. Planners and disclosure personnel must collaborate during mission analysis to identify disclosure requirements and obtain necessary disclosure support for all relevant categories of classified military information.

For more information on foreign disclosure, see DODD 5230-11, Disclosure of Classified Military Information to Foreign Governments and International Organizations, *DODI 5200.01,* DOD Information Security Program and Protection of Sensitive Compartmented Information, *and CJCSI 5221.01C,* Delegation of Authority to Commanders of Combatant Commands to Disclose Classified Military Information to Foreign Governments and International Organizations.

8. Protection

a. For the joint force, **force protection is a high priority.** Even in a permissive environment, the joint force can expect to encounter banditry, vandalism, and various levels of violent activities from criminals or unruly crowds. It is imperative that the joint force be trained and equipped to mitigate threats to US personnel, resources, facilities, and critical information. All deploying members should be provided with threat and force protection briefings prior to and throughout the duration of the operation.

b. As in any operation, **force protection in FHA is enhanced by establishing effective** CI support and by practicing strict OPSEC.

CI support will be conducted in accordance with JP 2-01.2, Counterintelligence and Human Intelligence Support to Joint Operations *(classified document).*

c. In addition to force protection and PR for the joint force, **a JFC may also be tasked to provide protection for other personnel and assets.** If not clearly stated in the mission, the extent of this security should be addressed in the ROE, to include protection of:

(1) Forces of other nations working jointly with US forces in a multinational force.

(2) USG, NGO, and IGO personnel and equipment.

(3) HA recipients.

(4) Affected country personnel and assets.

(5) Humanitarian relief convoys, supplies, and main supply routes.

(6) Relief distribution centers.

(7) Stocks of HA supplies.

(8) Ports and airfields.

(9) Hospitals and medical clinics.

d. **Nonlethal Weapons.** Nonlethal weapons provide an additional tool for force protection that may be particularly useful during FHA operations in which the use of lethal force may jeopardize strategic objectives. Nonlethal weapons are weapons, devices, and munitions that are explicitly designed and primarily employed to incapacitate targeted personnel or materiel immediately, while minimizing fatalities, permanent injury to personnel, and undesired damage to property in the target area or environment. Nonlethal weapons are intended to have reversible effects on personnel and material.

e. **ERW.** When conducting FHA operations in an area affected by war or civil strife, **security missions may include counter-IED operations, mine-clearing, and other ordnance disposal efforts.** These types of missions may be necessary in order to facilitate the protection of FHA personnel, LOCs, mission-related facilities, and designated areas. Explosive ordnance disposal personnel, special agent bomb technicians from the Department of Justice, or other explosive experts may provide this critical capability for the JFC. There are also a number of joint assets that can provide exploitation and analysis on collected ordnance and weapons.

For more information on the exploitation of improvised weapons, including IEDs, see JP 3-15.1, Counter Improvised Explosive Device Operations, *and the* Weapons Technical Intelligence Handbook.

f. Regardless of the environment, security must be factored into force requirements and support capability. In FHA operations, sustainment forces will require a substantial amount of their troops to protect unit and individual property.

g. During the conduct of FHA operations there is a potential for US military forces to operate in the proximity of CBRN contaminated sites. Commanders force protection plans must take this into account (including utilization of personal radiation exposure monitoring devices).

For further guidance on the sources of CBRN hazards (to include toxic industrial materials, their effects, and force protection against radiological hazards [to include setting and managing operational exposure guidance), refer to the Office of the Secretary of Defense (Policy) Revised Radiological Clearance Criteria Guidelines for Platforms and Materiel.

h. PR is one of the highest priorities in the DOD. Even in a permissive environment, a joint force can expect to encounter threats that can isolate its personnel. JFCs are responsible for including PR capabilities as a means to protect the force.

PR will be conducted in accordance with JP 3-50, Personnel Recovery.

9. Engineer Operations

a. FHA operations can be extremely engineer-intensive. In such cases, the JFC may opt to establish a subordinate JTF to control extensive engineer operations and missions. Such a JTF may be formed around an existing engineer command or naval construction group or regiment. Engineer forces could be placed under OPCON, TACON, or in a supporting role. The engineer assets attached to the subordinate JTF will normally be made up of a mix of engineer assets drawn from the entire force's engineer resources. If the subordinate JTF is to provide a common support capability, it will require a specific delegation of directive authority from the CCDR for the common support capability that is to be provided.

b. In addition to USG departments and agencies, the joint force engineer and staff may have to coordinate engineering activities with NGOs. NGOs may have unique engineering capabilities that can be leveraged as part of the overall operational effort. One example of great interest to engineers is their ability to conduct humanitarian demining operations. These organizations may also request extensive military engineer support for their activities and programs. It is critical to establish an effective engineer liaison in the CMOC to coordinate and execute engineering support with these organizations.

c. Typical engineer missions for FHA include:

(1) Training.

(2) Construction of rudimentary surface transportation systems.

(3) Well drilling.

(4) Clearing debris.

(5) Construction of relief centers and camps for dislocated civilians.

(6) Sanitation.

(7) Potable water production and distribution.

(8) Emergency power and lighting.

(9) Restoring public facilities and transportation routes.

(10) Reestablishing rudimentary utilities.

(11) Support to urban SAR.

(12) Construction of temporary facilities.

(13) Specialized underwater services to include clearing of obstacles, survey of port facilities, and salvage of vessels.

d. The level of assistance can vary from limited, highly specialized teams to complete engineer units. Limited teams are used to assess damage or estimate engineering repairs and can assist in specialized support such as power supply and distribution, utilities repair work, water purification, and well drilling operations. In large FHA operations, engineer units provide essential general engineering support including facility construction, structural repair, and camp construction for deployed forces. Initially, US military forces may be the only organization in the JOA capable of providing assistance, and military engineers could potentially be tasked to provide extensive cleanup and construction services. Requests for military support, including engineering support, should be initiated and coordinated through the LFA.

For additional information on engineer operations, refer to JP 3-34, Joint Engineer Operations.

10. Rules of Engagement

ROE are the directives issued by competent military authority that delineate the circumstances and limitations under which US forces will initiate and/or continue combat engagement with other forces encountered. **ROE define when and how force may be used.** CJCSI 3121.01, *Standing Rules of Engagement/Standing Rules for the Use of Force for US Forces* (classified document), provides ROE that apply to US forces during all military operations, unless directed otherwise by SecDef. **For each specific operation the JFC, in conjunction with the J-3 and the SJA, develops ROE** (as soon as possible after notification of the deployment) **within the framework of the standing rules of engagement (SROE).** The ROE should specifically address nonlethal force options and employment considerations. The proposed JTF ROE must be forwarded to the Joint Staff for SecDef review and approval prior to promulgation. In many situations, the mission may require specific ROE measures in addition to the basic SROE. Supplemental measures in the SROE enable the commander to obtain or grant those additional authorities or restraints necessary to accomplish the mission. The JFC must submit the changes through the appropriate approving official. **When multinational forces are under US control, US commanders need to ensure that those forces interpret the ROE in the same manner as US forces.** When multinational forces not under US control are involved, US commanders should request that those forces adopt or agree to ROE similar to or compatible with those in effect for US forces. ROE are a national responsibility and reflect domestic policy and laws, and the international law obligations of a PN. While desirable, it may not always be possible to align all PN ROE for this reason. Therefore as a minimum, US commanders must understand the differences in the various participating countries' ROE and the impact on operations.

For additional information on ROE, see Appendix A, "Legal Issues."

11. Legal Considerations

Many aspects of FHA operations require scrutiny by legal experts. Key members of both the planning and operations staffs and **SJAs should review and assist in analyzing and preparing SOFAs, ROE, fiscal law guidance, plans and orders, and especially any agreements or memoranda of understanding** established between US forces, multinational forces, and the affected country or nonmilitary organizations involved in FHA operations.

12. Liaison

Direct, early liaison with UN and other humanitarian relief agencies is a valuable source of accurate, timely information on many aspects of the crisis area. USG, UN, NGO, or IGO involvement is likely to precede that of US or multinational forces and presents an opportunity to enhance early force effectiveness significantly. A key additional benefit is an opportunity to build working relationships based upon trust and open communications among all organizations. For that reason, **ongoing liaison with other multinational forces** participating in the operation is equally important. Early in the operation FHA planners should ensure that sufficient, competent linguists be available for translation and interpretation requirements by the HN and the multinational forces. Regionally aligned CA personnel are well suited for liaison tasks.

For further details concerning LNOs, refer to JP 3-33, Joint Task Force Headquarters.

13. Communication Synchronization

a. For specific situations, the USG provides top-down strategic guidance relative to using the informational instrument of national power in specific situations. Implementation of the strategic guidance and synchronizing communications is facilitated through defense support to public diplomacy (DSPD) and military diplomacy activities.

b. Demonstrating US involvement in FHA operations can be extremely valuable to the image of the US supporting the achievement of US goals as well as those of the GCC's TCP. Activities that support communication synchronization inform affected populations about ongoing efforts and assist in achieving JTF objectives. Communication activities are also key in achieving strategic objectives in the region by reinforcing themes and messages regarding US goodwill evidenced by ongoing FHA operations. Care should be taken not to raise expectations about the speed or amount of assistance that may be provided, as US involvement in an operation may automatically result in unrealistic expectations of assistance among the population. Unmet expectations may result in suspicion, resentment, and mistrust of HA providers. Many NGOs prefer to avoid perceptions of being aligned or affiliated with DOD forces in any case. Likewise, JFCs and their staffs must exercise care in communication so that, in their attempts to demonstrate DOD responsiveness, concern, and assistance, they do not preempt the authority of the HN political leadership or appear to be taking credit for successes at the expense of other contributing parties.

c. Effective coordination and collaboration among all the information-related capabilities are necessary to ensure unity of effort and consistency in the information being disseminated. The COM, as the senior US representative in each HN, controls the release of official US information in country. To facilitate unity of effort and coordinated content, the PA staff should coordinate all themes, messages, and press releases impacting an FHA operation through the respective US embassy channels.

d. **IO.** When conducting an FHA mission, generating goodwill for the services rendered and departing with a favorable impression of US activities becomes a secondary objective. Effective employment of MISO and OPSEC is important in FHA operations:

(1) MISO are a vital part of the broad range of US activities to influence foreign audiences directly through the use of radio, print, and other media. To be effective, peacetime MISO are conducted in accordance with DODD 3600.01, *Information Operations,* and require interagency coordination and authorization at the national level.

(2) **OPSEC.** JFCs provide OPSEC guidance and identify critical information to all supporting commands, subordinate commands, other agencies, and appropriate PA offices. JFCs also coordinate OPSEC measures and their execution with other commands and agencies of those activities.

e. **Synchronization.** Synchronized planning of IO, MISO, PA, visual information (VI), and DSPD is essential for effective communication synchronization. Interagency efforts provide and promote international support for nations in the region and provide an opportunity to advance regional and global partnerships. JFCs should ensure that their IO, MISO, PA, VI, and DSPD planning is consistent with theater strategic objectives and overall USG objectives. These objectives are established and approved by SecDef, and are supported by the CCDRs. All activities must support these objectives to ensure a clear and concise message is conveyed to the HN at all levels of interaction. Since PA, VI, MISO, and IO support the dissemination of information themes and messages to their respective audiences, their activities must be closely coordinated and synchronized to ensure consistency and to avoid loss of credibility by the joint force and other USG PA spokespersons. All forces engaging with the HN population and entities must also understand these objectives. Planning considerations should address the fact that NGOs, IGOs, and other civilian organizations may have competing messages within the operational area.

> *"JPASE [joint public affairs support element] teams were an essential part of our mission in Pakistan following the earthquake that devastated that country. They explained our mission to both Pakistani and International audiences, and above all, communicated our commitment to help the people of Pakistan. Their ability to get our messages was a top factor in the overall success of the mission."*
>
> **Rear Admiral Mike LeFever, US Navy**
> **Commander, Combined Disaster Assistance Center—Pakistan**
> **April 2006**

14. Public Affairs

a. **Overview.** PA should be involved during initial FHA operational planning because disseminating information to the public and engaging with the news media are critical to mission success. Keeping domestic and international audiences informed of US support for FHA can also assist in communication, synchronization, and security cooperation goals. However, publicizing assistance efforts should not impede relief operations nor put aid workers or beneficiaries at risk. Coordination with the HN via the country team is critical to ensure public information activities do not undermine or conflict with the efforts of the HN. The PA staff performs the following functions:

(1) Provides advice to the CCDR and staff on the public implications of potential and actual FHA operations.

(2) Identifies force structure, equipment, and logistics requirements for PA support to specific operations.

(3) Evaluates the need for JPASE support and facilitates requests.

(4) Establishes liaison with PA counterparts (i.e., country team, HN, NGOs, IGOs) in the operational area.

(5) Participates in planning.

(6) Plans and synchronizes US military public information strategies and resources in order to communicate timely, factual, unclassified information about FHA operations.

(7) Participates in all applicable cross-functional staff organizations (e.g., IO cell).

(8) Provides media support/operates the MOC.

(9) Conducts analysis and assessment of public communication efforts.

b. **Organization.** The size and organization of the PA staff for FHA will depend on mission and operational requirements and the anticipated media interest. Generally, the PAO and staff are located in the JFC HQ, while the MOC is located in a secure area that is both convenient to the media and has good connectivity and access to JFC's PA staff. There may be existing media centers set up by other agencies with opportunities for partnerships.

c. **Public Information.** FHA operations generate substantial media interest for which the JFC, PAO, and staff must be prepared. Mass distribution of information via the media is critical to creating public awareness of US and PNs' policies and objectives. Explaining what the US intends to achieve and why it is important helps gain public understanding and support for the operation and also counters efforts to portray US and partner activities and intentions in a negative light.

(1) The media will endeavor to get to the scene of relief activities as soon as possible and cover operations. Supporting their efforts supports the JFC's public information mission. Media should have as much access as possible throughout the operation. Information shall be made fully and readily available and shall be withheld only when disclosure would adversely affect national security or threaten the safety or privacy of the members of the Armed Forces. If access is not available, the media will turn to the military for imagery of operations; therefore it is critical that the joint force have a robust combat camera capability. Combat camera and unclassified imagery should be shared with and through the country team when possible.

(2) The establishment of a MOC at the outset of operations serves as a logistics and information base for the press and facilitates media coverage. The MOC staff manages media requirements and conducts the following functions:

(a) Establishes ground rules for press coverage of operations.

(b) Provides credentials to the media.

(c) Coordinates media logistics requirements.

(d) Escorts media.

(e) Coordinates PA imagery requirements and activities with J-3 and combat camera.

(f) Provides operational updates.

(g) Coordinates interview requests.

(h) Conducts press briefings.

(i) Collaborates with HN, NGOs, and IGOs on media operations.

(j) Disseminates news releases.

(k) Posts information about relief operations on DOD and ReliefWeb and social media sites as appropriate.

(l) Provides media training as required.

(m) Monitors the information environment for the joint force themes, messages, and misinformation.

(3) In the interest of NGO and IGO safety, permission must be obtained to publish their participation.

d. **Command Information Program.** Keeping military personnel informed of operations is key to their understanding of the mission and the value they place on their contribution to operations. At the outset of operations, the PA staff will provide the same information being disseminated publicly to the command for internal consumption. A more formal command information program may be established if the length of the FHA operation warrants and the PA staff is sufficient to support the endeavor. The JFC and staff should expect and prepare for extensive media coverage during FHA operations. Visual media in particular can significantly influence public opinion. Positive press coverage serves as a force multiplier; therefore, media coverage of improved conditions will help sustain public support and also increase morale. Some images may have negative connotations for the media if they are not used to cover FHA operations. For example, barbed wire used to maintain a secure area to keep groups of dislocated civilians segregated from each other and the local population could be perceived as concentration camps by media not familiar with FHA operations. Therefore, the reasons and problems associated with this should be explained to the media.

Refer to JP 3-61, Public Affairs, *for additional information.*

15. Dislocated Civilians

a. When there is a humanitarian requirement that the US military is uniquely able to address, DOD may be requested to provide FHA support to dislocated civilians, including IDPs and refugees. The joint force role in providing for and protecting these groups will depend on the mission. In rare instances, joint forces may be called upon to establish dislocated civilian camps in an HN. In these cases, the JTF must take into account legal considerations regarding availability and ownership of land for camps; coordination with the HN, other USG departments and agencies, UN, NGOs, and IGOs; logistic factors connected with shelter, food, sanitation, and medical care; and construction, any of which may be accomplished via contract support. If called upon to establish and operate camps, the joint force can refer to Air Force Handbook 10-222, Volume 22, *Camp Planning for Displaced Persons,* UNHCR *Handbook for Emergencies,* and *Tactics, Techniques, and Procedures (TTP) for Migrant Camp Operations,* as excellent references. **The general policy of the UN is that where refugees are present, the affected country will provide security, safety, assistance, and law and order.** Additionally, military forces are not normally present in camps run by UNHCR. UNHCR will, upon government request, normally provide material assistance and protection to refugees. **US forces may be tasked to provide any portion of this assistance.**

b. The term dislocated civilian is unique to DOD and not used by DOS, NGOs, or IGOs. These organizations use the term IDPs for civilians displaced within their country and "refugees" for people who flee their country of origin and cross an international border. The following distinctions exist among the various categories of dislocated civilians.

(1) **Displaced persons** is a term used to refer to internally and externally displaced persons collectively.

(a) **Returnees** are displaced persons who have returned voluntarily to their former place of residence.

(b) **Resettled persons** are a subset of displaced persons—civilians who have been able to resettle in a third country, usually with the assistance of UNHCR and the government of their new country of residence, rather than returning to their previous home or land within the country or area of original displacement. Resettled persons are usually a very small subset of the original displaced population as opportunities for third country resettlement are rare.

(2) **Evacuees** are civilians who are removed from their places of residence by military direction for reasons of personal security or the requirements of the military situation. Note: The term "evacuee" is unique to DOD and not used by DOS (except for NEOs), NGOs, or IGOs.

(3) **IDPs** are any persons who have been forced or obliged to flee or to leave their home or place of habitual residence, in particular as a result of or in order to avoid the effects of armed conflict, situations of generalized violence, violations of human rights or natural or man-made disasters, and who have not crossed an internationally recognized state border.

(4) **Migrants** are persons who belong to a normally migratory culture who may cross national boundaries or have fled their native country for economic reasons rather than fear of political or ethnic persecution. Migrants travel to escape economic stagnation and poverty. This is in contrast to refugees, who travel to escape persecution, conflict, and perhaps death.

(5) Refugees are any persons who, owing to a well-founded fear of being persecuted for reasons of race, religion, nationality, membership of a particular social group or political opinion, are outside the country of their nationality and are unable or, owing to such fear, are unwilling to avail themselves of the protection of that country. It is important to understand the differences among refugees and other categories because of associated legal ramifications. Refugees are entitled to special protection because they can no longer avail themselves of the protection of their country of nationality. International law prohibits the forcible return of refugees to their country of origin or to any country where life or freedom would be threatened based on race, religion, nationality, membership of a particular social group, or political opinion. (DOS provides guidance as to what groups of people are classified as refugees. This description is provided as general guidance.) DOD personnel

should request specific DOS guidance when involved in operations that require the classification of groups of displaced persons. Further, per Article 33 of the Refugee Convention and agreed to by the 1967 Protocol to the Refugee Convention, it is not permitted to forcibly return a refugee to a place where his or her life or freedom may be threatened (nonrefoulment).

(6) **Stateless persons** are civilians who either have been denationalized, whose country of origin cannot be determined, or who cannot establish their right to the nationality claimed.

c. While the following are not categories of dislocated civilians, they are categories of civilians with whom military members may come in contact in an operational area and should be part of this discussion for FHA.

(1) **Trafficking victims** are persons subjected to sex trafficking (i.e., recruitment, harboring, transportation, provision, or obtaining of a person for the purpose of a commercial sex act) in which a commercial sex act is induced by force, fraud, or coercion, or in which the person induced to perform such act has not attained 18 years of age; or the recruitment, harboring, transportation, provision, or obtaining of a person for labor or services, through the use of force, fraud, or coercion for the purpose of subjection to involuntary servitude, peonage, debt bondage, or slavery. Simply stated, trafficking in persons (TIP) is modern-day slavery, involving victims who are forced, defrauded, or coerced into labor or sexual exploitation.

(a) DOD opposes prostitution, forced labor, and any related activities that may contribute to the phenomenon of TIP as inherently harmful and dehumanizing. TIP is a violation of US law and internationally recognized human rights and is incompatible with DOD core values.

(b) Commanders should deter activities of DOD Service members, civilian employees, indirect hires, contract personnel, and command-sponsored dependents that would facilitate or support TIP, domestically and overseas.

(c) Commanders provide support to HN authorities involved in the battle against TIP. Commanders and military police should meet periodically with NGOs to review TIP-related issues and prevention initiatives.

(d) Commanders incorporate anti-TIP and TIP-protection measures for vulnerable populations, in particular for women and children, into post-conflict and humanitarian emergency assistance programs.

(2) **Vulnerable persons** are persons who may not have equal access to HA because of physical, cultural, or social barriers (e.g., women, children, elderly, disabled, ethnic minorities, and people living with an incurable virus or disease). While this is not a legal distinction, it is important to describe this population, as it is the most vulnerable with often the greatest needs.

Appendix A, "Legal Issues," provides additional information regarding the legal aspects of dislocated civilians.

d. PRC assists HN governments in retaining control over their population centers, thus precluding complicating problems that may hinder mission accomplishment. PRC measures seek to reduce, relocate, or access population resources that may impede or otherwise threaten FHA operation success.

(1) FHA operations can be disrupted by:

(a) Uncontrolled and uncoordinated movement of frightened civilians.

(b) Uncontrolled and uncoordinated movement of civilians conducting legitimate activities.

(c) Illegal or illegitimate activities such as insurgent operations or black-market activities.

(d) Uncontrolled outbreak of disease among dislocated civilians.

(2) PRC consists of two distinct, yet linked, components: populace control and resources control.

(a) **Populace control** provides for security of the populace, mobilization of human resources, denial of personnel availability to the enemy, and detection and reduced effectiveness of enemy agents. Populace control measures include curfews, movement restrictions, travel permits, registration cards, and resettlement. Dislocated civilian support operations are a subset of populace control.

(b) **Resources control** regulates the movement or consumption of materiel resources, mobilizes materiel resources, and denies materiel to the enemy. Resources control measures include licensing, regulations or guidelines, checkpoints (e.g., roadblocks), ration controls, amnesty programs, and inspection of facilities.

(3) Normally these controls are a responsibility of indigenous civil governments. PRC measures implemented by a joint force are necessary when HN civil authorities or agencies are either unable or unwilling to undertake that responsibility. They are further defined and enforced during times of civil or military emergency.

More detailed information may be found in JP 3-57, Civil-Military Operations, *which provides specific guidance on PRC.*

16. Health and Medical Support

a. Medical forces typically have three missions in FHA operations: force health protection (FHP), care for disaster victims, and assisting in reestablishing indigenous public health resources and institutions affected by the disaster. Medical planning should be integrated into overall response early and prior to deployment.

b. JFCs have overall responsibility for the health readiness of forces assigned or attached to their command. FHA operations may place US forces in situations that may substantially increase the risk of disease; food, water, blood products, high levels of industrial pollution, stress, fatigue, and indigenous diseases combine to provide a high-risk environment for all assigned personnel. This requires that the JTF have robust preventive medicine assets to perform medical and environmental health risk assessments and identify effective preventive medicine measures to counter the threat to US forces.

OPERATION SHINING HOPE

In the spring of 1999, Serbian aggression in the Balkans forced hundreds of thousands of ethnic Albanians to flee their homes in Kosovo and seek refuge in neighboring countries. US European Command established Joint Task Force SHINING HOPE to support refugee humanitarian relief. Planning, design, and construction of three camps in southern Albania capable of supporting 60,000 refugees began almost immediately. US Air Forces in Europe engineers, using contractor support through the Air Force Contract Augmentation Program and along with US Navy Seabee forces, completed one 18,500-person camp in just 51 days with two additional camps well underway. Lessons learned from this experience stress the importance of early, active, and continuing involvement of the United Nations High Commissioner for Refugees, the Department of State, US Agency for International Development, and the nongovernmental organizations that will eventually operate the camp. This is essential to appropriately balance and incorporate the needs of the refugee population to be supported.

Various Sources

---

c. Specific to humanitarian missions, medical forces are usually asked to support local military and civilian health systems and provide direct public health care to include primary medical, dental, veterinary, and other needed care. These missions must always be coordinated closely with the HN medical authorities, NGOs and IGOs. Primary consideration must be given to supporting and supplementing existing medical infrastructure. **The JFC must ensure that no operation is considered that could have the effect of supplanting the existing medical infrastructure.** If authorized, US forces may also provide health care to foreign civilian populations on an urgent or emergent basis (within resource limitations) and return them to their national health systems at the earliest opportunity or when services can be provided by other agencies and organizations; such operations, however, pose the greatest risk for supplanting the existing medical infrastructure.

d. Medical personnel may be called on to assist in reestablishing and supporting indigenous medical infrastructure, optimizing existent health systems, or identifying future foreign medical infrastructure improvements, particularly those affected by disaster. Improving the medical systems near US and multinational forces fosters self-sufficiency and may contribute to accomplishing the US military mission sooner. Care must be taken to ensure that re-established health care standards are appropriate for the local population and at a level that can be maintained by the existing HN medical infrastructure.

HEALTH AND MEDICAL SUPPORT DURING THE 2005 PAKISTAN EARTHQUAKE

During the Pakistan earthquake relief effort in 2005, two US military medical units treated tens of thousands of patients, conducted nearly 500 surgeries, and administered over 10,000 immunizations. Following the earthquake, the US had its first relief supplies on the ground within 24 hours of the initial quake. However, it took 16 days before the first medical unit was fully operational. Some assets were not fully operational until 40 days after the initial earthquake.

With no international health specialist or medical planning guidance from Combined Disaster Assistance Center—Pakistan (CDAC-PAK), the standard of care for the theater was not determined or published until weeks into the operation. CDAC-PAK medical units provided a quality of care in excess of the pre-earthquake host nation capabilities and, unfortunately, this direct medical assistance negatively impacted local economies.

Without realizing the negative impact that it would have, CDAC-PAK medical units continued seeing patients for almost five months after there were no more victims with wounds resulting from the earthquake. Free medications undermined local pharmacies and created a pharmaceutical black market in the local towns. Local physicians and pharmacists lost patients and closed their offices/shops and left their local communities due to the presence of the no-cost US medical care.

Condensed from:
Lt Col William A. Mosier and Walter H. Orthner,
Military Medical Support for Humanitarian Assistance and Disaster Relief:
Lessons Learned From the Pakistan Earthquake Relief Effort
Joint Center for Operational Analysis Journal, June 2007

e. US military medical personnel do not routinely care for dislocated civilians unless specifically authorized. The joint force surgeon should develop medical engagement protocols and standards of care prior to deployment and ensure all providers understand the circumstances under which urgent and non-urgent patients should be evaluated, evacuated, and treated in military treatment facilities. UNHCR normally coordinates the care of refugees by NGOs.

f. In some FHA missions, health services may be the primary capability employed. During an FHA mission, a hospital or medical command may be the principal unit deployed, and the commander also may be the CJTF.

For additional considerations for providing health and medical support in FHA operations, see Appendix E, "Health and Medical Support in Foreign Humanitarian Assistance Operations."

17. Mortuary Affairs

a. GCCs are responsible for giving authoritative direction and guidance on providing mortuary affairs (MA) support to all assigned and attached forces within their AORs. They designate a Service component to serve as the lead Service for the theater MA support program at the AOR level and, as necessary, designate a lead Service at selected subordinate levels and assign responsibilities, tasks, assets, and organize commands as necessary to execute the lead Service MA mission. GCCs assume lead responsibility and coordination for fatalities occurring within the command's AOR and assign tasks, assets, and organize commands as necessary to execute the MA mission. They establish a joint mortuary affairs office (JMAO) to provide oversight of MA support within their AOR and provide MA support to other CCMDs when appropriate. It is the responsibility of unit commanders sustaining losses to recover the human remains and evacuate them to the nearest MA collection point. Every effort will be made to identify human remains and account for unrecovered human remains of US military personnel, government employees, government contractors, their dependents, and others who die in military operations, training accidents, and other multiple fatality incidents.

b. Upon notification of an FHA mission, the responsible GCC should task the J-4 to develop a staff estimate and provide planning guidance for MA operations based on the overall mission analysis and COAs. During the analysis phase, the staff officer should contact the J-4 of the Joint Staff to determine if any cooperation agreements exist between the supported foreign government and multinational partners. During this phase, the GCC's J-4 logistics planners should coordinate with subordinate and supporting commands to determine their MA force structure and capabilities.

c. **JMAO.** If determined necessary, the GCC may delegate MA support authority to the subordinate JFC, which will allow the commander to designate a lead Service component (usually the Army) to handle MA for the command. Additionally, the subordinate JFC (i.e., CJTF) may direct the J-4 to establish and operate a JMAO.

For more detailed information, see JP 4-06, Mortuary Affairs.

d. **Considerations**

(1) In general terms, legal obligations depend on whether the JTF is dealing with a deceased person that was simply found within the operational area or if the death was associated with JTF actions. The JTF's obligations concerning dead or buried bodies found in the operational area derive from the commander's responsibility for health and public hygiene of US forces. An example of this is contamination of water supplies from mass graves, or bodies washed from shallow graves, constituting a health hazard. In this consideration, reinterment should be facilitated. As with the handling of all disaster casualties, reinterment of remains should be conducted following local religion and culture to the extent possible. Insensitive actions (such as the use of black colored body bags in Muslim countries) can do serious damage to the desired FHA message. Sufficient information must be maintained to identify burial sites and, where possible, the names of persons reinterred. Upon termination of reinterment operations, records should be turned

over to the affected country government representatives. The death of a person associated with JTF actions requires an in-depth investigation. Processing of these remains will be in accordance with guidance provided by the SJA. Deaths of persons under the care of the JTF, such as dislocated civilians seeking help at a site under JTF control, create other obligations, such as medical certification and recording of death. In countries where a governmental infrastructure is in place, death records should be registered with that government. Where there is no government, the JTF should maintain appropriate records for later disposition. The JMAO is responsible for maintaining these records.

(2) In an FCM or nonpermissive situation, casualties may have died as a result of infectious or weaponized agents, or might be booby-trapped, regardless of the apparent cause of death. In order to prevent further casualties among those caring for the deceased, mortuary facilities should be designed with these possibilities taken into account when planning for casualty flow procedures.

(3) The JTF should attempt to coordinate with the International Red Cross and Red Crescent Movement for the return of deceased local nationals to local governmental control. These organizations can provide invaluable assistance in locating the next of kin of the deceased.

(4) Multinational partners and other non-US dead will be processed in accordance with international agreements or guidance from the supported GCC. In cases of foreign nationals or relief organizations requesting MA support, the JMAO will coordinate with the DOS representative through the CMOC or OSOCC in the affected area.

18. Religious Affairs

a. Religious affairs in joint operations include a range of professional duties a joint force chaplain (JFCH) performs in the dual role of religious ministry professional and staff officer.

b. Religion often plays a pivotal role in understanding the culture, requirements, attitude, and desires of a population and its government and may have a significant impact on the goals, objectives, nature of support, and CONOPS for the FHA operation.

c. Commanders and their staffs may also consider religion, other cultural issues, and ideology while developing schemes of maneuver and ROE or planning CMO, MISO, IO, and PA activities. Commanders must weigh the benefit of working with organizations that provide conditional aid vis-à-vis the risk of alienating the population.

d. Chaplain involvement during the planning process ensures that the religious needs of US forces are met. The JFCHs may assist the staff in developing an engagement strategy by providing advice within the scope of their expertise on these organizations and the influence of religion in the operational area. In a religiously diverse operational area, the JFCHs may provide relevant information on the religions of multinational partners and the adversary, which includes issues of national, regional, and sect or group religious customs, traditions, organizations, communities, symbols, facilities, and sensitivities.

e. When appropriate, and in coordination with the CMOC, **chaplains may serve as liaison** to NGOs that have a religious affiliation. The USG supports faith-based organizations, but USG policy strictly states that USG assistance must be distributed based on need, not based on religious affiliation or for the purpose of influencing the religious beliefs of a population. Reports of USG assistance being distributed in violation of this policy should be reported to the embassy, DOS, and/or USAID. Additionally, chaplains may accompany elements of the joint force as they distribute relief supplies or have other interactions (e.g., security patrols) with the local populace. This provides an opportunity to expand or enhance community outreach and allows the chaplain to evaluate and experience firsthand the OE and its impact on the morale of the unit and individual service members. This experience will be useful when advising the commanders and counseling those members of the joint force that may seek the chaplain's advice.

f. In coordination with CA personnel, chaplains may provide **pastoral support to dislocated civilians** only when directed by the JFC after consulting the SJA. In such cases, it is critical to avoid any activities which may be construed as proselytizing among dislocated civilians for one particular faith. The chaplain pastoral mission generally is limited to US military and DOD civilian personnel and, if required by the circumstances, to fulfill any obligation the JFC may have to protected persons under international law.

For more detailed information on religious support, refer to JP 1-05, Religious Affairs in Joint Operations.

19. Environmental Considerations

a. Environmental issues can have strategic, operational, or tactical implications and should be incorporated into planning and operations. Natural resources protection can be a key strategic mission objective, important to HN reconstruction. Failure to recognize environmental threats can result in significant health risks to the JTF, adversely impacting readiness. If not appropriately addressed, environmental issues have the potential to impact negatively local community relations, affect insurgent activities, and create diplomatic problems for the JTF.

b. **Joint Environmental Management Board (JEMB).** The CCDR or subordinate JFC may establish a JEMB to assist in managing environmental requirements. The JEMB is a temporary board, chaired by the CCMD or subordinate joint force engineer, with members from the joint force staff, components, and any other required special activities (e.g., legal, medical, CA, and weather). The board establishes policies, procedures, priorities, and the overall direction for environmental management requirements in a JOA. The JEMB will coordinate its activities with the CCMD or subordinate joint force engineering staff. The JEMB also provides guidance on development of annex L (Environmental Considerations) of plans and orders, and, if appropriate, assumes responsibility for preparation and updates of this annex.

c. **Environmental Support Operations.** The intent of environmental support operations is to minimize adverse environmental impact, ensure the safety and health of personnel, and reduce post-deployment environmental cleanup. While deployed engineering units may have the capability to provide environmental support, the use of contractors is usually required for long-term or large-scale projects. Typical environmental support operations include:

(1) Initial environmental baseline surveys.

(2) Site surveys to determine environmental and cultural conditions.

(3) Integration of environmental considerations into plans.

(4) Recommendations for nontoxic, environmentally benign material substitution.

(5) Emergency response plans, training, and initial actions.

(6) Establishment of solid and liquid waste disposal systems.

(7) Establishment of hazardous materials distribution centers.

(8) Establishment of hazardous waste collection, long-term storage, and shipment center.

(9) Sampling of water sources for contaminates.

(10) Closure environmental baseline surveys and removal of waste and excess supplies.

For additional information on environmental considerations, refer to JP 3-34, Joint Engineer Operations.

20. Change of Mission

Periodic review of the mission statement will determine whether the force's actions still support SecDef and supported GCC's intent. The JFC must be prepared to react to a change of mission during an FHA operation, as directed by the chain of command. The JFC must also guard against an unintentional change of mission, sometimes referred to as "mission creep." A **clearly articulated end state and appropriate MOEs** help the JFC protect against this phenomenon. Other organizations involved in the operation may have differing views of the end state, and request support from the joint force that falls outside the stated mission. Although these requests may seem logical and within the joint force's capabilities, the JFC must be pragmatic when dealing with these organizations' attempts to change the joint force's mission without SecDef direction.

21. Transition or Termination

a. **The termination of military FHA operations will normally involve a transition of relief activities to US, intergovernmental, or HN relief organizations. Termination occurs when the relief efforts have been successfully transitioned or**

when SecDef directs, or at the discretion of the HN. Planning for transition should be incorporated as early as possible in all aspects of operational planning for FHA.

b. Criteria for transition may be based on **events, MOEs, availability of resources,** or a **specific date.** Examples of events that may be included in termination criteria include restoration of critical facilities in the crisis area; an acceptable drop in mortality rates; or a certain percentage of dislocated civilians returned to their homes. When other organizations (such as USAID, UN, NGOs, and IGOs) have marshalled the necessary capabilities to assume the mission, US forces may execute a transition plan.

c. **Transition may occur between the joint force and a variety of elements,** such as the HN, the UN, or other nations' forces. A detailed plan addressing the various FHA functions and to whom they will transition will greatly reduce the turmoil typically associated with transition. A **comprehensive transition plan** includes specific requirements for all elements involved in the transition, summarizes capabilities and assets, and assigns specific responsibilities. When transitioning to nonmilitary organizations, an unclassified transition plan written in easily understood terms suitable for a nonmilitary audience is required. Organizing the plan by specific FHA functions, humanitarian clusters, or sectors (such as provision of food, restoration of facilities, and medical care) also enhances the transition. **The joint force staff should periodically review the transition plan** with all organizations that have a part in it. This will help ensure that planning assumptions are still valid, and determine if changes in the situation require changes in the transition plan.

d. Termination plans should cover transition to post-disaster or emergency activities and conditions as well as disposition of military forces. Operation and termination plans should be prepared simultaneously and in conjunction with the deployment plan, with the termination plan serving as a supporting plan to the OPLAN.

e. **Mission transition planning will be continuous and will be accorded equal priority with execution planning.** At the outset, the joint force will work in close cooperation with the HN and LFA and other participating agencies to define the desired end state of the involvement of US military forces in FHA operations. Universally understood and accepted MOPs will be developed that indicate achievement of each element of the end state and provide the basis for timely and orderly redeployment of the joint force, while preserving continuity in the long-term relief operations.

f. **Concept of Transition.** Mission transition planning will be continuous throughout the operation. Specifically, it identifies the functions and tasks being performed by the joint force and determines which functions may be terminated when either the requirement no longer exists or is transferred to the HN or others. The transition plan consists of four phases: Phase A–Assessment, Phase B–Observation and Orientation, Phase C–Integration, and Phase D–Handover.

g. **Phasing the Transition**

(1) **Phase A—Assessment**

(a) **Concept.** The assessment phase consists of a review of the functional tasks being performed by the joint force and determines whether these tasks can be terminated or transferred. This process is conducted in conjunction with, and with the concurrence of, the DOS through the COM. This phase also identifies the organizations and agencies (e.g., HN, NGOs, IGOs) most capable and willing to assume the functional tasks performed by the joint force. This phase is complete when all functional tasks have been identified for either transfer or termination and the HN, NGOs, and IGOs have been identified and accept responsibility for performing that functional responsibility.

(b) **Intent.** The purpose of this phase is to review the functional tasks performed by the joint force and determine which long-term tasks will be handled by the HN, NGOs, and IGOs. The method is to identify functional tasks for either transition or termination. Once determined for transition, the appropriate HN agency, NGO, or IGO is identified to assume that functional responsibility. The end state is attained once the long-term transfer tasks have been identified and affiliated with the agency or organization willing to accept responsibility.

(2) **Phase B—Observation and Orientation**

(a) **Concept.** This phase builds on the analysis and agreements obtained in Phase A. The organizations identified for transfer duties will observe the functional tasks that the joint force is currently performing. The objective is to accomplish a seamless transfer of functional tasks from the joint force to transfer organizations without any loss of support or international commitment. This phase is complete when transfer organizations have their required assets in place in accordance with the timeliness previously agreed upon. **Care should be taken during this phase to ensure that the nonmilitary audiences involved do not perceive joint force efforts as a way to impose military procedures on their own time-tested approaches.** In some cases, joint force elements may be performing civilian tasks because of a lack of civilian resources.

(b) **Intent.** The purpose of this phase is to orient and familiarize transfer organizations with the functional tasks being performed by the joint force. When necessary for use, the method is to educate, orient, and train or familiarize the HN, NGO, and IGO leadership on the functional tasks and methods employed by the joint force. The end state is the alignment of the HN or appropriate NGO or IGO with the component of the joint force currently performing the assigned function.

(3) **Phase C—Integration**

(a) **Concept.** Integration is defined by participation of the HN, NGOs, or IGOs in functional tasks supporting the HN, not by the integration of the HN, NGOs, and IGOs into the joint force. The integration phase initiates the direct involvement of the HN, NGOs, and IGOs in the functional tasks being performed by the joint force that will require long-term continuation. The objective is to increase HN, NGO, and IGO levels of support (within their capabilities) until they assume full responsibility for the functional support. Progress is quantified by the percentage of functional task support provided by each agency over time. This phase incrementally increases the level of involvement by the HN, NGOs, or IGOs while proportionately decreasing the level of involvement by the JTF. The use of universally understood and mutually accepted MOEs will facilitate integration of the HN, NGOs, and IGOs by building mutual support for the functional tasks. This phase ends when all functional elements performed by the joint force are capable of being transferred to properly trained, equipped, and capable organizations.

(b) **Intent.** The purpose of this phase is to initiate and progressively increase the level of support provided by the HN, NGOs, and IGOs until they are capable of sustained operations in a designated cluster or humanitarian sector. Critical to this integration is the continual monitoring of the MOPs to ensure no lag or loss of support to the HN. The method is to progressively increase levels of HN, NGO, and IGO involvement in performing joint force-run functional tasks. The end state is realized when all functional tasks are being performed by non-joint force organizations, fully trained, equipped, and capable of performing sustained operations.

(4) **Phase D—Hand Over**

(a) **Concept.** The hand over phase culminates with the end of joint force direct involvement in humanitarian support to the HN. The objective is a seamless transfer of responsibility for functional tasks from the joint force to the HN, NGOs, and IGOs. These organizations must be fully trained, equipped, and capable of assuming their functional tasks over the long term. These organizations must also be perceived by the public as being credible and capable of performing their designated functional tasks. Progress is marked by the handover of specified functional tasks to non-joint force organizations. This phase ends when all functional areas performed by the joint force have been successfully assumed by either the HN, NGOs, or IGOs.

(b) **Intent.** The purpose of this phase is to hand over all functional tasks performed by the joint force to either the HN, NGOs, or IGOs. The method is to train capable HN agencies, NGOs, and IGOs, incrementally increase their involvement, then disengage when they reach a mission-capable state. The end state is realized when all functional tasks are being performed by non-joint force organizations without the presence of the joint force.

h. **Incremental Transition.** While the four phase transition model may be appropriate in most FHA operations, the OE may drive a more incremental transition. A gradual transition may occur with a shrinking military footprint across both geographical areas and humanitarian clusters.

OPERATION UNIFIED ASSISTANCE: TSUNAMI TRANSITIONS

Military-to-civilian transition planning was challenging, and determining when military assistance was sufficient and complete was particularly difficult. Because of the unfamiliar operating environment, deciding when to transition relief efforts from military to civilian forces initially boggled military planners' minds. Nongovernmental organizations' (NGOs') and Intergovernmental organizations' (IGOs') participation in the planning process was particularly valuable. NGO and IGO representatives were impressed that we were developing a transition plan early in the operation. Planning for transition involved two steps: mission analysis and course of action (COA) development.

Mission analysis. The transition was actually a continuous operation, moving from military assistance to international response efforts to a final long-term host nation (HN) effort. The United Nations (UN) representative emphasized that the transition would not move from a well-defined military structure to a well-defined, centrally controlled civilian structure, but more likely flow outward from the military structure to numerous NGOs and IGOs and HN governments. The transition would be quite different from the usual battle handover familiar to military planners and not at all like the detailed process joint doctrine describes. The UN planner recommended transferring stored supplies to other organizations for distribution (to prevent waste) and identifying incomplete tasks to be handed over on transition. Two transitions occurred, one from military to international assets and the other from international to HN assets. The handovers occurred not at specific times, but in windows or periods of transition during which relief providers performed simultaneous, overlapping missions in their areas of operation. HN approval of the transition plan was also critical.

COA development. While mission analysis went fairly smoothly, the Combined Support Force (CSF) had a difficult time formulating COAs. COA development for a transition that was somewhat ambiguous led planners to develop just one COA—a rough list of tasks for the subordinate elements to complete or pass on to other agencies as the CSF slowly shrank and eventually redeployed. The transition occurred in three phases: assessment, transition, and disengagement. Identifying the desired effects for the transition and then developing a process to measure the CSF's progress were critical steps in determining when the transition could begin. CSF commanders did not develop an effects list because they did not want to commit the force to effects that might eventually prove to be unrealistic or too costly. The CSF bogged down in discussion because there were too many different sets of standards (e.g., Sphere, number of requests for assistance [RFAs]) that could be applied.

The CSF directed that the military footprint would slowly shrink when RFAs for military assistance decreased or were passed to aid agencies.

The end of military operations does not mean the end of relief operations; it only means that civilians are in control. The CSF was able to leverage into its transition plan the wealth of knowledge and experience NGO and IGO aid workers and partner nations brought to the operation. In the end, gaining civilian and partner-nation perspectives on the transition plan was key to the CSF's successful transition and redeployment.

Adapted from
Operation UNIFIED ASSISTANCE: Tsunami Transitions
Lieutenant Colonel James Daniel, US Army
January-February 2006, Military Review

22. Redeployment

Redeployment planning should be conducted simultaneously with joint force deployment. Redeployment considerations depend upon mission accomplishment and diminished requirements for military support. FHA functions conducted by the joint force should be transferred to the HN, UN, NGOs, or IGOs when the capability exists for transition without support degradation. Redeployment by function is efficient and ensures that **each FHA requirement is met or responsibility is assumed by other entities** (HN, UN, NGOs, or IGOs). Commanders should continually evaluate mission requirements and redeploy unnecessary forces as soon as possible. Personnel rotation plans should also be considered for operations conducted over extended time periods.

OPERATION UNIFIED ASSISTANCE REDEPLOYMENT

What was noted on several occasions was also the duration of stay—military forces came in, performed their tasks and departed—thus fulfilling one maxim for perceived success— "leave whilst the audience is still applauding."

Source: Tsunami Evaluation Coalition
Coordination of International
Humanitarian Assistance in Tsunami-
Affected Countries Evaluation
Findings-Sri Lanka

Intentionally Blank

APPENDIX A
LEGAL ISSUES

1. General

Significant and complex legal issues that surround FHA operations make it important that the JFC understand international and domestic legal principles associated with the mission. International law issues include the law of war, the law of the sea, the status of persons encountered during the mission, ROE, and HN law, while domestic legal issues include such subjects as fiscal law, military justice, claims, and intelligence oversight. These topics are discussed in this appendix. Commanders should consult their SJA on addressing these complex and interrelated issues.

2. Law of War

DOD policy is to comply with the law of war during all armed conflicts. However, such conflicts are characterized in all other military operations in accordance with DODD 2311.01, *DOD Law of War Program*. In the context of FHA, perhaps the most important obligations are to treat humanely persons taking no active part in hostilities, and to "respect and protect" certain persons, such as wounded and sick combatants, and the medical units and personnel assigned to care for them. Such medical units and personnel could include the staff of national Red Cross societies and that of other voluntary aid societies, duly recognized and authorized by their government, as long as they are exclusively engaged in medical duties, and they are subject to military laws and regulations. Law of war standards requiring "humane treatment" of persons taking no active part in hostilities should be considered as minimum standards, regardless of the nature of the operation or type of conflict. However, the laws and rules under which FHA forces operate may be significantly more restrictive than law of war standards, particularly those rules relating to the use of force by military personnel.

The following publications provide guidance on the law of war: CJCSI 5810.01, Implementation of the DOD Law of War Program; *Navy Warfare Publication (NWP) 1-14M,* The Commander's Handbook on the Law of Naval Operations; The Operational Law Handbook *published by the US Army Judge Advocate General's Legal Center and School;* Air Force Handbook 10-222, Volume 22, *Camp Planning for Displaced Persons; and Field Manual (FM) 27-10,* The Law of Land Warfare.

3. Laws and Jurisdictions for Foreign Humanitarian Assistance Forces and the Host Nation

All US Armed Forces participating in FHA operations remain subject to the *Uniform Code of Military Justice* and other applicable US laws. JFCs are responsible for the discipline and administration of personnel assigned to the joint organization, and may be delegated courts-martial authority by SecDef. In addition, a CCDR may prescribe procedures by which the senior officer of a Service assigned to the HQ element of a joint organization may exercise administrative and nonjudicial punishment authority over personnel of the same Service assigned to the same joint organization. Commanders have only limited administrative and disciplinary options for civilians, such as other USG employees and US contractors who accompany the FHA force, which may result in difficult issues relating to both HN law and good order and discipline within the force. Absent international agreement provisions to the contrary, members of FHA forces both military and civilian, and activities of the FHA force, are most likely subject to HN law and jurisdiction. For example, the FHA force might be subject to HN import laws; duties and taxes; procurement laws; prohibitions or restrictions on carrying and use of weapons; and health, safety, and labor laws. Members of the FHA force are subject to actions in HN criminal and civil courts, unless a SOFA or other international agreement limits HN jurisdiction.

More detailed information may be found in JP 1, Doctrine for the Armed Forces of the United States, *and the* Manual for Courts-Martial.

4. Status-of-Forces Agreements

A SOFA defines the legal status of a military force when deployed in the territory of a friendly state. A SOFA does not itself authorize the presence or activities of those forces. The purpose of a SOFA during FHA operations is to define how the sending and receiving states will share their sovereign prerogatives. SOFAs seek to define the rights, immunities, and duties of the force and its members. If no treaty or SOFA exists with the affected country, DOD must become involved in establishing the status of US forces. Authority to negotiate and conclude SOFAs must be obtained from DOS under its Circular 175 Procedure (US Department of State Foreign Affairs Manual, Volume 11, Political Affairs, chapter 720). These agreements/arrangements should be in place in each country where forces will transit and/or stage in support of FHA operations. In cases where time or circumstances do not permit the negotiation of a full SOFA, adequate protection for US forces may be obtained by an exchange of diplomatic notes between the US and the HN. The DOS will have the lead for this action.

DODD 5530.3, International Agreements, *provides guidance regarding the negotiation and conclusion of SOFAs, and the electronic* DOD Foreign Clearance Guide *provides current requirements for DOD personnel to enter and exit each nation.*

5. Legal Status of Nongovernmental Organizations

NGOs, like other private actors, are generally subject to HN laws and jurisdiction. Except for a regionally oriented Convention of the Council of Europe, no international treaty grants NGOs legal personality or authority.

6. International Human Rights

International laws pertaining to human rights may obligate governments to recognize and protect the human rights and fundamental freedoms of persons within their territory and subject to their jurisdiction. Customary international law, multinational treaties such as the International Covenant on Civil and Political Rights, and regional treaties provide a broad framework of protections for individuals. These include prohibitions on torture and cruel, inhuman, or degrading treatment or punishment; arbitrary interference with family, home, or privacy; discrimination on the basis of race, gender, and other factors; and arbitrary detention. Commanders should be aware that interpretations of laws pertaining to human rights, including the applicability of the International Covenant on Civil and Political Rights, vary from country to country. For example, forces of countries who are party to the European Convention on Human Rights may be required to act differently to US forces in circumstances where Articles of the Convention apply. Questions in this area should be directed to the CCMD SJA.

7. Refugees and Asylum Seekers

Under international law a refugee is a person who, owing to a well-founded fear of being persecuted for reasons of race, religion, nationality, membership of a particular social group or political opinion, is outside the country of his nationality and is unable or, owing to such fear, is unwilling to avail himself of the protection of that country. The 1951 Convention Relating to the Status of Refugees and its 1967 Protocol remain the principal international instruments benefiting refugees.

DODI 2000.11, Procedures for Handling Requests for Asylum and Temporary Refuge, *provides more information regarding this issue.*

8. Civilian Detainee Procedures

During FHA operations, commanders are likely to have extremely limited authority to detain non-DOD personnel. When detention is authorized, pursuant to specified ROE, or made necessary during lawful exercise of unit or individual self-defense, commanders must be prepared to control, maintain, protect, and account for all categories of detainees in accordance with applicable US policy, domestic law, and applicable international law. DODD 2310.01, *Department of Defense Detainee Program,* establishes the overarching DOD detainee policy and directs that all detainees, regardless of the status of the detainee or the characterization of the conflict, shall be treated humanely at all times while in the care, custody, or control of any member of the DOD components. Civilian internees are civilians who are interned during an international armed conflict or belligerent occupation for security reasons, for protection, or because they have committed an offense against the detaining power.

For more details concerning detainee operations, refer to JP 3-63, Detainee Operations.

9. Eligibility for Medical Care

A determination of eligibility for care in a US medical treatment facility (MTF) must be made by the CCMD surgeon in conjunction with the supporting SJA and in accordance with the law of war. This authority may be delegated to the JTF level. Each category of personnel who might seek emergency or routine treatment (such as DOD contractors; USG civilian employees; multinational or HN forces; and others) in a US theater MTF should be determined prior to initiation of the operation and updated as required. During FHA operations, the demands for military medical support to civilian populations may be so substantial that at the beginning of the operation the GCC must establish the scope of care to be rendered to civilian populations.

10. Claims

A single-Service component may be assigned responsibility for processing claims against the USG. Unless otherwise stated in the JFC's guidance, unit level commanders are responsible for investigating incidents of foreign property damage and personal injury or death to foreign nationals alleged to have been caused by US military personnel. Command legal personnel should be appointed to the foreign claims commission(s) with authority to adjudicate and pay foreign claims in accordance with procedures established in departmental regulations. Responsibility for adjudicating such claims is assigned to the Military Departments by DODI 5515.08, *Assignment of Claims Responsibility*. The supported CCDR may assign interim responsibility for resolving claims in countries where such assignment has not been made under the directive.

11. Environment

a. As a rule, US environmental laws have no application overseas. For environmental compliance (e.g., day-to-day activities), where country specific final governing standards (FGSs) have been established, abide by them. In a foreign nation where FGSs have not been established, applicable international agreements and the Overseas Environmental Baseline Guidance Document (OEBGD) govern. Particular attention should be paid to the disposal of hazardous waste. However, the OEBGD applies only to DOD-controlled or operated installations and facilities. They do not apply to off-installation operational deployments. See DOD 4715.05-G, *Overseas Environmental Baseline Guidance Document*, for a detailed list of exemptions. Such off-installation activities are governed by applicable, international agreements and environmental annexes to operation plans and orders. Such annexes should be as consistent with the OEBGD as circumstances and operations dictate, but should always be informed by the needs of the mission.

b. Environmental restoration is not conducted outside the US except to take prompt action to address a substantial impact to human health and safety due to environmental contamination that is caused by DOD activities and is located on a DOD installation. Environmental restoration is never performed to return a facility. Distinction should be made between cleanup of a spill and environmental restoration. Cleanup of a spill is an action taken contemporaneously, i.e., within days or weeks of the release and is considered environmental compliance.

12. Overflight and Law of the Sea

a. Customary international law, as reflected in the 1982 United Nations Convention on the Law of the Sea (UNCLOS), provides that the sovereignty of each nation extends to its territorial sea, including the airspace above, to a maximum breadth of 12 nautical miles from the shoreline. UNCLOS also confirmed the freedom of overflight rights through international airspace and the right of ships and aircraft to transit international straits and archipelagic sea lanes without requiring prior permission or consent from any nation. Although the US is not a party to UNCLOS, it considers many provisions in UNCLOS to reflect customary international law, including, but not limited to, the provisions concerning freedom of navigation. USG policy is that all DOD aircraft entering the legally recognized sovereign territory of another nation will first receive an aircraft diplomatic clearance signifying the HN's permission to enter.

b. US embassies become involved when an HN challenges USG policy that all nations can fly through international airspace unchallenged. Some countries claim airspace beyond the 12 nautical mile limit while others claim that the flight information regions that they have designated require both an air traffic control clearance and an aircraft diplomatic clearance. As long as DOD aircraft remain in international airspace, they do not require a diplomatic clearance.

c. The duty to rescue those in distress at sea is firmly established in customary and conventional international law (e.g., Article 98, UNCLOS). Asylum seekers have been escaping by sea for many years. If persons are rescued at sea, decisions with regard to disembarkation should be consistent with Section 2242 of the Foreign Affairs Reform and Restructuring Act of 1998 (US policy that prohibits the transfer of a person to a country where he or she is more likely than not to be tortured).

13. **National Sovereignty**

a. National sovereignty issues can impact FHA mission planning from operational, legal, and fiscal perspectives.

b. In addition to recognition of national sovereignty of territory under UNCLOS, the 1944 Convention on International Civil Aviation (also known as the Chicago Convention) codified airspace "rules of the road" for the international community and recognized the principle that state aircraft enjoy "sovereign immunity," similar to the immunity enjoyed by naval vessels. Specifically, parties to the Chicago Convention agreed on principles and arrangements to facilitate the safe and orderly development of international civil aviation. For example, Article I of the Chicago Convention recognizes that each state has complete and exclusive sovereignty over the airspace above its territory (including territorial sea). Accordingly, the aircraft of one state may not enter the airspace of another state without authorization. Under Article III, "state aircraft," which includes aircraft used by the military, customs agencies, and police, is generally exempt from the provisions of the Chicago Convention.

c. When cleared to overfly or land in a foreign territory, US military aircraft are, as a matter of international custom and practice, generally exempt from duties and taxation; not subject to search, seizure, and inspection (boarding); and immune from judicial process and exercise of jurisdiction by an HN without prior consent. US policy, consistent with international custom and practice, is that flights or aircraft operated by sovereign states in or through another state will not be required to pay navigation or overflight fees; not be required to pay landing or parking fees at government airports; but will pay reasonable charges for services requested and received, whether at governmental or nongovernmental airports. The USG is willing to pay landing and parking fees at commercial airports, if required to do so. In many countries, bilateral agreements or other arrangements explicitly provide that US state aircraft are not to be charged fees at either governmental or nongovernmental airports. Every effort should be made not to undermine these arrangements. US embassies are directed to reject billings for overflight and navigation fees, charges for aircraft operating in international airspace, and parking and landing fees assessed at government airports.

d. DOD often contracts commercial aircraft to perform airlift or other missions. The USG has consistently taken the position that DOD contracted commercial aircraft do not qualify as military or other state aircraft unless the USG specifically designates them as such. DOD contracted commercial aircraft are not subject to the same exemptions that are generally provided to military aircraft as a matter of international customs and practice.

For additional information, see the electronic DOD Foreign Clearance Guide.

14. Rules of Engagement

a. ROE are a C2 tool. They provide implementation guidance on the application of force for mission accomplishment and the exercise of self-defense. The sensitive political and international nature of FHA operations requires that ROE be established and coordinated with other forces involved in the operation. CJCSI 3121.01B, *Standing Rules of Engagement/Standing Rules for the Use of Force for US Forces*, provides fundamental policies and procedures for US commanders. It is US policy that ROE never limit a commander's inherent authority and obligation to take appropriate actions in self-defense of the unit or other US forces. ROE for FHA operations will commonly be characterized by restraint, consistent with an evaluation of the threat. Whenever possible, all allied and PNs operating within a humanitarian relief area should do so under a commonly established ROE. This is essential to assure consistency of response for all participating forces.

b. In addition to force protection, ROE may address the range of authorized actions in the event there is looting, rioting, or other criminal conduct in the relief area and should incorporate any limitations found in the applicable SOFA or other relevant international agreements.

c. Ideally, ROE should provide a quick process to request ROE amendments in response to FHA requirements. The use of joint fires, the ability to act in defense of non-US persons, and the use of riot control agents (RCAs) should be specifically addressed in the ROE. Consult CJCSI 3110.07, *Guidance Concerning Employment of Riot Control Agents and Herbicides (U)*, for the appropriate approval authority for the use of RCAs. Additionally, authority for the use of RCAs may be obtained pursuant to Enclosure I to CJCSI 3121.01, *Standing Rules of Engagement/Standing Rules for the Use of Force for US Forces.*

d. During FHA operations, the use of force, especially lethal force, is typically reserved for unit or individual self-defense, and is therefore normally a measure of last resort. Consistent with CJCSI 3121.01, *Standing Rules for Engagement/Standing Rules for the Use of Force for US Forces,* when time and circumstances permit, forces committing hostile acts or demonstrating hostile intent toward US forces should be warned and given the opportunity to withdraw or cease threatening actions. Employment of MIS assets and capabilities and nonlethal weapons should be considered toward this end. However, the availability of nonlethal weapons and MIS assets and capabilities shall not limit a commander's inherent authority and obligation to take appropriate action in self-defense. Neither the presence nor the potential effect of nonlethal weapons shall constitute an obligation for their employment or a higher standard for employment of force than provided for by applicable law. In all cases, US forces retain the option for immediate use of lethal weapons, when faced with a lethal threat.

e. ROE should be coordinated in detail and may change as the operation evolves. Early and frequent coordination between the JFC and the embassy COM will be essential to proper ROE development. Changes to ROE must be rapidly disseminated to all personnel. Commanders at all levels may request changes to the ROE through the chain of command. Figure A-1 is provided as a sample ROE card, which summarizes ROE applicable to the individual. These example ROE were established for forces conducting FHA operations in an uncertain or hostile environment. All personnel may carry such a card for reference.

f. In limited circumstances, standing rules for the use of force (SRUF) may apply instead of ROE. SRUF generally apply to DOD law enforcement and security duties within US territory or installations. However, SRUF may be appropriate for law enforcement and DOD security functions related to FHA operations off of installations outside the US. See CJCSI 3121.01, *Standing Rules of Engagement/Standing Rules for the Use of Force for US Forces,* for guidance.

15. Intelligence Oversight and Operational Law

Intelligence oversight regulations should be reviewed for applicability, especially with regard to relationships between intelligence personnel and US citizens who work for NGOs

---

Sample Rules of Engagement Card

Nothing in these rules of engagement limits your rights to take appropriate action to defend yourself and your unit.

- You have the right to use force to defend yourself against attacks or threats of attack.
- Hostile fire may be returned effectively and promptly to stop hostile acts.
- When US forces are attacked by hostile elements, mobs, and/or rioters, US forces should use the minimum force necessary under the circumstances and proportional to the threat.
- You may not seize the property of others to accomplish your mission.
- Detention of civilians is authorized for security reasons or in self-defense.

Remember:

- The United States is not at war.
- Treat all persons with dignity and respect.
- Respect local customs and traditions of the host nation.
- Use minimum force to carry out the mission.
- Always be prepared to act in self-defense.

Figure A-1. Sample Rules of Engagement Card

---

and IGOs. A legal review should be conducted prior to the initiation of intelligence operations to ensure that there is no unforeseen impact upon the mission from the conduct of planned intelligence or information gathering operations.

16. Fiscal Law

a. The basic fiscal law principles that apply to all military operations also apply to FHA operations. However, as the authorizations applicable to FHA missions are very specific with respect to purpose and are often funded at relatively low levels, legal issues related to the funding of FHA missions can be complex.

b. It is a basic tenet of fiscal law that all expenditures in an FHA operation must be for an authorized purpose, must be made within applicable time periods, and must be for authorized and appropriate amounts. Congress has provided authority for DOD to conduct OHDACA operations, but authorizations are normally narrowly focused and appropriations can be very limited with specific expenditures validated by OFDA. As a result, it can be difficult to find the correct authorization and appropriation from which to fund an FHA mission legally. Generally, costs incurred by DOD for authorized support to FHA efforts, at the request of another department or agency may be reimbursed by the supported federal agency. However, reimbursement will generally not be available if US forces act prior to receiving the request.

c. It is essential that the SJA be involved with FHA mission planning from the outset to ensure funding is handled correctly.

For information on authorizations that may be applicable to FHA operations, refer to Appendix B, "Department of Defense Foreign Humanitarian Assistance Tasking, Funding Procedures, and Humanitarian Assistance Programs."

17. Preventing Terrorist Financing and Material Support to Terrorists

a. Preventing terrorist financing and material support to terrorist groups is a critical component of the war on terrorism. Terrorists may exploit organizations working in emergencies and areas of conflict to raise and move funds, provide logistic support, encourage terrorist recruitment, or otherwise support terrorist organizations and operations. This abuse threatens to undermine donor confidence and jeopardizes the integrity of the relief sector. Charities operating overseas in areas of high risk are especially vulnerable to this abuse. Since the terrorist attacks of September 11, 2001, the US has designated several charities worldwide as supporting terrorist activity. A list of these charities can be found at http://www.treasury.gov/resource-center/terroris-illicit-finance/Pages/protecting-fto/aspx. In addition, the US has designated several foreign terrorist organizations that have operated under aliases that appear to be for the purpose of establishing potential fundraising front organizations for terrorist activity. DOS and USAID try to ensure all organizations they fund and their subcontractors comply with US Executive Order 13224 and other laws and regulations, which prohibit transactions with and the provision of support to organizations associated with terrorism.

b. Terrorist and insurgent abuse of the charitable sector can take many forms, including:

(1) Establishing front organizations or using charities to raise funds in support of terrorist organizations.

(2) Establishing or using charities to transfer funds, other resources, and operatives across geographical boundaries.

(3) Defrauding charities through branch offices or aid workers to divert funds to support terrorist organizations.

(4) Leveraging charitable funds, resources, and services to recruit members and foster support for terrorist organizations and their ideology.

c. The Office of Foreign Assets Control of the US Department of the Treasury has primary responsibility for administering and enforcing economic and trade sanctions based on US foreign policy and national security goals against targeted foreign countries, terrorists, international narcotics traffickers, and those engaged in activities related to the proliferation of weapons of mass destruction (WMD) and other areas addressed in particular statutes and executive orders. They act under Presidential national emergency powers, as well as authority granted by specific legislation, to impose controls on transactions and freeze foreign assets under US jurisdiction. Many of the sanctions are based on UN and other international mandates, are multilateral in scope, and involve close cooperation with allied governments.

Intentionally Blank

ANNEX A TO APPENDIX A
PRINCIPLES IN THE LAW OF WAR

1. General

The law of war regulates the conduct of states and combatants engaged in armed conflict hostilities, and is often referred to as the law of armed conflict. The law of war is inspired, in part, by a humanitarian desire to diminish unnecessary suffering during armed conflict. It provides protections for all classes of persons recognized by the law of war including combatants, noncombatants, and civilians from unnecessary suffering, and establishes safeguards for civilians, prisoners of war, and the wounded and sick. The law of war also attempts to prevent degeneration of conflicts into savagery and brutality, thereby facilitating the restoration of peaceful relations which must, at some point, follow the conclusion of hostilities. It is DOD policy that US forces follow the law of war in all military operations.

For additional legal considerations, see JP 1-04, Legal Support to Military Operations.

2. Basis

Much of the law of war has been codified by treaties, such as the 1907 Hague Convention IV on Land Warfare and the four 1949 Geneva Conventions. Generally, the Hague Convention prescribes rules regarding the methods and means of warfare and establishes humanitarian requirements, such as the prohibition on the use of poison weapons. The 1949 Geneva Conventions define and prescribe the treatment of the wounded, sick, shipwrecked at sea, prisoners of war, civilians, and protected persons. Some of the law of war has never been incorporated in any treaty or convention to which the US is a party but is nonetheless reflected in customary international law. Customary international law results from the general and consistent practice of states under the belief that the practice is required by law. Countries may disagree on the application of customary international law.

3. Minimum Standards

The law of war includes minimum standards to be applied during armed conflict. Humanitarian considerations underlie much of the law of war. For example, the requirement for combatants to distinguish themselves from the peaceful civilian population such as by the use of uniforms and carrying their arms openly, exists to reinforce the protections secured to the peaceful civilian population. The law of war also seeks to protect prisoners of war, wounded and sick, and the peaceful civilian population from suffering during war to the maximum extent possible. The international community has sought to identify situations in armed conflict in which humanitarian principles can be invoked to minimize unintended harm, while allowing appropriate attacks on military objectives without sacrificing material military advantages.

4. Legal Principles

a. The principles of the law of war are military necessity, discrimination, proportionality, and unnecessary suffering. The principle of military necessity states a belligerent is justified in applying compulsion and lawful force, of any kind, to the extent necessary for the realization of the purpose of war, that is, the complete or partial submission of the enemy at the earliest possible moment with the least expenditure of its personnel, resources, and money. The principle of *discrimination*, sometimes referred to as the principle of *distinction*, is the international law obligation of the parties to a conflict to distinguish between the civilian population (or individual civilians not taking a direct part in the hostilities) and combatant forces when engaged in military operations, directing the application of force solely against personnel belonging to the latter. Similarly, military force may be directed only against military objects or objectives, and not against civilian objects. The principle of *proportionality* requires a balancing of the anticipated military advantage of conducting the attack (military necessity) with potential for civilian casualties or damage to civilian property as such. The principle of *proportionality* requires that the incidental injury to civilians, and/or damage to civilian property anticipated in the attack, must not be excessive in relation to the concrete and direct military advantage anticipated in conducting the attack. The "military advantage" is not restricted to tactical gains, but is linked to the full context of a war strategy. The principle of *unnecessary suffering* stems from the international law prohibition to employ arms, projectiles, or material calculated to cause unnecessary suffering. The prohibition against the use of weapons calculated to cause unnecessary suffering constitutes acknowledgement that suffering to combatants is lawful and expected, and may include severe injury or loss of life.

b. Law of war principles, like other universal legal principles, are part of international law. Legal principles, however, are not as specific as rules, and thus interpretations of how principles apply to a given situation may vary. Nonetheless, understanding law of war principles helps practitioners interpret specific treaty or customary rules; apply these rules to novel or complex situations; and understand how the law of war, combined with ROE, establishes a coherent system to regulate the conduct of hostilities.

c. When no specific rule applies, the principles of the law of war form the general guide for conduct during war. The law of war principles work as interdependent and reinforcing parts of a coherent system.

5. Cruelty and Excesses

The armed forces of a state act on behalf of its government and its citizens; unnecessary cruelties and excesses during armed conflicts may weigh heavily on the conscience of governmental leaders and citizens. Moreover, every nation is sensitive, to some degree, to the reaction of others to its policies; the good will and support of other governments and peoples are important in the overall conduct of foreign policy and achievement of national goals. Reciprocity, in retaliation for cruelties suffered, is a critical factor. For example, the positive treatment and well-being of one's own forces when captured by an opposing force serves as an incentive for the positive treatment of captured enemy forces. Reciprocity is not, however, a legitimate legal argument for mistreatment of enemy forces, of civilian populations or other noncompliance with the law of war. If a state fails in the first instance to comply with the law of war, its conduct may provoke violations by an adversary. Additionally, international standing to complain of violations by an adversary would be seriously compromised. Civilian loyalties may be at stake and compromised by excesses and cruelty. History demonstrates also that the successful negotiation or termination of hostilities may be prolonged or complicated by antagonisms and alienation heightened by serious violations of the law of war.

6. Training

Commanders have a responsibility to ensure that their subordinates understand the principles of the law of war. Even the appearance of improper behavior by US military personnel can have a significant effect on military operations and may cause a loss of international and domestic support. The command SJA should be tasked to conduct training in accordance with DODD 2311.01E, *DOD Law of War Program,* and CJCSI 5810.01, *Implementation of the DOD Law of War Program,* and any relevant Service regulations, for all personnel within the command in order to ensure full compliance with the law of war.

7. Individual Responsibility

Every Service member is responsible for compliance with the law of war. To avoid violations of the law of war, commanders must ensure that its principles and requirements are known and understood by all subordinate personnel.

Intentionally Blank

APPENDIX B
DEPARTMENT OF DEFENSE FOREIGN HUMANITARIAN ASSISTANCE TASKING, FUNDING PROCEDURES, AND HUMANITARIAN ASSISTANCE PROGRAMS

1. General

The Office of the ASD (SO/LIC) and DSCA execute a number of assistance programs. This appendix provides a brief overview of these programs and authority for their implementation in support of FHA operations.

2. Approval Authority for Foreign Disaster Relief

Except in cases of emergencies where the on-site commander (OSC) with assigned or attached forces at or near the immediate scene determines prompt action to save human lives as required (see paragraph 5, "72 Hour Authority for Prompt Action Saving Human Lives"), DOD components will participate in FDR operations only at the direction of the President or SecDef or a designee approves, with the concurrence of the Secretary of State, an RFA from another USG department or agency. FDR is not authorized without a request for assistance, or an indication of a willingness to accept assistance, from the affected country. Generally speaking, USAID must also validate the HA requirement before FDR is authorized. ASD (SO/LIC) is the normal approval authority for DOD resource and services commitment to FDR. The DOD lead for management of budget allocations in this area is DSCA. The main point of contact for the Joint Staff is the J-3 Joint Operations Division.

3. Responsibilities

DOD provides supplies and services from the most expedient source, which normally is the CCDR. The CCDR, when directed, assumes the primary coordinating role for provision of DOD supplies and services. For humanitarian relief supplies for use during FHA, CCDRs should first source from EP warehouses managed by DSCA before purchasing from DOD/Defense Logistics Agency (DLA) stock (see paragraph 7, "Excess Property Program"). The Joint Staff, USTRANSCOM, and DSCA, if EP is transported, coordinate transportation requirements. The Military Departments and Joint Staff support the designated CCDR by coordinating interdepartmental approval and funding processes with ASD(SO/LIC), DSCA, and the Office of the Under Secretary of Defense (Comptroller) (OUSD[C]). If items requested are not available in the CCMD, DSCA will locate resources through DLA, the Services, or a supporting CCDR. DLA's Joint Contingency Acquisition Support Office mission support team may be required to implement, synchronize, integrate, and manage OCS among the different USG departments and agencies to support the CCDR's objectives in an FHA operation.

4. Funding

a. DOD activities associated with FDR may be sourced using OHDACA appropriation funds, service operations and maintenance funds during immediate response (see paragraph 5, "72-Hour Authority for Prompt Action Saving Lives") or under some specific legal authority (e.g., drawdown authority), the Combatant Commander Initiative Fund, funds from other agencies, or a combination of these, depending on the nature of the operation.

b. USTRANSCOM calculates transportation system shipping costs (normally, using the DOD rate), and conveys that information to ASD(SO/LIC) and DSCA and the Joint Staff J-4. ASD(SO/LIC) and DSCA forward cost information to USAID (OFDA) and other agencies, as required.

c. After cost acceptance by the appropriate agencies (e.g., DOS, USAID, ASD[SO/LIC], and OUSD[C]), formal approval to commit DOD materials and services is forwarded from the Office of ASD(SO/LIC) to the Director, Joint Staff. This approval contains funding and billing information (including, if possible, fund cites), as well as resource disposition instructions. Fund cites should be provided for each DOD support item. The Joint Staff then forwards the fund cites and other relevant information to the affected Service(s), agency supplier, or USTRANSCOM for each action at the time of request. The Joint Staff J-4 (or J-3, as appropriate) develops tasking messages, which should contain fund cites, funding limits, billing addresses, and Joint Staff points of contact, if possible, for each DOD element tasked. Tasking messages will require tasked units to provide clear text itemized billing information and the tasked unit point of contact. The messages should also advise tasked elements that approval must be obtained before exceeding the funding limit; that agencies, such as OFDA, will only reimburse for those items or services requested; and that all bills must be submitted in the next monthly billing cycle following completion of the service or activity.

d. In the event military units and personnel are required to deploy, the Joint Staff Director for Force Structure, Resource and Assessment assists OUSD(C) in obtaining rough order of magnitude cost estimates from the CCDR or Service(s). Following receipt of funding approval from the Office of ASD(SO/LIC), the Joint Staff J-3 prepares a CJCS deployment order for SecDef approval.

e. **Economy Act.** The Economy Act of 1932 provides agencies the authority to provide services to, or secure the services of, another Executive agency for in house performance or performance by contract where there is no other statutory authority. The head of an agency or major organizational unit within an agency may place an order with a major organizational unit within the same agency or another agency for goods or services if the agency has available funds; the order is in the best interests of the USG; the agency filling the order can provide, or acquire by contract, the ordered goods or services; and the ordered goods or services cannot be provided by contract as conveniently or cheaply (See Title 31, USC, Section 1535[a]).

(1) The FAR [*Federal Acquisition Regulation*] Subpart 17.5 and the DFARS [*Defense Federal Acquisition Regulation Supplement*] Subpart 217.5 govern use of the Economy Act of 1932. It can be a valuable tool if used correctly. However, misuse can lead to criminal violations of the law.

(2) The regulations require two primary documents. The first is a determination and findings that establish the Economy Act of 1932 as the authority for the transaction.

The second document is the order constituting the agreement between the requiring and servicing agencies on the statement of work, payment for supplies or services, and related terms and conditions.

5. 72-Hour Authority for Prompt Action Saving Human Lives

A military commander with assigned forces at or near the immediate scene of a foreign disaster may take prompt action to save human lives. In cases in which this authority is invoked, the commander should obtain the concurrence of the HN and COM of the affected country before committing forces. The OSC should report the action taken at once and request guidance. Also, the CCDR will follow up as soon as possible, but no later than 72 hours after the start of relief operations, to secure SecDef or Deputy Secretary of Defense approval for continuing assistance. CCDRs must also obtain SecDef approval in order to obtain reimbursement with OHDACA funds. Reimbursement of funds expended under these circumstances is not assured. Such assistance during the first 72 hours does not include the authority to provide military assistance that does not contribute to urgent life-saving efforts, therefore, it is particularly important to avoid mission creep in this scenario. The more time that passes, the less likely that the assistance will be deemed critical to saving human lives. Responding elements must track incremental costs incurred by maintaining detailed records of expenditures, and provide detailed billing information to support their reimbursement efforts. The DOD Financial Management Regulation, Volume 12, Chapter 12, and DODD 5100.46, *Foreign Disaster Relief,* contain guidelines for DOD elements to bill for cost reimbursement for supplies and/or services provided in support of FDR.

6. Excess Property Program

a. The DOD EP Program is managed by DSCA and refers to nonlethal EP made available to donate for HA and FHA purposes. EP donations typically include furniture, medical and school equipment and supplies, vehicles (e.g., fire trucks, ambulances), tools, and construction equipment. DSCA has one continental United States (CONUS) EP warehouse in Albany, Georgia, and two outside the continental United States (OCONUS) warehouses located in Livorno, Italy, and Okinawa, Japan, respectively. Oversight of warehouse operations is executed by the DSCA Warehouse Manager located in the CONUS warehouse. Warehouse personnel process, refurbish, store, arrange, and track transportation of the property.

b. DOD EP provided, pursuant to the authority of Title 10, USC, Section 2557, must be transferred to the Secretary of State, typically via the US embassy (or the ambassador's designated representative), which is responsible for distribution to the intended recipient, normally through an HN government ministry, charitable organization, or an NGO/IGO that supports the population on behalf of the HN government. The DOD EP Program enables the transfer of such property in a manner that ensures quality control and proper coordination, and that is consistent with legal and policy requirements.

See DOD 5105.38-M, Security Assistance Management Manual, Chapter 12, for more information on program process, acquiring EP, and reporting requirements.

7. Presidential Drawdown Authority

Pursuant to Sec 506(a)(2) of the FAA of 1961, as amended, the President may direct the drawdown of defense articles or services of DOD for various activities including international disaster assistance. This provides authority to make available materials and services from existing stock up to a $75 million aggregate value.

Note: Drawdowns are not actual funds, and the organization providing the material or service may or may not be reimbursed at a later date. DSCA is the DOD entity responsible for processing drawdowns in conjunction with DOS.

See DOD 5105.38-M, Security Assistance Management Manual, *Chapter 11, for more information on program process and reporting requirements.*

8. Funded Transportation Program

a. The Funded Transportation program is conducted under Title 10, USC, Section 2561, Humanitarian Assistance, which authorizes DOD to use funds appropriated to DOD to be used for transportation of humanitarian relief supplies. DSCA administers the application process and works with the donor, DOD contracted commercial carriers (through USTRANSCOM's Surface Deployment and Distribution Command) and the DOD/DSCA contracted cargo inspector to facilitate the transportation process.

b. Cargo must be humanitarian in nature and may not include any hazardous, political, or religious material. Interested donors submit requests for transportation of humanitarian supplies using the Humanitarian Assistance Transportation website http: hatransportation.ohasis.org. Additional guidance may also be found at this website.

c. After an application is approved, the contracted commercial carrier arranges transportation of the cargo from point of origin to final destination. DSCA tracks the shipment and provides updates with regard to HA transportation-related activities. The DSCA (Programs Directorate) transportation specialist, in coordination with the DSCA Comptroller's office, validates the transportation costs billed by the contracted commercial carrier.

d. Donations are transported primarily via surface transportation; exceptions may be considered on a case-by-case basis.

e. **EP Transportation.** EP warehouse personnel arrange contracted transportation in accordance with parameters set by the CCMD EP program manager and implementing project managers as per DSCA-approved EP project submissions. In most cases, mode(s) of transportation will be selected based on the best interests of the USG, usually surface transport. However, exceptions will be granted when the occasion warrants a faster mode of shipping, such as during FHA efforts.

f. **FDR Transportation.** When OHDACA is determined to be the appropriate funding source for relief efforts, the Funded Transportation Program is used to transport personnel and relief materials and can be via air, surface, or both. Upon notification of a disaster, DSCA will establish contact with USTRANSCOM, the appropriate CCMD JDDOC, and Joint Staff J-4 to ensure information sharing and coordination concerning potential or actual OHDACA funded transportation missions. The DSCA (Program Directorate) transportation specialist will coordinate the establishment of transportation account codes with the DSCA Comptroller's office. Under FHA operations, a SecDef waiver is required for DOD to transport non-DOD personnel and supplies on DOD assets. Language requesting SecDef waiver is included in each disaster response Executive Secretary package that is ultimately approved by SecDef.

9. Space Available Transportation Program

a. DSCA coordinates the overall execution of transportation of humanitarian relief supplies to foreign countries (Title 10, USC, Section 402, commonly referred to as the Denton Program). The Denton Program employs USTRANSCOM resources to provide space available transportation, primarily by air, for the FHA supplies furnished by nongovernmental sources. Denton Program transportation is coordinated from port to port, at no cost to the donor. Cargo must be humanitarian in nature and may not include any hazardous, political, or religious material. Cargo cannot be sent to military or paramilitary organizations, unless the organization provides a specific service to the civilian population.

b. DSCA coordinates with the donor, DOS, USAID, and USTRANSCOM to facilitate the process. USAID and the DOS review and submit valid requests to DSCA for action. Applicant requests must be formally submitted through USAID for clearance and forwarded to DSCA. DSCA provides final approval, establishing a transportation control number for each shipment and forwards it to USTRANSCOM in order to arrange the space available mission.

c. During FHA operations, transportation under the Denton Program to countries affected by a disaster may be suspended until after response operations have ceased.

10. Department of Defense Humanitarian Demining Assistance

a. Humanitarian demining assistance is the detection and clearance of land mines and other ERW, including activities related to the furnishing of education, training, and technical assistance with respect to the detection and clearance of land mines and other ERW. DOD humanitarian demining assistance is authorized by Title 10, USC, Section 407. The USG HMA program assists countries in relieving the suffering from the adverse effects of uncleared land mines and other ERW while promoting US interests. The DOD HMA program assists nations plagued by land mines and ERW by executing train-the trainer programs of instruction designed to develop indigenous capabilities for a wide range of HMA activities.

b. The USG PCC for Democracy, Human Rights, and International Operations Subgroup on HMA approves support for PNs. The DOD representative to this interagency

PCC is the Chief, HMA(ASD[SO/LIC]). DOD humanitarian demining assistance is a critical component of the overall USG mine action program.

c. HMA activities are a legitimate training opportunity for US military units that have demining tasks on their mission-essential task list (METL). The operational requirements for deployment of US military personnel in support of HMA activities are identical to the deployment process for other similar training operations. The training requirements on a unit's METL for wartime training and deployments may be met during HMA training. HMA training activities are also a key security cooperation tool available to a CCDR to gain training and other engagement opportunities in a specific country. Specifically, HMA activities can improve DOD visibility in the context of providing assistance to address a humanitarian need; build the capacity of the PN government; reduce or eliminate ERW; and build relationships with the PN government and its populace that can improve DOD access within a PN and/or region. DOD HMA activities typically include training PNs in the procedures of land mine clearance, mine risk education, and victims' assistance.

d. US forces carry out humanitarian demining assistance when the assistance promotes either the security interests of both the US and HN or the specific operational readiness skills of the members of the armed forces who participate in the activities. Humanitarian demining assistance must be approved by DOS and shall complement, and may not duplicate, any other form of social or economic assistance which may be provided to the country concerned by other USG departments or agencies.

e. By law, DOD personnel are restricted in the extent to which they may actively participate in ERW clearance and physical security and stockpile management operations during HCA. Under Title 10, USC, Section 401(a)(1), Military Departments may carry out certain HCA activities in conjunction with authorized military operations of the armed forces in a foreign nation. Title 10, USC, Section 407(e)(1), defines the term humanitarian demining assistance (as part of HCA activities) as detection and clearance of land mines and other ERW, and includes the activities related to the furnishing of education, training, and technical assistance with respect to explosive safety, the detection and clearance of land mines and other ERW, and the disposal, demilitarization, physical security, and stockpile management of potentially dangerous stockpiles of explosive ordnance. However, under Title 10, USC, Section 407(a)(3), members of the US Armed Forces while providing humanitarian demining assistance shall not engage in the physical detection, lifting, or destroying of land mines or other ERW, or stockpiled conventional munitions (unless the member does so for the concurrent purpose of supporting a US military operation). Additionally, members of the US Armed Forces shall not provide such humanitarian demining and civic assistance as part of a military operation that does not involve the armed forces. Under DOD policy, the restrictions in Title 10, USC, Section 407, also apply to DOD civilian personnel.

f. A country experiencing the adverse effects of uncleared ERW may request US assistance. The country must formally request help from DOS through the US embassy. The country team provides a copy of the request to the pertinent GCC. DSCA assists the CJCS, USSOCOM, GCCs, host countries, and other organizations in planning for, establishing, and executing mine action programs.

g. All requests for DOD HMA training and activities, including testing of new demining technology in foreign countries, will be vetted through Chief, HMA(ASD[SO/LIC]). This office will conduct all interagency coordination as required.

h. DOD HMA activities are funded from the OHDACA appropriation. The CCMDs may purchase limited demining equipment and supplies necessary for the conduct of the trainer program and transfer the equipment to the PN or designated agent upon completion of the DOD training program.

Further information may be obtained from CJCSI 3207.01, Military Support to Humanitarian Mine Actions, *JP 3-15,* Barriers, Obstacles, and Mine Warfare for Joint Operations, *and DOD Humanitarian Demining Research and Development Homepage: http://www.humanitariandemining.org, and the United Nations Electronic Mine Information Network: http://www.mineaction.org.*

i. Expenses incurred as a direct result of providing humanitarian demining assistance to a foreign country shall be handled in accordance with guidance in Title 10, USC, Section 407, *Humanitarian Demining Assistance and Stockpiled Conventional Munitions Assistance: Authority; Limitations.*

11. Humanitarian and Civic Assistance

a. Military personnel participate in HCA activities to create strategic, operational, and/or tactical effects that support GCC's objectives in theater security cooperation or designated contingency plans, while at the same time reinforcing skills required for the operational readiness of the forces executing the HCA mission.

b. HCA deployments enhance US military operational readiness and provide unique training opportunities in remote and austere environments. US forces practice deployment activities, C2 procedures, and logistics operations and sustainment over extended distances. US military personnel also become familiar with the command's AOR, learn about the HNs' economy and culture, and hone foreign language skills. HCA missions also enhance interagency coordination and complement efforts of the DOS's integrated country strategy mission resource request and the USAID's country development cooperation strategy. HCA projects consists of rudimentary engineering, medical, dental, or veterinary activity in the HN. HCA activity is distinct from development and not designed to drastically change the conditions found in local environments.

c. Funding for HCA activities is provided by the annual National Defense Authorization Act and obligated for incremental expenses such as costs for consumable materials, supplies, and services, if any, that are reasonably necessary to execute HCA activities. Funding does not include costs associated with the military operation (e.g., transportation, personnel expenses, petroleum, oils and lubricants, repair of equipment), which would likely have been incurred whether or not the HCA was provided.

d. HCA projects are planned and developed through normal security cooperation protocols. The country team in coordination with the HN develops project nominations. When the plan is developed it is coordinated through USAID to determine no duplication of efforts and is approved by the US ambassador to the country. Recommended HCA projects are then submitted to the GCCs for prioritization and funding; they in turn submit their projects to the Joint Chiefs of Staff for coordination with legal counsel, country desk officers, the Department of State Bureau of Political and Military Affairs, and the Office of the USD(P) who finally approves project nominations. Messaging within the HN is achieved in coordination with and through the US embassy.

See DODI 2205.02, Humanitarian and Civic Assistance (HCA) Activities, *for more information on process, policy, and reporting requirements.*

12. Humanitarian Daily Rations

OHDACA funds are used to procure and provide low cost, nutritional, daily rations for use in foreign countries to alleviate hunger after man-made or natural disasters. HDRs are stored at DSCAs EP Warehouse in Albany, Georgia, in a climate-controlled bay for use in support of FHA efforts and may be requested from DSCA via the CCMD. HDRs are a temporary feeding measure designed to be easily transported to meet requirements of mobile populations until conventional, longer term relief programs can resume. HDRs are designed to be suitable for consumption by all cultures and have no less than 2,200 calories, contain no animal byproducts, are meatless, fortified with vitamins, and provide a single day's worth of nutrition per unit. Use of HDRs should be coordinated with, and validated by, the appropriate USAID/OFDA representative to ensure the accomplishment of desired effects and to avoid unintended consequences.

13. United States National Guard State Partnership Program

The National Guard's (NG's) State Partnership Program (SPP) is a DOD security cooperation program under which a military-to-military relationship is established between the NG of a US state and a PN's military forces for the complementary purposes of promoting mutual understanding, interoperability, and furtherance of the GCC's theater security cooperation program objectives. The SPP builds enduring relationships with, and, to the extent authorized by law, the capacity of, PN military forces and promotes the readiness of NG forces. The program is administered by the NG Bureau, guided by DOS foreign policy goals and executed by the state adjutants general in support of GCC and COM security cooperation objectives and DOD policy goals.

a. SPP began in 1993 as a direct response to the collapse of the former Soviet Union to enable the US to take an active role in shaping the new international security environment by strengthening emerging nations, promoting civilian control of the military, fostering prosperity, and enhancing democratic security. The program provides valuable international engagement experience and interoperability for US NG members and foreign partners.

b. SPP provides significant benefits to the US whole-of-government efforts to meet national security needs through building partner capacity globally. It provides unique, niche capabilities in direct support to the GCCs and COMs in meeting theater and country engagement objectives as authorized under Title 10, USC, and Title 22, USC, respectively. NG capabilities addressed through SPP include critical areas such as emergency management and disaster response; border and port security; medical capacities; economic security; natural resource protection; peacekeeping operations; leadership development; counter illicit trafficking; counter proliferation; and, counterterrorism.

c. Through SPP, the NG conducts military-to-military engagements in support of defense security goals but also leverages relationships and capabilities to facilitate broader interagency and corollary engagements in accordance with existing authorities. Corollary engagements are funded through the state, NGO, or private resources, or by another federal agency outside DOD. Such engagements might include education, medical, legal, business, and professional exchanges. Through these capabilities, SPP spans the military, government, economic, and social realms of society.

d. SPP offers recognized capabilities to the GCCs and Service components in meeting their TCPs and objectives outside of what active-duty forces can provide. SPP activities are approved by the appropriate GCC and are certified to meet stated objectives of the relevant TCP. SPP events are also normally approved by the relevant COM and certified to meet stated objectives of the appropriate DOS authored integrated country strategy.

e. SPP continues to evolve and has expanded partnerships between US states and territories and partner countries, the latter of which fall within the AORs of the six GCCs. The NG currently has 65 partnerships with 71 countries around the world. The unique and enduring relationships between SPP countries and partner states have established trust between partners. Providing HA with SPP units offers an opportunity to significantly enhance partnerships, thereby furthering the objectives of the National Military Strategy.

For further information on SPP, see DODI 5111.20, State Partnership Program (SPP).

Intentionally Blank

APPENDIX C
DEPARTMENT OF STATE AND UNITED STATES AGENCY FOR INTERNATIONAL DEVELOPMENT ORGANIZATIONS

1. Department of State

a. **The mission of DOS is to create a more secure, democratic, and prosperous world for the benefit of the American people and the international community.** American diplomacy in the 21st century is based on fundamental beliefs: our freedom is best protected by ensuring that others are free; our prosperity depends on the prosperity of others; and our security relies on a global effort to secure the rights of all. Millions of the world's poor have not yet benefited from globalization, increasing their risk of alienation. Furthermore, transnational threats have emerged from globalization, spreading disease via the most mobile population in history. Famines and civil conflicts have erupted in countries steeped in poverty or constrained by autocratic rulers, creating waves of refugees and swelling the ranks of internally displaced populations.

b. DOS and USAID will work with US NGOs, institutions of higher learning, and private sector partners who share USG objectives and help leverage our resources. By providing vital links to the American people and to counterpart organizations and institutions overseas, DOS's US partners help represent the best in America's technical, humanitarian, and management skills.

c. In meeting their strategic objectives and goals, DOS and USAID are committed to protect US national interests and advance peace, security, and sustainable development. DOS will work with USAID and other agencies to ensure US resources support our goals of saving lives, safeguarding people's health, and advancing regional stability. The US is committed to find longer-term solutions to food insecurity and working in partnership with developing countries to address this global problem, which affects millions of people. Viable early warning systems and assessments will help mitigate disasters and increase preparedness and response.

2. Bureau of Population, Refugees, and Migration

PRM has primary responsibility for formulating policies on population, refugees, and migration, and for administering US refugee assistance and admissions programs. PRM coordinates US international population policy and promotes its goals through bilateral and multilateral cooperation. It works closely with USAID, which administers US international population programs. PRM also coordinates US international migration policy within the USG and through bilateral and multilateral diplomacy. PRM administers and monitors US contributions to NGOs and IGOs to assist and protect refugees abroad. PRM also oversees admissions of tens of thousands of refugees to the US for permanent resettlement. The USG funds protection and life-sustaining relief for millions of refugees and victims of conflict around the globe; PRM is central to these efforts.

3. Bureau of Political-Military Affairs

a. **PM is the principal link between DOS and DOD.** PM provides policy direction in the areas of international security, security assistance, military operations, defense strategy and plans, and defense trade.

b. The **Office of Weapons Removal and Abatement (WRA)** creates local, regional and international conditions conducive to peace, stability, and prosperity by curbing the illicit proliferation of conventional weapons of war such as light automatic weapons, rocket propelled grenades, and by removing and destroying others, such as persistent land mines and abandoned stocks of munitions, that remain and pose hazards after the cessation of armed conflict.

(1) WRA develops, implements, and monitors policy, programs, and public engagement efforts that further US foreign policy goals through the development and implementation of comprehensive solutions to the harmful humanitarian effects caused by the existence of public hazards from conventional weapons following cessation of armed conflict. WRA works closely with USG departments and agencies as well as NGOs, IGOs, and private enterprises.

(2) WRA serves as the lead organization in coordinating US HMA activities worldwide.

(a) The USG HMA program assists selected countries in relieving human suffering and in developing an indigenous mine action capability while promoting US interests. The program provides increased HMA assistance to countries suffering from the presence of persistent land mines, which maim and kill innocents, obstruct emergency assistance activities, hamper economic development, and impede free movement of citizens.

(b) WRA develops and implements country-specific HMA programs and oversees the interagency strategic planning and policy development processes supporting US global demining activities. It directly supports the work of the PCC Subgroup on HMA.

c. The **Office of International Security Operations** is the primary interface between DOS and DOD on operational military matters. Specifically, it:

(1) Initiates and coordinates exceptional requests from DOS to DOD for the provision and transport of HA in the event of disasters or pressing humanitarian crises abroad. Requests may be on a reimbursable or non-reimbursable basis and are normally conveyed through Executive Secretary channels.

(2) Coordinates DOS review and approval of DOD excess nonlethal supplies donations, HCA, and certain other types of HA overseas. The Office of International Security Operations ensures assistance proposals are consistent with US foreign policy and meet relevant statutory requirements regarding HA.

(3) Ensures assistance proposals are consistent with US foreign policy and meet relevant statutory requirements regarding HA.

(4) Coordinates DOS review of Denton Program applications to ensure that they are consistent with US foreign policy objectives.

(5) Reviews applications for the Funded Transportation Program to ensure that they are consistent with US foreign policy.

d. The **Office of Security Negotiations and Agreements** facilitates the worldwide deployment of US military forces and protects current or former Service members from surrender to the International Criminal Court (ICC) without the consent of the USG. It negotiates SOFAs, defense cooperation agreements, burden-sharing agreements, and Article 98 agreements. The first three types of agreements support the deployment of US forces abroad while Article 98 agreements address the ICC. Article 98 agreements are bilateral non-surrender agreements protecting American citizens from the ICC.

e. **Office of the POLAD Coordinator** supports the community of POLADs to the US Service Chiefs and principal US military commanders in the US and overseas. The POLADs are senior DOS officers (flag/general office-rank equivalent) detailed as personal advisors to leading US military leaders/commanders to provide policy support regarding the diplomatic and political aspects of the commanders' military responsibilities. The Office of the POLAD Coordinator also supports DOS's participation in the DOS-DOD Officer Exchange Program. In addition, the Office of the POLAD coordinator supports DOS representatives in JIACGs at select military commands.

4. Bureau of Conflict and Stabilization Operations

a. The **core mission** of the CSO strengthens US national security by breaking cycles of violent conflict and mitigating crises in priority countries. Guided by local dynamics, CSO acts quickly to devise sustainable solutions to address the full spectrum of conflict, from prevention to crisis response to stabilization. Failing and post-conflict states pose one of the greatest national and international security challenges of our day, threatening vulnerable populations, their neighbors, our allies, and ourselves. Struggling states can provide breeding grounds for terrorism, crime, trafficking, and humanitarian catastrophes, and can destabilize an entire region. Experience shows that managing conflict, particularly internal conflict, is not a passing phenomenon. It has become a mainstream part of our foreign policy. Until now, the international community has undertaken stabilization and reconstruction operations in an ad hoc fashion, recreating the tools and relationships each time a crisis arises. To ensure that countries are set on a sustainable path towards peace, democracy, and a market economy, new, institutionalized foreign policy tools are required that can influence the choices countries and people make about the nature of their economies, their political systems, their security, and, indeed, in some cases about the very social fabric of a nation.

b. **Civilian Response Corps (CRC).** The CRC is a group of civilian federal employees and, eventually, volunteers from the private sector and state and local governments, who will be trained and equipped to deploy rapidly to countries in crisis or emerging from conflict, in order to provide reconstruction and stabilization assistance. They are diplomats, development specialists, public health officials, law enforcement and corrections officers, engineers, economists, lawyers, public administrators, agronomists, and others–offering the full range of skills needed to help fragile states restore stability and the rule of law, and achieve economic recovery and sustainable growth as quickly as possible. Because no single government entity has all of the relevant expertise, the CRC is a partnership of eight departments and agencies: DOS, USAID, Department of Agriculture, Department of Commerce, Department of Health and Human Services, Department of Homeland Security, Department of Justice, and Department of the Treasury. Pilot Active and Standby components of the CRC within DOS have deployed members to Sudan, Chad, Haiti, Lebanon, Kosovo, Iraq, and Afghanistan to assist with conflict prevention and mitigation.

5. Bureau of International Security and Nonproliferation

a. The Bureau of International Security and Nonproliferation (ISN) is responsible for managing a broad range of nonproliferation, counterproliferation, and arms control functions. ISN supports efforts of foreign partners to respond to the use of WMD.

b. Within ISN, the Office of Weapons of Mass Destruction Terrorism develops policy and plans, directs initiatives, and coordinates partner capacity building activities to prevent, protect against, and respond to the threat or use of WMD by terrorists. The office will coordinate USG support to manage and mitigate the consequences of incidents occurring in foreign jurisdictions that involve the use of CBRN contaminants. Key functions include:

(1) Supporting the needs of FCM missions.

(2) Collaborating with other elements of the USG to provide diplomatic support for FCM responsibilities and activities.

(3) Coordinating USG engagement with foreign governments and IGOs regarding FCM planning and capacity building.

(4) Improving the USG's management architecture for FCM support.

c. FCM provides a critical element in a layered defense in depth against WMD terrorism. The Office of Weapons of Mass Destruction Terrorism is responsible for the security policy framework that integrates FCM activities of the USG into a strategic architecture for planning and response. In this capacity, the office carries out the following activities:

(1) Cooperates with foreign governments in their planning, capabilities, and response development.

(2) Negotiates international FCM cooperation and planning agreements with foreign governments.

(3) Provides FCM expertise and support to the DOS FEST and appropriate DOS task forces.

6. Office of the Coordinator for Counterterrorism

a. The mission of the Office of the Coordinator for Counterterrorism is to develop and lead a worldwide effort to combat terrorism.

b. The FEST is the USG's only interagency, on-call, short-notice team poised to respond to terrorist and other incidents worldwide. The FEST is a rapid-response interagency team sent to support the COM.

c. The FEST's mission is to advise, assist, assess, and coordinate. Specifically, the FEST provides the COM, HN leaders, and incident managers guidance concerning US capabilities to mitigate the consequences of an incident/attack. The FEST brings unique FCM assistance capabilities not normally available at an affected US mission.

7. Humanitarian Information Unit

a. HIU serves as a USG interagency center to identify, collect, analyze, and disseminate unclassified information critical to USG decision makers and partners in preparation for and response to humanitarian emergencies worldwide, and to promote best practices for humanitarian information management.

b. To accomplish this mission, the HIU performs the following tasks:

(1) Identifies key sources of geospatial and georeferenced data best suited to meet the information requirements of its consumers.

(2) Collects timely, verifiable, and relevant data utilizing an extensive network of information partnerships.

(3) Analyzes data using multiagency expertise and applying proven technologies to determine significant trends and relationships.

(4) Disseminates information of value to all levels of consumers, from national-level policymakers to operational field managers.

c. The HIU is part of the Bureau of Intelligence and Research and receives oversight from a USG interagency executive steering committee. Its staff is composed of personnel from DOS, USAID, DOD, and NGA.

8. United States Agency for International Development

a. USAID plays a vital role in promoting US national security and foreign policy. It does so by addressing poverty fueled by lack of economic opportunity, one of the root causes of violence today. As stated in the President's National Security Strategy, USAID's work in development joins diplomacy and defense as one of three key pieces of the nation's foreign policy apparatus. USAID promotes peace and stability by fostering economic growth, protecting human health, providing emergency HA, and enhancing democracy in developing countries. These efforts to improve the lives of millions of people worldwide represent US values and advance US interests for peace and prosperity.

b. USAID provides assistance in sub-Saharan Africa, Asia and the Near East, Latin America and the Caribbean, and Europe and Eurasia. With HQ in Washington, DC, USAID's strength is its field offices in many regions of the world. The agency works in over 100 developing countries and in close partnership with NGOs, IGOs, IPI, universities, American businesses, other governments, trade and professional associations, faith-based organizations, and other USG departments and agencies. USAID has working relationships, through contracts and grant agreements, with more than 3,500 companies and over 300 US-based NGOs.

For more information on USAID, see USAID Primer.

c. Within USAID, DCHA provides technical leadership and expertise in coordinating USAID's democracy programs, international disaster assistance, emergency and developmental food aid, aid to manage and mitigate conflict, and volunteer programs. DCHA provides technical leadership, support, and advice in developing policy and programs to assist countries transitioning out of crisis and administers disaster assistance, preparedness, and mitigation. DCHA also provides capacity building for US NGOs and aid to American schools and hospitals abroad. DCHA provides technical advice and support to the USAID Administrator, regional bureaus, field missions, and other offices with regard to these programs.

(1) CMC works to align defense and development policies, plans, and programs to achieve US foreign policy goals and developmental goals, leveraging the unique capabilities of DOD and USAID. CMC accomplishes this goal by addressing areas of common interests between defense and development through a personnel exchange and communication information exchange at various levels. CMC manages and facilitates USAID's day-to-day interface with DOD, interprets and implements USG civilian-military policies, and coordinates joint planning, training, conferences, exercises, and communications. A key feature of CMC's staffing is the exchange of senior military and development personnel. USAID's senior development advisors (SDAs) and deputy development advisors (DDAs) in CCMDs outside the US and USSOCOM, and the Joint Staff ensure collaboration with USAID's bureaus and offices. SDAs are senior Foreign Service Officers who provide advice and counsel to CCDRs regarding development, relief, reconstruction, and stabilization issues. DDAs are Foreign Service Officers who work more at the action officer level. Many SDAs and DDAs have experience implementing development and stabilization programming in collaboration with DOD and DOS in conflict countries. Complementing USAID SDAs and DDAs are CCMD LNOs assigned to DCHA/CMC, who ensure access at each level of their commands. In addition, USAID hosts LNOs from the US Navy, US Marine Corps, and the US Army Corps of Engineers. CMC builds on DCHA's strong links with the military and its lead role in quick response to conflict, reconstruction, transition, famine, and disaster situations. CMC has links with USAID's bureaus and offices to ensure that all of USAID's interface needs with DOD are coordinated and informed. Headed by a director and deputy director, CMC has three divisions supported by an administrative support staff.

(a) The Planning Division manages the day-today aspects of the USAID-military relationship and conducts civilian-military planning and analysis with DOD, DOS, and other USG departments and agencies. These planning activities are accomplished with teams comprised of USAID employees, CCMD LNOs, SDAs, and DDAs who foster the relationship between USAID and the commands.

(b) The Operations, Learning, and Outreach Division serves, as the USAID's primary point of contact, for civilian-military training and coordinates interagency training, education, and exercise requirements; develops training and education programs and curricula; and delivers training and education programs to a wide variety of audiences. This division also serves as the point of contact for USAID briefings to military audiences visiting USAID and at DOD venues, and it provides operations support to the CMC office mission.

(c) The Policy Division coordinates USAID civilian-military policy and strategy with DOD, and other USG departments and agencies and the NGO community. This division develops USAID policies related to civilian-military cooperation, facilitates DOD input into USAID policy development and implementation processes, and provides coordinated USAID inputs into DOD policies, strategies, planning and programming guidance, and doctrine.

(2) **Office of Transition Initiatives (OTI)** supports local partners to advance peace and democracy in priority conflict-prone countries. At the request of and in coordination with the Congress, DOS, and the appropriate in-country US ambassadors and USAID field missions, OTI seizes critical windows of opportunity to provide on-the-ground, fast, flexible, catalytic short-term assistance that promotes movement toward political and social stability and democracy. OTI programs in such countries should continue until reasonable stability is established and an effective hand-off is completed to longer-term institutional development efforts.

(a) The **management and program operations team** enhances and facilitates OTI activities worldwide by contributing to OTI's strategic plan and managing OTI's policy formulation; monitoring and evaluation of activities; internal communications and public outreach; budget formulation; tracking and reconciliation; procurement planning and processing; and general operations support and administrative services.

(b) The **field operations team** develops and oversees OTI country programs, including country strategies, program design, implementation, and donor coordination; and conducts liaison with USAID bureaus, field missions, and USG departments and agencies to ensure policy compliance and coordination.

(3) **Office of Food for Peace (FFP)** provides leadership, coordination, and operational support for international food activities. It develops USG policy, formal positions, and funding levels for grants to and cooperative agreements with the WFP, NGOs, and, in selected instances, government implementing food programs. It provides assistance for emergency operations and support for USAID food security and developmental objectives. FFP implements legislation and policies governing the donation of US agricultural commodities. FFP manages a budget of over a billion dollars annually, and also

oversees the procurement and shipping of over two million metric tons of food annually. The Famine Early Warning System is also part of FFP.

d. **OFDA** is delegated the responsibility to provide international disaster and HA and coordinate the USG response to declared disasters in foreign countries. USAID/OFDA's mandate is to save lives; alleviate human suffering; and reduce the economic and social impact of disasters. OFDA provides technical support to the Administrator of USAID, who serves as the President's Special Coordinator for International Disaster Assistance. OFDA formulates US foreign disaster assistance policy in coordination with other USG departments and agencies. It coordinates with USAID offices and others to provide relief supplies (e.g., blankets, plastic sheeting, sanitation hygiene kits), funds implementing partners (e.g., UN agencies, NGOs, Red Cross) to provide direct support and HA and develops and manages logistical, operational, and technical support for disaster responses. Besides its coordination activities within the USG, USAID/OFDA carries out these response options in coordination with the affected state, other donor countries, UN, NGOs, and IGOs. There are three divisions within OFDA.

(1) The **Disaster Response and Mitigation Division** coordinates with USAID offices and others to provide relief supplies and HA. It plans for the level of response needed for an emergency and implements and manages USG disaster relief and rehabilitation programs worldwide. It devises, coordinates, and implements program strategies for the application of the most current science and technology to prevention, mitigation, and national and international preparedness for a variety of natural and man-made disaster situations. It evaluates the impact of previous disaster response initiatives/programs and ensures the integration of this information into future planning and response activities. It coordinates with other USAID geographic bureaus' donor organizations, UN agencies, and NGOs.

(2) The **Operations Division** develops and manages logistical, operational, and technical support for disaster responses. It identifies sources for procurement of relief supplies and manages the stockpiling and transportation of those supplies. It maintains readiness to respond to emergencies through several mechanisms, including managing SAR teams, maintaining the operational status of the ground operations team, and developing and maintaining the capability to field DART and RMTs in Washington. It develops and maintains OFDA's relationship with the DOD, the Federal Emergency Management Agency, DOS, and the Department of Energy. Within the Operations Division is the Military Liaison team, which provides technical assistance, guidance, and military liaison for CBRN events. It also provides overseas support to OFDA offices and personnel and to other sectors necessary to ensure OFDA's capacity to execute and coordinate USG HA and response to natural disasters and complex emergencies.

(3) The **Program Support Division** provides programmatic and administrative support, including budget/financial services, procurement planning, contract/grant administration, general administrative support, and communication support for both OFDA Washington and its field offices. It supports the OFDA mission by providing centralized control of funds, resources, and procurement to facilitate the time-sensitive

delivery of relief assistance. It also maintains and develops administrative and programmatic policy as it relates to OFDA programs.

(4) Each fiscal year (FY), DOS releases a cable, "Subject: USAID/DCHA Office of US Foreign Disaster Assistance's Guidance for Disaster Planning and Response FY XXXX." This cable provides guidance to all posts concerning support from USAID/DCHA's OFDA before, during, and after the occurrence of natural and complex disasters abroad in FY XXXX. USAID/OFDA's mission, capabilities, and support capacities in coordinating and managing USG assistance in response to disasters are also outlined. Procedures highlight the need for both continuous USAID/OFDA and USAID mission collaboration in the planning process for disasters as well as regular and sustained communication between MDROs and USAID/OFDA regional advisors and coordinators to ensure timely, appropriate, and effective USG emergency assistance. The guidance provided in the cable should be used in conjunction with Automated Directives System 251 on international disaster assistance. This is an important reference for planning FHA operations.

9. Disaster Assistance Response Team

a. The DART was developed by USAID's OFDA to provide rapid response to foreign disasters as mandated by the FAA. A DART provides a variety of trained specialists to assist US embassies and USAID missions with managing the USG response to foreign disasters. DART activities vary according to the nature, magnitude, and complexity of each disaster and are staffed accordingly.

b. **Immediate Action.** During the initial onset of disasters, the DART focuses upon:

(1) Coordinating needs assessments.

(2) Recommending USG response.

(3) Managing USG on-site relief activities, including SAR and air operations.

(4) Managing receipt, distribution, and monitoring of USG-provided relief supplies.

(5) Liaison with NGOs and IGOs.

c. During long-term, complex disasters, the DART focuses upon:

(1) Collecting situational and general data on the disaster.

(2) Monitoring effectiveness of USG-funded relief activities.

(3) Reviewing relief proposals for potential funding by OFDA.

(4) Recommending follow-on strategies and actions to OFDA, Washington, DC.

d. During either type of disaster response, DARTs coordinate their activities with the affected country, NGOs, IGOs, other assisting countries, and deployed US military resources, including HASTs formed by the GCC.

e. **Structure.** The DART is structured according to the size, complexity, type, and location of the disaster as well as the needs of the affected country. DART staffing is based upon personnel numbers and skills needed to carry out the strategy and meet mission objectives. The DART is designed as a highly flexible, mobile organization capable of adapting to changing disaster requirements; therefore, the DART structure will vary considerably from operation to operation.

f. **Functional Areas.** The DART operates in five functional areas:

(1) **Management.** Manages overall DART activities including liaison with the affected country, NGOs, IGOs, other assisting countries, and US military. Develops and implements plans to meet strategic objectives.

(2) **Operations.** Manages DART operational activities, including SAR activities, technical support, medical and health response, and aerial operations coordination. This function is most active during the initial onset of a disaster.

(3) **Planning.** Collects, evaluates, tracks, and disseminates disaster information. Reviews activities, recommends actions, and develops its OPLAN.

(4) **Logistics.** Supports OFDA and DART personnel by managing supplies, equipment, and services. Orders, receives, distributes, and tracks personnel and USG-provided relief supplies.

(5) **Administration.** Manages team fiscal activities and DART cost accounting and contracts and procures OFDA DART-required goods and services.

(6) **Contracting.** Manages grant and contracting activities of the DART for victim needs.

g. **Organization.** Decisions related to DART activation, composition, and mission are made at an OFDA disaster response planning meeting in Washington, DC, by the OFDA Director. An OFDA-selected team leader organizes and supervises the DART. The OFDA Assistant Director for Disaster Response (or designee) delegates authority to and supervises the team leader. The delegation lists DART objectives, priorities, constraints, and reporting requirements. Based on this list and in conjunction with the assistant Director for Disaster Response and Operations Division, the team leader identifies other positions needed.

h. **Coordination with the USAID Representative to the Embassy.** Prior to departure, the team leader will contact the USAID representative in the affected country to discuss the situation, review DART objectives and capabilities, and obtain additional instructions or authority. While in the affected country, the team leader advises and may receive directions from the USAID representative. Directions will be followed to the extent that they do not conflict with OFDA policies, authorities, and procedures. The team leader maintains direct communications with OFDA to coordinate policies, authorities, and procedures. The team leader maintains direct LOCs with OFDA, Washington throughout the operation.

i. **Coordination with the JFC.** Neither the DART nor JFC is subordinate to the other; a successful relationship is based upon close coordination and mutual understanding of each element's respective mission. Both have a common purpose and, accordingly, have much to gain through close coordination and unity of effort. In some cases it will be appropriate to have a DART member attached to the JTF HQ. An exchange of personnel can bring clarity to a situation where planning and execution are met with the fog of operations. In most cases the DART will use the MITAM to identify tasks to be executed by the appropriate organization or agency. The JTF can use the MITAM as a record of RFAs that will become JTF and component level tasks. Although the DART represents OFDA, which is the USG lead for the FDR response, the JFC should be aware that the COM is in charge of all USG activities in the disaster-affected country.

j. **Duration.** The DART leader and OFDA will review the disaster situation and DART progress in achieving mission objectives. The DART leader and OFDA set the duration of the DART accordingly.

For more information on the DART, see USAID Field Operations Guide for Disaster Assessment and Response.

Intentionally Blank

APPENDIX D
HUMANITARIAN INTERGOVERNMENTAL
AND NONGOVERNMENTAL ORGANIZATIONS

1. General

By nature, responses to humanitarian emergencies are difficult to manage. Many actors—governments, NGOs, and IGOs—seek to respond simultaneously to complex emergencies. The roles of NGOs and IGOs in humanitarian action have their foundation in international law, laws pertaining to human rights, and refugee law and various multilateral legal and policy frameworks agreed upon by the UN General Assembly regarding international humanitarian action. Humanitarian actors operate on the basis of the principles of humanity, neutrality, impartiality, and independence. In practical terms, adherence to these principles is essential to their ability to establish and maintain humanitarian operations, including access to all affected populations, particularly in situations of armed conflict or other situations of violence and political controversy. Creating a coherent framework within which everyone can contribute promptly and effectively to the overall effort is a daunting task. The UN is the major provider and coordinator of HA around the world. The UN has strengthened cooperation with other organizations, both governmental and nongovernmental, and has taken actions to speed its emergency response capability. If and as requested, US military personnel will most likely operate with some of the primary IGOs and NGOs described in this appendix.

More detail is provided in JP 3-08, Interorganizational Coordination During Joint Operations.

2. The United Nations

a. Since it first coordinated humanitarian relief operations in Europe following the devastation and massive displacement of people in the Second World War, the international community has relied on the UN to respond to natural and man-made disasters that are beyond the capacity of national authorities alone. Today, the UN is a major coordinator of international humanitarian efforts, provider of emergency relief and longer-term assistance, a catalyst for action by governments and relief agencies, and an advocate on behalf of people struck by emergencies. This section provides information regarding UN organizations and programs that have worldwide HA mandates that a commander may encounter during FHA operations.

b. **UNOCHA.** The mission of UNOCHA is to mobilize and coordinate effective and principled humanitarian action in partnership with national and international actors to alleviate human suffering in disasters and emergencies, advocate for the rights of people in need, promote preparedness and prevention, and facilitate sustainable solutions. As the UN focal point for civil-military coordination of HA activities within UNOCHA, the Civil Military Coordination Section ensures the effective use of military and civil defense assets in disaster relief and HA operations, establishes civil-military coordination mechanisms to facilitate interaction and cooperation, and upholds humanitarian principles in support of humanitarian coordinators and UNOCHA's mandate.

c. **UNDAC** is a stand-by team of disaster management professionals who are nominated and funded by member governments, UNOCHA, UNDP, and operational humanitarian UN agencies such as WFP, United Nations Children's Fund (UNICEF), and World Health Organization (WHO). Upon request of a disaster-stricken country, the UNDAC team can be deployed within hours to carry out rapid assessment of priority needs and to support national authorities and the UN resident coordinator to coordinate international relief on-site. The team is responsible for providing first-hand information on the disaster situation and priority needs of the victims to the international community through UNOCHA.

d. **OSOCC,** run by the UNDAC team, assists local authorities with coordinating international response teams during disasters. In addition, an internet-based virtual OSOCC facilitates information exchange between responding governments and organizations throughout the relief operation. Establishing an OSOCC is one of the functions an UNDAC team will frequently be asked to perform. The size and functions of the OSOCC will vary in each emergency. However, its basic structure is described in the *UNDAC Handbook*. The UNDAC team should modify this to suit the requirements of the situation.

(1) An OSOCC has three main objectives:

(a) To provide a system for coordinating and directing the activities of an international relief effort at the site of a disaster/emergency; this is especially the case in an earthquake scenario to coordinate the activities of international urban SAR teams.

(b) To provide a framework/platform for cooperation and coordination among the international humanitarian entities at a disaster/emergency site.

(c) To act as a link between such entities and the affected country's authorities.

(2) An OSOCC is designed to facilitate the coordination of the international relief community in a disaster/emergency. The emergency management principles behind the OSOCC's scope, structure, and procedures make the OSOCC a valid tool in any sudden-onset disaster involving international relief resources. The OSOCC system is designed as a rapid response tool. To be effective, it should be initiated in the immediate aftermath of a disaster/emergency and before, or simultaneously with, the arrival of international relief resources. It is expected that an OSOCC in some form would be operational during the relief phase of an emergency until the national/local authorities or the traditional UN structure can cope with the coordination of international resources or until the international relief resources meeting emergency requirements have been withdrawn.

e. **The *UNDAC Handbook*** is a reference guide for the use of members of the UNDAC team undertaking an emergency mission. The handbook contains a variety of useful information, checklists, and a description of coordination structures in the field. It has been designed and written in the form of a typical UNDAC mission cycle with chapters commencing with the UNDAC members' preparation prior to a mission, through various stages of a mission until the termination of the mission and debriefing. It also attempts to assist UNDAC members in accomplishing any of the various tasks they may be expected to perform on missions. These include a range of issues such as staffing an OSOCC for urban

SAR teams during an earthquake and to working with military contingents in humanitarian emergencies. It also contains useful data for everyday use on a mission such as composition of medical kits, security precautions, and characteristics of operating in different climatic conditions and terrain. The handbook has been compiled utilizing information from a wide spectrum of acknowledged sources.

f. **ReliefWeb** is the world's leading online gateway to information (documents and maps) on humanitarian emergencies and disasters. An independent vehicle of information, designed specifically to assist the international humanitarian community in effective delivery of emergency assistance, it provides timely, reliable, and relevant information as events unfold, while emphasizing the coverage of "forgotten emergencies" at the same time. ReliefWeb is administered by UNOCHA.

g. **HICs** aim to ensure that individuals and organizations at field and strategic levels have access to the benefits of information management tools to assess, plan, implement, and monitor HA. HICs are an interorganizational resource, reporting to the humanitarian/resident coordinator, whose products and services are available to the entire humanitarian community. HICs provide surge capacity to the humanitarian community, and particularly to the coordination function, usually (but not exclusively) in the context of complex emergencies.

h. **International Search and Rescue Advisory Group (INSARAG)** is a global network of more than 80 countries and disaster response organizations under the UN umbrella. INSARAG deals with urban SAR related issues and aims at establishing standards for international urban SAR teams and methodology for international coordination in earthquake response. The INSARAG SAR Directory provides an overview of INSARAG member countries and their urban SAR teams in the INSARAG regional groups Africa/Europe, Asia/Pacific, and the Americas.

i. **Office of the United Nations High Commissioner for Refugees.** UNHCR is mandated to lead and coordinate international action to protect refugees and resolve refugee problems worldwide. UNHCR's primary purpose is to safeguard the rights and well-being of refugees. In its efforts to achieve this objective, UNHCR strives to ensure that everyone can exercise the right to seek asylum and find safe refuge in another state, and to return home voluntarily. UNHCR promotes three durable solutions for refugees: voluntary return to their country of origin; local integration in the country of first asylum; and resettlement in a third country. As a humanitarian, nonpolitical organization, UNHCR has two basic and closely related aims—to protect refugees and to seek ways to help them restart their lives in a normal environment. UNHCR additionally leads coordinated humanitarian efforts in relation to protection, camp management and coordination, and emergency shelter in situations of internal armed conflict.

(1) The great majority of today's refugees would prefer to return home willingly once the situation stabilizes. In these circumstances, UNHCR encourages voluntary return by providing transportation, financial incentives, and practical help such as seeds, farming equipment, and building materials.

(2) Sometimes, when it is impossible for civilians to go home, UNHCR helps them either to integrate in countries where they first sought asylum or to go to one of 16 states that regularly accept refugees for permanent resettlement.

j. **WFP.** WFP's objectives are to establish international procedures for meeting emergency food needs and emergencies inherent in chronic malnutrition; assist in preschool and school feeding programs; and implement food-for-work pilot projects in support of social and economic development. WFP's primary task is to furnish food in support of economic and social development projects in developing countries. In addition, substantial resources may be provided to meet emergency food needs. WFP purchases and ships food needed in emergencies on behalf of donor governments or the affected countries. WFP staff may assist, when required, in coordinating the reception and utilization of food aid received from all sources. The WFP can be regarded as the de facto logistic arm of the UN in disaster situations. The WFP also hosts the Humanitarian Early Warning Service (HEWSweb). HEWSweb (www.hewsweb.org) is an interagency partnership project aimed at establishing a common platform for humanitarian early warnings and forecasts for natural hazards. The main objective of HEWSweb is to bring together and make accessible in a simple manner the most credible early warning information available at the global level from multiple specialized institutions. Within the WFP, the UN Humanitarian Air Service provides civilian passenger and cargo air transport services for humanitarian and development agencies. In the early stages of disaster response this is often the primary and preferred means of NGOs reaching remote areas that have become isolated due to lack of or damaged infrastructure.

k. **UNICEF.** UNICEF is mandated to advocate for the protection of children's rights, to help meet their basic needs, and to expand their opportunities to reach their full potential. UNICEF responds in emergencies to protect the rights of children. In coordination with UN partners and humanitarian agencies, UNICEF makes its unique facilities for rapid response available to its partners to relieve the suffering of children and those who provide their care. UNICEF uses materials from emergency stockpiles in the UNICEF warehouses in Copenhagen to meet emergency requirements. UNICEF can also procure relief supplies on behalf of other UN agencies and relief organizations. In the first six to eight weeks following the outbreak of a crisis, UNICEF, with its national UN and NGO partner organizations, will work to:

(1) Assess, monitor, report, and communicate the situation of children and women: conduct a rapid assessment, including determination of severe or systematic abuse, violence, or exploitation; and report through the appropriate mechanisms.

(2) Provide vaccination, essential drugs, and nutritional supplements: vaccinate children between 6 months and 14 years of age against measles, providing vitamin A supplementation as required; provide essential drugs, basic and emergency health kits, oral rehydration, fortified nutritional products, and micronutrient supplements; provide post-rape-care kits, including post-exposure prophylaxis for human immunodeficiency virus, where appropriate; and provide other emergency supplies such as blankets and tarpaulins.

(3) Provide child and maternal feeding and nutritional monitoring: with the WFP and NGO partners, support infant and young child feeding, therapeutic, and supplementary feeding; introduce nutritional monitoring and surveillance.

(4) Provide safe drinking water, sanitation, and hygiene: emergency water supply and purification, provision of basic family water kits, safe disposal of feces, and hygiene education.

(5) Assist in preventing the separation and facilitate the identification, registration, and medical screening of children separated from their families: ensure family tracing systems are put in place and provide care and protection; and prevent sexual abuse and exploitation of children and women.

(6) Initiate the resumption of schooling and other child learning opportunities: set up temporary learning spaces and reopen schools, start reintegrating teachers and children (with a focus on girls), and organize recreational activities.

l. **UN Food and Agriculture Organization (FAO).** With most communities dependent on agriculture and related enterprises for their food security and livelihoods, FAO's expertise in farming, livestock, fisheries, and forestry is crucial in emergency response and rehabilitation efforts. In responding to an emergency, FAO collaborates with many partners, including governments, other UN organizations, and humanitarian groups. During these crises, assistance is required to restore local food production and reduce dependency on food aid, an essential part of the recovery process. This is where FAO plays a vital role. The Emergency Operations Division of the Technical Cooperation Department of the FAO, working jointly with the WFP, sends missions to the affected areas to assess the crop and food supply situation. During these missions, experts consult closely with the farmers, herders, fishers, and local authorities. Once the assessment mission is finished, FAO designs a relief and rehabilitation program and mobilizes funds for its implementation. In response to emergencies, FAO distributes material assets, such as seeds and fertilizer, fishing equipment, livestock, and farm tools.

m. **WHO.** The WHO's Emergency Response and Operations group is responsible for developing operational and logistic capacity in support of countries in acute crises. It also develops standard operating procedures for emergencies, to ensure a uniform approach across WHO to crises that demand an immediate response.

(1) WHO's key functions in a crisis are to:

(a) Promptly assess health needs of populations affected by crises and measure ill-health, identifying priority causes of ill-health and death.

(b) Support member states in coordinating action for health.

(c) Ensure that critical gaps in health response are rapidly identified and filled.

(d) Support restoration of essential public health functions.

(e) Revitalize health systems and build up their capacity for preparedness and response.

(2) WHO's mobile response teams bring together expertise in epidemic response, logistics, security coordination, and management. They are combined with mobile teams provided by the UN as a whole. They will empower the UN organizations in the affected country to better address the health aspects of crises.

n. **UNDP.** Following disasters and armed conflict, UNDP assists national governments and communities to lay the foundation for sustainable development. UNDP's expertise and resources focus on several areas. However, early recovery will be the initial effort. Early recovery focuses on restoring the capacity of national institutions and communities after a crisis. Early recovery begins in a humanitarian relief setting, immediately following a natural disaster or armed conflict. Guided by development principles, the early recovery phase aims to generate self-sustaining, nationally owned processes to stabilize human security and address underlying risks that contributed to the crisis. Early recovery encompasses a wide range of areas such as governance, livelihoods, shelter, environment, and social dimensions, including the reintegration of displaced populations.

o. **United Nations Environment Programme (UNEP).** The Post-Conflict and Disaster Management Branch extends UNEP's work in areas of the world where the environment is impacted by conflicts and disasters, or where the environment is a factor contributing to conflicts and disaster impacts. Because conflicts and disasters are so closely intertwined with the environment, proper environmental management and governance is essential for long-term peace, stability, and security in any conflict- or disaster-prone country. It conducts environmental assessments in crisis affected countries and strengthens national environmental management capacity through institution building, promoting regional cooperation, technical legal assistance, environmental information management, and integrating environmental concerns and risk reduction measures in reconstruction programs. Field-based assessments are conducted to identify the impacts of a conflict or disaster on environmental systems and the possible, indirect impacts on human health. UNEP delivers technical support for environmental cleanup or to mitigate environmental risks caused by disasters or conflicts, including those posed by chemical contamination or severe environmental damage to human health or livelihoods.

3. **International Red Cross and Red Crescent Movement**

a. The Red Cross and Red Crescent Movement is the largest humanitarian network in the world. It is composed of the ICRC, the IFRC, and the 188 individual national societies. Its mission is to alleviate human suffering, protect life and health, and uphold human dignity especially during armed conflicts and other emergencies. It is present in every country and supported by millions of volunteers. Each has its own legal identity and role, but they are all united by seven fundamental principles: humanity, impartiality, neutrality, independence, voluntary service, unity, and universality.

b. **ICRC.** ICRC is an impartial, neutral, and independent organization with an exclusively humanitarian mission to protect the lives and dignity of victims of war and internal violence and to provide them with assistance. During conflicts, it directs and coordinates the international relief activities conducted by the movement. It also endeavors to prevent suffering by promoting and strengthening humanitarian principles.

(1) Its specific tasks applicable to FHA include:

(a) Visits and interviews, without witness, to prisoners of war and detained or interned civilians.

(b) Search for missing persons.

(c) Transmission of messages between family members separated by conflict, including from prisoners of war and detained civilians.

(d) Reunification of dispersed families.

(e) Provision of basic health care services.

(f) Provision of urgently needed food, water, sanitation, and shelter to civilians without access to these basic necessities.

(g) Monitoring compliance with and contributing to the development of international humanitarian principles.

(h) Spreading knowledge of international humanitarian principles.

(2) The ICRC has a permanent international mandate for its work. This derives from the 1949 Geneva Conventions and from the statutes of the Red Cross and Red Crescent Movement, which encourage it to undertake similar work in situations of internal violence, where the Geneva Conventions do not apply.

(3) Despite often being referred to as an IGO, the ICRC remains a private organization governed by Swiss law and strictly independent in its governance and operational decisions.

(4) The ICRC receives its funding from voluntary contributions from governments, other IGOs, national Red Cross and Red Crescent Societies, and private sources.

c. **IFRC.** The IFRC is a global humanitarian organization that coordinates and directs international assistance following natural and man-made disasters in non-conflict situations. The International Federation comprises 188 member Red Cross and Red Crescent societies, a Secretariat in Geneva, and more than 60 delegations strategically located to support activities around the world.

(1) The vision of the International Federation is to strive, through voluntary action, for a world of empowered communities, better able to address human suffering and crises with hope, respect for dignity, and a concern for equity.

(2) Its mission is to improve the lives of vulnerable people by mobilizing the power of humanity. Often, these are victims of natural disasters, those in poverty brought about by socio-economic crises, refugees, and victims of health emergencies.

(3) The International Federation carries out relief operations to assist victims of disasters, and combines this with development work to strengthen the capacities of its member national societies. The International Federation's work focuses on four core areas: promoting humanitarian values, disaster response, disaster preparedness, and health and community care. The unique network of national societies—which covers almost every country in the world—is the IFRC's principal strength. Cooperation between national societies gives the IFRC greater potential to develop capacities and assist those most in need. At a local level, the network enables the IFRC to reach individual communities.

(4) *The Code of Conduct for The International Red Cross and Red Crescent Movement and NGOs in Disaster Relief* was developed and agreed upon by eight of the world's largest disaster response agencies in 1994. The code of conduct is voluntary and establishes ten points of principle for humanitarian actors in their disaster response work, describing the relationships that agencies working in disasters should seek with donor governments, host governments, and the UN system. International Federation of the Red Cross uses the code of conduct to monitor its own standards of relief delivery and to encourage other agencies to set similar standards. It is being used by the International Federation to monitor its own standards of relief delivery and to encourage other agencies to set similar standards. The code of conduct is voluntary and applicable to any NGO. The code of conduct lays down 10 points of principle to which all NGOs should adhere in their disaster response work, and goes on to describe the type of relationships with donor governments that agencies working in disasters should seek.

(5) Emergency response units (ERUs) are standardized packages of trained personnel and modules of equipment, ready to be deployed at short notice. The units are fully self-sufficient for one month and can be deployed for up to four months. ERUs are part of the global International Federation of Red Cross disaster response system and therefore used in large emergency response operations, when global assistance is needed and the federation's delegation(s) and the affected national society cannot respond alone. ERUs provide specific services where local infrastructure is damaged, temporarily out of use, or insufficient to cope with the needs. There are eight types of ERU: logistics; information technology and telecommunication; water and sanitation; basic health care; referral hospital; rapid deployment hospital; relief; and base camp.

(6) The International Federation has developed the field assessment and coordination teams (FACTs) concept. The methodology has been developed in close cooperation with UNOCHA, and the assessment and coordination systems are compatible with UNOCHA's UNDAC system.

(a) A core group of experienced Red Cross/Red Crescent disaster managers from within the International Federation and from the national societies with different expertise in relief, logistics, health, nutrition, public health and epidemiology, water and sanitation, finance, administration, psychological support, as well as language capabilities, have become members of FACT, and are able to support national Red Cross and Red Crescent Societies in major disaster response. They are ready to participate in a FACT deployment with 12-24 hours notice for 2-4 weeks anywhere in the world.

(b) In the case of a humanitarian emergency, the national society in the affected country may request assistance from the International Federation. In this case, FACT members all over the world are alerted using automated systems and their availability within 12-24 hours is requested. The Operations Support Department, in consultation with the Regional Department at the Secretariat, composes a team that is deployed to the disaster area immediately. The FACT works with counterparts from the local national society, and with members of regional disaster response teams, members of the Federation regional or country delegation, and the ICRC.

(c) In coordination with local authorities, UN organizations, and NGOs, the FACT carries out an assessment of the situation and identifies the most urgent needs. The team compiles an assessment report, a plan of action that recommends the most appropriate Red Cross/Red Crescent intervention, and drafts an appeal, which is then launched by the Federation Secretariat in Geneva to the member national societies and other donors.

(d) The FACT also facilitates and coordinates the startup of relief activities. It may request ERUs and coordinate their deployment, advise on and request other human and material resources, and coordinate the assistance provided by the Red Cross Movement in response to the disaster.

(e) After assisting in the implementation of the plan of action, the FACT hands over the relief operation to the host national society, the delegation, and the delegates who have been recruited to support them.

d. **National Red Cross and Red Crescent Societies.** National Red Cross and Red Crescent Societies form the basic units and constitute a vital force of the International Red Cross and Red Crescent Movement in nearly all countries. National societies act as auxiliaries to the public authorities of their own countries in the humanitarian field and provide a range of services including disaster relief, health, and social programs. During wartime, national societies assist the affected civilian population and support the army medical services where appropriate. To participate in the movement, a national society must first be recognized by the ICRC and then admitted to the International Federation. There are ten conditions for recognition listed in the statutes of the movement. They include such requirements as autonomous status recognized under national legislation, the use of a recognized emblem, and adherence to the fundamental principles. There can only be one society in each country, and it must be constituted in the territory of an independent state.

4. International Organization for Migration

IOM is the principal IGO in the field of migration. IOM is dedicated to promoting humane and orderly migration for the benefit of all. As an intergovernmental body, IOM acts with its partners in the international community to assist in meeting the operational challenges of migration; advance understanding of migration issues; encourage social and economic development through migration; and uphold the human dignity and well-being of migrants. It does so by providing services and advice to governments and migrants. IOM works to help ensure the orderly and humane management of migration, to promote international cooperation on migration issues, to assist in the search for practical solutions to migration problems, and to provide HA to migrants in need, be they refugees, displaced persons, or other uprooted people. IOM works in the four broad areas of migration management: migration and development, facilitating migration, regulating migration, and addressing forced migration. IOM works closely with governmental, IGO, and NGO partners. With offices and operations on every continent, IOM helps governments and civil society through:

    a. Rapid humanitarian responses to sudden migration flows.

    b. Post-emergency return and reintegration programs.

    c. Assistance to migrants on their way to new homes and lives.

    d. Facilitation of labor migration.

    e. Assisted voluntary return for irregular migrants.

    f. Recruitment of highly qualified nationals for return to their countries of origin.

    g. Aid to migrants in distress.

    h. Training and capacity-building of officials.

    i. Measures to counter TIP.

    j. Migration medical and public health programs.

    k. Mass information and education on migration.

    l. Research related to migration management and other services for migrants.

5. Euro-Atlantic Disaster Response Unit

    a. The Euro-Atlantic disaster response unit (EADRU) was created by NATO to coordinate disaster relief efforts for the member countries of the Euro-Atlantic Partnership Council (EAPC) in case of a natural or technological disaster in the EAPC geographical area.

    b. EADRU is located at NATO HQ in Brussels, Belgium, and is headed by the Director Civil Emergency Planning with additional staff from NATO and partner countries. The EADRU is also open to representatives from the UN and the NATO Military Authorities. In close consultation with the UNOCHA, the EADRU is responsible for coordinating the response of EAPC countries to a disaster occurring within the EAPC geographical area.

    c. EADRU is a non-standing, multinational mix of national civil and military elements (qualified personnel of rescue, medical and other units, equipment and materials, assets, and transport) which are volunteered by EAPC countries. The EADRU can be deployed in case of a major natural or technological disaster in an EAPC country upon request from the stricken country or in support of a relevant international organization. The composition and size of this multinational EADRU will be determined by the requirements based on an international assessment of each particular disaster. National elements will remain under national control while deployed in the stricken country as an asset of the local emergency management agency. The area of deployment of the EADRU will be limited to the EAPC member countries. In exceptional circumstances, should there be an RFA for a stricken non-EAPC country, political guidance will be obtained immediately before initiating any disaster response via the EADRU.

6. American Council for Voluntary International Action

a. InterAction is the largest coalition of US-based international NGOs focused on the world's poor and most vulnerable people. Collectively, InterAction's more than 165 members work in every developing country. Based in Washington, DC with a staff of 40, InterAction's member agencies are large and small, faith-based and secular, and are headquartered across 25 states.

b. InterAction exercises leadership in conflict prevention, the peaceful resolution of disputes, and peace building initiatives in post-conflict situations. InterAction members respond to natural disasters all around the world.

c. InterAction leverages the impact of US private support by advocating for the expansion of USG investments and by insisting that policies and programs are responsive to the realities of the world's poorest and most vulnerable populations.

d. InterAction brings the values and experience of the NGO community into the broader development and HA community through strategic alliances with key partners around particular issues and objectives.

7. European Commission Directorate General for Humanitarian Aid and Civil Protection

The European Union as a whole (i.e., the Member States and the Commission) is one of the world's main humanitarian aid donors; the European Commission Directorate General for Humanitarian Aid and Civil Protection (ECHO) is the service of the European Commission responsible for this activity. The objective of European Union humanitarian aid is to provide a needs-based emergency response aimed at preserving life, preventing and alleviating human suffering, and maintaining human dignity wherever the need arises if governments and local actors are overwhelmed, unable, or unwilling to act. ECHO's task is to ensure goods and services get to crisis zones fast. Goods may include essential supplies, specific foodstuffs, medical equipment, medicines, and fuel. Services may include medical teams, water purification teams, and logistical support. Goods and services reach disaster areas via ECHO partners.

8. Other Organizations

a. The **Caribbean Disaster Emergency Management Agency (CDEMA)** serves the Caribbean community. CDEMA's main function is to make an immediate and coordinated response to any disastrous event affecting any participating state, once the state requests such assistance. Other functions include:

(1) Securing, collating, and channeling comprehensive and reliable information on disasters affecting the region to interested governmental and NGOs.

(2) Mitigating, or eliminating as far as possible, the consequences of disasters affecting participating states.

(3) Establishing and maintaining on a sustainable basis adequate disaster response capabilities among participating states.

(4) Mobilizing and coordinating disaster relief from governmental and NGOs for affected participating states.

b. **Reuters AlertNet** (www.alertnet.org) is a humanitarian news network based around a popular website. It aims to keep relief professionals and the wider public up to date on humanitarian crises around the globe. It provides operation-critical information to relief charities worldwide; encourages relief charities to swap information with one another; and raises awareness of humanitarian emergencies among the general public. AlertNet focuses its resources on covering fast-moving humanitarian emergencies and on the early warning of future emergencies.

9. United Nations Cluster Approach

a. The UN cluster approach is the principle construct, utilized by the international humanitarian community, to facilitate a coordinated humanitarian response to an affected state. The cluster approach ensures predictability and accountability in international responses to humanitarian emergencies, by clarifying the division of labor among organizations, and better defining their roles and responsibilities within the different sectors of response.

b. The UN cluster approach designates lead entities to coordinate response efforts for specific mission areas. Requirements are identified by participating organizations, in collaboration with the affected state, and UN member organizations volunteer to fulfill them. Cluster leads have no authority to assign missions; they must meet requirements using coordination, collaboration, cooperation, and communication. The cluster sector activities and respective leads are reflected in Figure D-1.

c. At a global level, the aim is to strengthen preparedness and capacity to respond to humanitarian emergencies by ensuring leadership and accountability in all main sectors.

d. At a country level, the aim is to ensure a more coherent and effective response by mobilizing groups of agencies, organizations, and NGOs to coordinate, share information,

United Nations Cluster Approach

Number	Sector or Area of Activity	Global Cluster Lead
1	Food Security	Food and Agricultural Organization of the United Nations and World Food Programme (WFP)
2	Camp Coordination and Camp Management	United Nations High Commissioner for Refugees (UNHCR), International Organization for Migration
3	Early Recovery	United Nations Development Programme
4	Education	United Nations Children's Fund (UNICEF) and Save the Children UK
5	Emergency Shelter	UNHCR and International Federation of Red Cross and Red Crescent Societies
6	Emergency Telecommunications	WFP (telecommunications provider)
7	Health	World Health Organization
8	Logistics	WFP
9	Nutrition	UNICEF
10	Protection	UNHCR
11	Water, Sanitation, and Hygiene	UNICEF

Figure D-1. United Nations Cluster Approach

and respond in a strategic manner. At the country level, sectors and sectoral groups have always existed and they will continue to exist. In the past, however, it was usually the case that only a limited number of sectors had clearly designated lead agencies accountable to the humanitarian coordinator. The cluster approach aims to rectify this by ensuring that, within the international humanitarian response, there is a clear system of leadership and accountability for all the key sectors or areas of humanitarian activity. The cluster approach is intended, therefore, to strengthen rather than to replace sectoral coordination under the overall leadership of the humanitarian coordinator, with a view to improve humanitarian response in emergency situations.

 e. Cluster lead organizations are responsible to:

  (1) Facilitate the coordination between the cluster members.

  (2) Encourage joint working.

  (3) Ensure that responses are in line with existing guidelines and standards.

  (4) Collate and share information.

  (5) Identify gaps in the response.

  (6) Stand in as the "provider of last resort" when there are no other options.

APPENDIX E
HEALTH AND MEDICAL SUPPORT IN FOREIGN HUMANITARIAN ASSISTANCE OPERATIONS

1. General

In addition to being responsible for health services for the deploying force, a CJTF may also be tasked to provide health and medical support to the affected population in an FHA crisis. This appendix lists considerations for providing such health and medical support as part of the mission. Essential tasks for this mission generally include the following:

a. Coordinating actions to prevent or control disease outbreak.

b. Evacuating or temporarily hospitalizing sick, wounded, and injured persons, and coordinating their return to civilian facilities or the parent nation.

c. Distributing supplies and equipment.

d. Assisting in reestablishing indigenous health sector resources and institutions. Primary consideration must be given to supporting and supplementing any existing medical infrastructure. **No operation should be considered that may supplant the existing medical infrastructure.**

Comprehensive guidance and information is provided in JP 4-02, Health Services.

2. Medical Concept of Operations

a. Based upon the mission requirements and medical and operational situation, the joint force surgeon and staff will develop a medical CONOPS that will (if possible) combine the efforts of the military health and medical forces, NGOs, and the existing medical infrastructure.

b. Following a disaster, there are generally three waves of medical assistance: trauma, control of disease and infection, and support to rebuilding HN medical capabilities. Initial responders, including forward deployed military forces that can be diverted, may assist in managing trauma, but most US health and medical support will be involved in the second and third waves. The JFC must ensure that US forces support and supplement HN capabilities, rather than replace or supplant them.

c. During an FHA operation, priority should be given to preserving the health of the forces supporting the operation. This is accomplished by an intensive medical intelligence analysis and implementation of a vigorous preventive medicine program, emphasizing medical surveillance activities.

d. Consistent with the mission and the GCC's intent, the CCMD surgeon should ensure that the level of care provided meets current US standards of care tempered by HN standards of care, available supplies, anticipated patient follow-up and hand off, as well as issues related to the HN's culture and ability to sustain the level of care provided. Once approved by the JFC, the JTF staff should initiate planning and action required to support the standard of care deemed appropriate. Upon execution, if a joint force surgeon thinks that modifications should be made to the established standard of care, a request may be made through the supported CCMD surgeon. The WHO has recommended that health care support include nutrition, sanitation, water standards, pre- and post-natal health care, disease treatment, prevention and control related to locally endemic diseases, immunization, and health education.

e. The senior deploying commander of a HAST should ensure that a predeployment vulnerability assessment has been conducted. These assessments should include health and medical personnel qualified to evaluate the safety and vulnerability of local food and water sources, perform an epidemiological risk assessment, evaluate local medical capabilities, perform a vector/pest risk assessment, determine adequacy of hygiene of local billeting and public facilities, and perform an environmental risk assessment. Assessments provide the necessary background data for sizing the force protection package required, thus reducing the threat to DOD force personnel and assets.

f. The HAST should include preventive medicine personnel that are trained to perform a detailed occupational and environmental health site assessment of the operational area that documents the conditions found at a site (base camp, bivouac site or outpost, or other permanent or semipermanent basing location) beginning at or near the time it is occupied initially. The assessment includes site history; environmental health survey results for air, water, soil, and noise; entomological surveys; occupational and industrial hygiene surveys; and ionizing and nonionizing radiation hazard surveys, if indicated. Its purpose is to identify hazardous agents that may affect the health of deployed personnel.

3. **Planning and Execution Considerations**

The JTF should anticipate that the health care delivery infrastructure may be austere to nonexistent. NGOs and IGOs may be able to compensate for some of the shortfalls. The following factors merit consideration when providing health and medical support to the affected population.

a. **Coordination and Collaboration.** Effective coordination and collaboration is a key element that is central to health and medical support.

(1) The JFC's staff must coordinate all health and medical activities with the USAID medical representative and/or DOS regional medical officer. Contact the respective USAID and/or DOS representative prior to commencing any operations.

(2) The UNOCHA, WHO, and NGOs/IGOs operating in the HN are valuable sources of regional medical information and coordination. Early identification of health and medical needs and cooperation by all or most of the parties involved will increase efficiency and reduce redundancy.

(3) The JFC should establish some type of central point or organization for collaboration of medical requirements with nonmilitary organizations. The OSOCC or CMOC is a logical place for this collaboration to occur. The differing policies and cultures

of individual NGOs and IGOs, military capabilities and procedures, and affected country requirements require a dedicated collaboration element to encourage and help enable unity of effort among all participants.

b. **Communications.** Effective operations require a constant effort to avoid gaps in services and redundant services. Uninterrupted communications between military elements, NGOs, IGOs, and affected HN personnel will help eliminate unnecessary suffering and apply resources to the operation more effectively.

c. **Cultural Aptitude.** Health professionals with foreign language, cultural competency, and interagency experience are valuable in an FHA operation (i.e., US Air Force international health specialists [IHSs]) and Army special operations medical personnel).

d. **Demographics.** The population at risk is an important planning factor to consider. Three specialties that are not typically included in a JTF deployment, but may be needed during an FHA operation, are obstetrics and gynecology, geriatrics, and pediatrics.

e. **Preventive Medicine.** In any FHA operation, preventive medicine is a critical consideration. Individual personal hygiene practices and procedures are key elements of a sound preventive medicine program. The provision of adequate food service sanitation, potable water supplies, vector control, disease and nonbattle injury (DNBI) prevention, and waste disposal facilities all contribute to the maintenance of a healthy and fit force. FHA operations may place US forces in situations that may substantially increase the risk of DNBI. Exposure to foreign civilian populations potentially carrying endemic diseases as well as disease outbreaks as a result of a natural disaster are both factors increasing the DNBI risk. DODD 6490.02, *Comprehensive Health Surveillance,* and DODI 6490.03, *Deployment Health,* mandate that DOD monitor and identify both long- and short-term health effects of US forces during deployments. This requires that the JTF have robust preventive medicine assets to perform medical and environmental health risk assessments and identify effective preventive medicine measures to counter the threat to US forces. In addition, the significant roles that public health and communicable disease control play in FHA missions further support the need for robust preventive medicine assets.

f. **Disease Prevention.** Natural and man-made disasters frequently give rise to substantial increases in endemic disease. While no parts of the world are immune to increases in diseases, some regions of the developing world are more susceptible to disease than others, and are impacted at devastating levels. Contributory factors in spreading disease to epidemic proportions during disasters include disruption of sanitation services, food and water contamination, and increased rodent and arthropod breeding habitats.

g. **Disease Control.** The risk of communicable diseases is increased in a post-disaster environment due to overcrowding, poor environmental conditions, and poor public health. For example, there is a close association between malnutrition and the effects of communicable disease, particularly childhood diarrhea. Expert advice should be obtained for communicable disease control and management of epidemics. Some communicable diseases have a seasonal pattern and timely measures must be taken to prevent a rapid increase in cases. The following are central to disease control:

    (1) Water supply and soap.

    (2) Proper disposal of sewage and refuse.

    (3) Vector control (pest control).

    (4) General public health education and awareness.

    (5) Medical surveillance.

    h. **Patient Evacuation.** The CCMD J-4 should advise and assist the CCMD surgeon in matters pertaining to patient evacuation from the operational area and help develop a plan to meet patient movement requirements. Considerations should include, but are not limited to:

    (1) Eligibility criteria.

    (2) Sponsorship guidelines (i.e., secretarial designation).

    (3) Available evacuation resources and routes.

    (4) Reimbursement procedures.

    (5) Capabilities of medical treatment facilities within (and adjoining) the operational area to receive evacuees requiring all levels of care.

    i. **Immunization.** There are strong reasons, both medical and practical, to resist pressure for an immediate mass immunization program. Although many of the most common causes of disease and death in developing countries are vaccine-preventable, immunization campaigns require considerable forethought and planning and should not be entered into lightly. Immunization programs/campaigns must be appropriately equipped and adequately staffed with workers to supervise and manage refrigerated vaccines through the entirety of the cold chain. Given the logistical challenges, these programs may not represent the best use of resources. The importance of specific immunizations will be dependent on the health threats and HN medical capabilities. The HN, WHO, UNICEF, or another NGO or IGO will likely lead or coordinate the program, and US military support to the implementing agency or organization must be requested and coordinated. Immunizations programs/campaigns may be conducted in conjunction with HCA missions.

    j. **Primary Care.** Often during disasters, the first wave of patients is trauma care, and the second wave is disease control. During the second wave, women's and children's care takes special planning to ensure the right mix of providers and medications are available. Due to cultural norms, the gender of both providers and interpreters should be considered. Primary care may be provided from fixed facilities or during remote medical missions by multinational forces. As above, coordination with appropriate HN organizations and NGOs must be accomplished to avoid unnecessary duplication and to ensure coordinated long-term capacity building is accomplished. Missions must involve US forces and HN providers, which gives bidirectional legitimacy to all involved.

k. **Veterinary Support.** Many societies where joint forces will operate are rural and their economies and personal health are often dependent on their domesticated animals. Capacity building exercises, public health, and direct treatment of animals can make as big an impact on the economy of a struggling country as the health of the animals' owners. Veterinary missions must also involve local animal health providers and the herdsmen themselves.

l. **Health System Capacity Building.** One of the first tasks to support capacity building should be to help health systems near US and multinational forces to improve their self sufficiency and eventually contribute to redeployment of US forces. Health systems should be periodically assessed to determine their status and effectiveness of previous capacity building efforts. Once assessments have been made, targeted improvements to the JTF capabilities must be accomplished after close coordination with the CMO and surgeon. Care must be taken to ensure that reestablished health care standards are appropriate for the local population and at a level that can be maintained by the existing HN medical infrastructure.

m. **Funding for Medical HA Activities.** To pay for the above programs, resources must be managed in accordance with congressional and GCC guidance.

4. Medical Intelligence

Medical intelligence is the product of the collection, evaluation, analysis, integration, and interpretation of available health information for a given nation or operational area. Medical intelligence addresses the medical aspects that are significant to military planning in general and to health and medical planning in particular. In addition to preparing commanders to protect their own forces from medical and environmental risks during an operation, medical intelligence also assesses the general health of the population, which is a significant factor in planning for FHA operations. Additionally, information related to HN health and medical capabilities is important in assessing whether medical care shortfalls exist for which US, NGOs, or IGOs must compensate. Sources of this information include the Joint Pathology Center, the National Center for Medical Intelligence, DIA, and established civilian organizations with longstanding resources in the operational area. Medical intelligence should include awareness of cultural differences that can impact medical care such as hygiene and religious norms.

5. Nongovernmental Organizations Medical Providers

a. In emergencies, urgent outside assistance in the health sector is almost invariably necessary. This is because the immediate and specialized attention needed represents a burden that existing local structures are not designed to bear. Local health and medical capabilities will almost never have the needed reserve capacity in terms of staff at all levels, infrastructure, medical supplies, and technical expertise. This capacity can be developed over time, with the support from the HN and other UN agencies.

b. NGOs must be chosen with care and this is usually done by the HN. However, it is also the responsibility of the UN to advise the government on which organizations have proven competence in emergencies. Some agencies have experience in long-term situations but less in emergencies; others may be too narrow in focus, preferring to do purely curative work to the exclusion of public health, prevention, sanitation, etc. Small NGOs, especially those created in response to a specific situation, should demonstrate appropriate competence before being engaged in the emergency phase.

c. During the early stages of an emergency it is essential that the numbers of NGOs involved should be kept to the minimum necessary, and that those chosen should be professional, capable of deploying experienced personnel, and with proven past experience in collaborating with both governments and UN in the effective management of an emergency.

6. Service Capabilities

a. **US Navy**

(1) **Hospital Ships.** Two hospital ships operated by Military Sealift Command are designed to provide emergency, on-site care for US forces deployed in war or tailored for other operations, such as FHA missions. The United States Naval Ship (USNS) Mercy (T-AH 19) and USNS Comfort (T-AH 20) have a maximum capacity of 12 operating rooms. When fully manned, casualty receiving can triage and provide treatment for 50 patients simultaneously. The frequency and volume of patients subsequently assessed may be limited by the staffing for inpatient hospitalization. The surgical suite throughput is determined by staffing, room turnover, case complexity, and availability of inpatient beds (intensive care unit and intermediate bed). Medical staffing for FHA and HCA missions aboard Navy ships is usually sourced with a combination of joint service component medical personnel, interagency USG personnel, credential holding foreign partners, and credential holding NGOs. Depending upon the location and nature of the FHA operation, transit time and distance considerations are key planning considerations. Capabilities include digital radiological services, invasive angiography, a diagnostic and clinical laboratory, a pharmacy, an optometry lab, a computerized axial tomography scan, two oxygen producing plants, and a blood bank. Both vessels have a helicopter deck capable of landing many military helicopters, as well as side ports to take on patients at sea.

For additional information, refer to Navy Tactics, Techniques, and Procedures (NTTP) 4-02.6, Hospital Ships.

(2) Some amphibious class ships have modern medical facilities, second only to the Navy's hospital ships. These facilities include four main and two emergency medical operating rooms, three dental operating rooms, x-ray rooms, a blood bank, laboratories, and patient wards. Additionally, casualty collecting and triage areas are located on the flight deck and in medical spaces, and can be set up on the well deck. When augmented with additional health and medical personnel and resources, they are capable of providing preventive, first responder, and forward resuscitative capabilities of care for up to 60 inpatients and numerous outpatients. They can provide sustained care to patients brought

aboard ship during humanitarian missions, while still providing ongoing care to crewmembers and embarked staff at the same time.

(3) **EMF and Expeditionary Medical Unit (EMU).** EMFs are a standardized, modular, flexible combat capability that provides health services to an advanced base environment throughout the full range of military operations. The EMF is designed in multiple configurations to support a wide spectrum of military health support. An EMU-10 is a stand-alone, 10-bed facility capable of being air-transportable or mobile loaded on vehicles for rapid response for FHA or immediate short duration surgical support. The EMF 150-bed facility is a modular, scalable design that allows for an initial setup of a 50-bed core module (all medical and surgical capabilities) capable of expanding with the addition of a 100 bed (ward) module creating the 150-bed EMF. The 250-bed EMF is the same design as the 150-bed EMF with the addition of another 100-bed (ward) module. While initially conceived and developed as war reserve facilities to provide health services during intense combat operations, EMFs can also be used in protracted low-intensity conflict scenarios and humanitarian operations, with design changes. EMFs and EMUs are pre-positioned in various CONUS and OCONUS locations, or deployed on MPF enhanced ships. Once transported to the desired location, the time frame for assemblage varies with the size and/or capability of the EMF/EMU. EMFs, depending on size, can provide theater hospitalization capability and capabilities similar to those on a hospital ship. However, they are not light and have a large footprint. Due to the size associated with some EMF platforms, significant logistical support is required to relocate these assets once assembly and activation have occurred. Smaller, task-organized EMFs are easier to relocate, post-activation, with much less logistical support.

For additional information, refer to NTTP 4-02.4, Expeditionary Medical Facilities.

(4) The FDPMU is a level four preventive medicine and public health capability with the primary mission of identifying and controlling health threats across the range of military operations, including FHA. The FDPMU consists of 11 UTCs staffed by public health experts and scientists who are trained to effectively communicate with NGOs, HN representatives, and military personnel. The UTCs allow DPMU personnel and equipment packages to be scaled to meet specific mission support to requirements. The modular design of the FDPMU provides for two adaptive force packages capable of providing robust preventive medicine and public health support for FHA missions. One adaptive force package is designed to build public health capacity within the HN. The second provides essential public health, preventive medicine, and consequence management support.

For additional guidance, refer to NTTP 4-02.8, Forward Deployable Preventive Medicine Unit.

b. **US Air Force**

(1) Expeditionary medical support (EMEDS) is a modular, rapidly deployable medical capability that can support FHA operations of various sizes and durations. The EMEDS health response team (HRT) is the first increment of EMEDS capability. Designed for rapid mobility and efficient setup, EMEDS HRT can deploy within 24 hours of

notification, establish emergency room capability within 2 hours, operating room capability within 4 hours, and critical care capability within 6 hours, and reach full operational capability within 12 hours of arrival. It can hold four patients (three of which can be critical) for up to 24 hours prior to evacuation to a larger medical facility. It has a patient throughput capability of 350-500 patients per day for 5 days without resupply. EMEDS HRT generally deploys with medical command/control and support services, surgical and critical care, primary care, dental, bioenvironmental engineering, public health, IHS, and specialty care support (OB/GYN [obstetrics and gynecology], pediatrics, internal medicine). It is expandable to an EMEDS 10-bed facility or an EMEDS 25-bed facility, which offer enhanced medical, surgical, and ancillary services capabilities. EMEDS is not a stand-alone capability. Base operating support (BOS) for EMEDS facilities and personnel will be provided using the host base's capabilities, deployable base systems, and contracted civilian support. BOS includes billeting, messing and other consumable materials, power, water, ice, latrines, showers, laundry, waste management, exterior lighting, transportation (to include ambulances and general purpose vehicles), fuels, vehicle maintenance, equipment maintenance, general supplies, contracting, information and communications systems support, MA, PA, chaplain, linguist, personnel and vehicle decontamination, and security. BOS requirements for FHA are tailored to the mission.

(2) The US Air Force IHS program serves combatant and component command surgeons by providing medics with proficiency in a second language, regional and cultural expertise, medical planning, medical diplomacy, CA, and knowledge of IGOs and NGOs. IHS personnel have specific training in HA and disaster response as well as other medical stability operations. IHS teams are assigned to CCMDs and can also serve on a joint force surgeon's staff and work at the strategic and operational levels to help plan, monitor, and guide FHA operations.

(3) The **preventive and aerospace medicine (PAM) team** consists of aerospace medicine specialists, public health, bioenvironmental engineering, flight medicine personnel, and independent duty medical technicians. The team oversees basic education and training to prevent disease and briefs commanders on actual threats, safety issues, current illness, and current health trends. The PAM team leader should be considered the functional expert in casualty prevention. The team consists of three UTCs, which can deploy both in phases and simultaneously.

c. **US Army**

(1) Army combat support hospitals are Role 3 medical treatment facilities capable of providing hospitalization and outpatient services for 248 patients when fully staffed and equipped. Capabilities include emergency treatment, triage, and preparation of incoming patients for surgery; general, orthopedic, thoracic, urological, gynecological, and oral maxillofacial surgical capability (surgical capacity based on six operating room tables staffed for 96 operating table hours per day); consultation services; pharmacy, psychiatry, community health nursing, physical therapy, clinical laboratory, blood banking, radiology, and nutrition care support; emergency dental treatment; medical administrative and logistical services; and laundry for patient linens. The modular design of the hospital provides the capacity to deploy as modules or multiple individual capabilities for incrementally increased

medical services. The hospital may also be augmented by one or more medical detachments, hospital augmentation teams, or medical teams designed to enhance the unit's ability to provide the Army Health System support to the operational area.

(2) Preventive medicine detachments provide preventive medicine support and consultation for the prevention of disease; field sanitation, entomology, sanitary engineering; occupational and environmental health surveillance; and epidemiology to minimize the effects of environmental injuries, and enteric diseases, vector-borne disease, and other health threats with deployed forces. Capabilities also include monitoring pest management; field sanitation; water treatment and storage; waste disposal; other environmental health-related problems; recommending corrective measures; medical surveillance activities to assist in evaluating conditions affecting the health of the supported force; and epidemiological investigations. The detachment also monitors casualties, hospital admissions, and reports of autopsies for exposure to harmful agents (such as radiation, chemical, and biological hazards). The preventive medicine detachment can deploy as a single unit, or configured into three mobile teams.

(3) The Army medical detachment veterinary service support provides dispersed veterinary Role 1 and Role 2 (medical and resuscitative surgical care); veterinary Role 3 (comprehensive canine medical and surgical care); evacuation and hospitalization support for military and contractor working dogs; endemic zoonotic and foreign disease epidemiological surveillance and control; animal holding facility and kennel inspections; commercial food source audits for DOD procurement; food safety, quality, and sanitation inspections; food defense vulnerability assessments; food and water risk assessments; food microbiological and chemical laboratory diagnostics for supported units; and FHA in support of all branches of the Service throughout the operational area.

(4) A medical company (area support) is deployable worldwide and capable of providing triage of mass casualties, initial resuscitation/stabilization, advanced trauma management, patient holding for up to 40 patients, preparation for evacuation of the ill or injured, and patient decontamination in support of the deployed force. Capabilities also include behavioral health consultation services (to include combat and operational stress control elements); pharmacy, laboratory, and radiological services; emergency dental care to include stabilization of maxillofacial injuries and limited preventive dentistry. When organized under the C2 of the company HQ, this unit can operate dispersed over a wide area in teams as small as one physician or physician's assistant and three medics with associated equipment and can provide training to local health professionals in reestablishing essential health services.

(5) A medical command (deployment support) or medical brigade can deploy worldwide in support of FHA operations to serve as the senior medical C2 element of assigned and attached medical forces as described above, or other US Army medical units/capabilities made available for FHA.

d. **US Marine Corps.** USMC FHA operations are typically centrally planned by the MAGTF staff for decentralized execution by assigned forces. Each MAGTF has organic air, ground, C2, and logistic capabilities that provide immediate and integrated FHA options to the JFC. Operational maneuver from the sea, implementing ship-to-objective maneuver and seabased logistics, enables rapid execution of USMC FHA, without the need to establish extensive infrastructure ashore.

APPENDIX F
PLANNING FACTORS FOR FOREIGN HUMANITARIAN ASSISTANCE AND FOREIGN DISASTER RELIEF OPERATIONS

1. General

a. Lessons learned during previous FHA operations can provide valuable insight for commanders and staffs preparing for a similar operation. The following factors include some of the key lessons from FHA operations and highlight areas that FHA forces have found to be extremely important.

b. Is DOD the LFA? If not, has the LFA required DOD assistance?

c. Is the mission stated in terms of working towards restoration to preemergency status? Is mission success stated in terms not strictly defined by US or western standards? Is the situation at end state sustainable by the affected country and organizations remaining in the operational area?

d. What is the legal authority for the operation? Do plans include SJA personnel and assets? What is the legal and fiscal authority to conduct civil action projects? Is there a SOFA in effect? If not, should a SOFA, or some other type of international agreement, be negotiated or implemented?

e. What coordination and collaboration is required with the supported GCC, supporting CCDRs, subordinate joint force commands, USAID, COM, country team, multinational partners, NGOs, IGOs, and USG departments and agencies? What are the command, coordination, and collaboration relationships?

f. Have civilian agencies involved in the operation been encouraged to contribute their valuable expertise and assistance? Have US forces recognized these agencies for their efforts in this regard?

g. What restrictions exist regarding the sharing of information (sensitive or otherwise) with other agencies and organizations? What information and OPSEC measures are required?

h. What are the liaison requirements? Are LNOs positioned in both higher and subordinate HQ as well as other USG departments and agencies, medical facilities, NGOs, and IGOs, as required?

i. Is sea port and aerial port infrastructure, to include road and rail access to the ports, in place before forces begin to arrive? Has USTRANSCOM been consulted as to transportation feasibility? Has the use of ports been deconflicted with HN, NGOs, and IGOs?

j. Are interpreters available for the JTF, GCC, and other USG departments and agencies?

k. Is adequate communications equipment available for essential basic services? Is additional equipment or connectivity reconfiguration needed to provide direct communications routing to principal destinations?

l. What is the communications plan for communicating with NGOs, IGOs, and multinational forces? Do these entities require equipment augmentation?

m. Are briefing formats appropriate for use in CMO? Do they emphasize conditions, activities, and population support requirements? Are other participants in the FHA effort (other USG departments and agencies, NGOs, and IGOs) included in the briefings?

n. What are the information gathering and dissemination requirements? Has MISO been brought into the planning process?

o. During the planning process, has the joint force surgeon identified the commander's critical information requirements, PIRs, and named AOIs pertaining to the health threat in the operational area and submitted requirements to the supporting intelligence element?

p. Have supplemental measures to the SROE been identified, approved, and published prior to deployment? Do multinational forces understand the ROE? Are they using the same or compatible ROE?

q. Are planned actions within the budgetary limitations of the operation?

r. Has a finance officer been identified and deployed early in the operation?

s. Have Service contracting teams been identified and deployed early in the operation?

t. What logistic requirements are needed to support the operation, and what mechanism is in place to continually monitor logistic resources to ensure that urgent needs are met?

u. Has a PAO and necessary staff been identified and deployed early in the operation?

v. Has PA guidance been developed and passed to all members of the joint force?

w. Has an MOC been established to support the media?

x. What means are available to provide information to the affected population about FHA operations?

y. What force protection, security, and PR measures are required? What is the legal status of DOD participants and those who may need to respond to a threat? What is the role/relationship of the local and national security forces to the US forces?

2. Sphere Project

a. Sphere is based on two core beliefs: first, that all possible steps should be taken to alleviate human suffering arising out of calamity and conflict, and second, that those affected by disaster have a right to life with dignity and therefore a right to assistance.

Sphere is three things: a handbook, a broad process of collaboration, and an expression of commitment to quality and accountability.

b. The aim of Sphere is to improve the quality of assistance to people affected by disaster and improve the accountability of states and humanitarian agencies to their constituents, donors, and the affected populations.

c. Sphere represents a unique voluntary initiative and reflects the collective will and shared experience of a broad array of humanitarian actors. The community of these actors includes NGOs, IGOs, the International Red Cross and Red Crescent Movement, donor agencies, host governments, and representatives from affected populations.

d. The *Humanitarian Charter and Minimum Standards in Disaster Response* handbook is designed for use in disaster response (www.sphereproject.org). While not a policy document, it is applicable in a range of situations where relief is required, including natural disasters as well as armed conflict. It is designed to be used in both slow- and rapid-onset situations, in both rural and urban environments, in developing and developed countries, anywhere in the world. The emphasis throughout is on meeting the urgent survival needs of people affected by disaster, while asserting their basic human right to life with dignity. Despite this focus, the information contained in the handbook is not prescriptive. Minimum standards and key indicators have been developed using broad networks of practitioners in each of the sectors. Most of the standards, and the indicators that accompany them, are not new but consolidate and adapt existing knowledge and practice.

Intentionally Blank

APPENDIX G
REFERENCES

The development of JP 3-29 is based upon the following primary references.

1. Public Law

a. Title 10, USC.

b. Title 22, USC.

c. *Uniform Code of Military Justice.*

2. Presidential Directives

a. Executive Order 12114, *Environmental Effects Abroad of Major Federal Actions.*

b. Executive Order 13224, *Blocking Property and Prohibiting Transactions with Persons Who Commit, Threaten to Commit, or Support Terrorism.*

3. Department of Defense Publications

a. DODI 6490.03, *Deployment Health.*

b. DOD O-2000.12-H, *DOD Antiterrorism Handbook.*

c. DOD 4715.05-G, *Overseas Environmental Baseline Guidance Document.*

d. DOD 5105.38-M, *Security Assistance Management Manual (SAMM).*

e. DODD 1300.22E, *Mortuary Affairs Policy.*

f. DODD 2000.13, *Civil Affairs.*

g. DODD 2010.9, *Acquisition and Cross-Servicing Agreements.*

h. DODD 2205.02, *Humanitarian and Civic Assistance (HCA) Activities.*

i. DODD 2310.01E, *The Department of Defense Detainee Program.*

j. DODD 2311.01E, *DOD Law of War Program.*

k. DODD 3000.03E, *DOD Executive Agent for Non-Lethal Weapons (NLW, and NLW Policy.)*

l. DODD 3002.01, *Personnel Recovery in the Department of Defense.*

m. DODD 3025.14, *Evacuation of US Citizens and Designated Aliens from Threatened Area.*

n. DODD 3150.08, *DOD Response to Nuclear and Radiological Incidents.*

o. DODD S-3321.1, *Overt Psychological Operations Conducted by the Military Services in Peacetime and in Contingencies Short of Declared War (U).*

p. DODD 4715.1E, *Environment, Safety, and Occupational Health (ESOH).*

q. DODD 5100.46, *Foreign Disaster Relief (FDR).*

r. DODD 5230.11, *Disclosure of Classified Military Information to Foreign Governments and International Organizations.*

s. DODD 5525.01, *Status of Forces Policies and Information.*

t. DODD 5530.3, *International Agreements.*

u. DODD 6050.7, *Environmental Effects Abroad of Major Department of Defense Actions.*

v. DODD 6200.04, *Force Health Protection (FHP).*

w. DODD 6490.02E, *Comprehensive Health Surveillance.*

x. DODI 2000.11, *Procedures for Handling Requests for Political Asylum and Temporary Refuge.*

y. DODI 2000.12, *DOD Antiterrorism (AT) Program.*

z. DODI 2000.21, *Foreign Consequence Management (FCM).*

aa. DODI 2200.01, *Combating Trafficking in Persons (CTIP).*

bb. DODI 2205.3, *Implementing Procedures for the Humanitarian and Civic Assistance (HCA) Program.*

cc. DODI 3000.05, *Stability Operations.*

dd. DODI 3003.01, *DOD Support to Civil Search and Rescue (SAR).*

ee. DODI 3020.41, *Operational Contract Support (OCS).*

ff. DODI 5111.20, *State Partnership Program (SPP).*

gg. DODI 5200.01, *DOD Information Security Program and Protection of Sensitive Compartmented Information.*

hh. DODI 5515.08, *Assignment of Claims Responsibility.*

ii. *Defense Federal Acquisition Regulation Supplement.*

jj. *Manual for Courts Martial.*

4. Chairman of the Joint Chiefs of Staff Publications

a. CJCSI 2120.01C, *Acquisition and Cross-Servicing Agreements.*

b. CJCSI 2300.01D, *International Agreements.*

c. CJCSI 3110.05E, *Military Information Support Operations Supplement to the Joint Strategic Capabilities Plan.*

d. CJCSI 3110.07D, *Guidance Concerning Employment of Riot Control Agents and Herbicides (U).*

e. CJCSI 3110.10F, *Communications Systems Supplement to the Joint Strategic Capabilities Plan (JSCP).*

f. CJCSI 3121.01B, *Standing Rules of Engagement/Standing Rules for the Use of Force for US Forces.*

g. CJCSI 3207.01B, *Military Support to Humanitarian Mine Actions.*

h. CJCSI 3214.01D, *Defense Support for Chemical, Biological, Radiological, and Nuclear Incidents on Foreign Territory.*

i. CJCSI 5221.01C, *Delegation of Authority to Commanders of Combatant Commands to Disclose Classified Military Information to Foreign Governments and International Organizations.*

j. CJCSI 5810.01D, *Implementation of the DOD Law of War Program.*

k. CJCSI 7401.01F, *Combatant Commander Initiative Fund (CCIF).*

l. CJCSM 3122.01A, *Joint Operation Planning and Execution System (JOPES), Volume I (Planning Policies and Procedures).*

m. CJCSM 3122.02D, *Joint Operation Planning and Execution System (JOPES), Volume III, Time-Phased Force and Deployment Data Development and Deployment Execution.*

n. CJCSM 3130.03, *Adaptive Planning and Execution (APEX) Planning Formats and Guidance.*

5. Joint Publications

a. JP 1, *Doctrine for the Armed Forces of the United States.*

b. JP 1-0, *Joint Personnel Support.*

c. JP 1-02, *Department of Defense Dictionary of Military and Associated Terms.*

d. JP 1-04, *Legal Support to Military Operations.*

e. JP 1-05, *Religious Affairs in Joint Operations.*

f. JP 1-06, *Financial Management Support in Joint Operations.*

g. JP 2-0, *Joint Intelligence.*

h. JP 2-01, *Joint and National Intelligence Support to Military Operations.*

i. JP 2-01.2, *Counterintelligence and Human Intelligence Support to Joint Operations.*

j. JP 2-01.3, *Joint Intelligence Preparation of the Operational Environment.*

k. JP 2-03, *Geospatial Intelligence in Joint Operations.*

l. JP 3-0, *Joint Operations.*

m. JP 3-05, *Special Operations.*

n. JP 3-07, *Stability Operations.*

o. JP 3-07.2, *Antiterrorism.*

p. JP 3-07.3, *Peace Operations.*

q. JP 3-08, *Interorganizational Coordination During Joint Operations.*

r. JP 3-11, *Operations in Chemical, Biological, Radiological, and Nuclear Environments.*

s. JP 3-13, *Information Operations.*

t. JP 3-13.2, *Military Information Support Operations.*

u. JP 3-14, *Space Operations.*

v. JP 3-15, *Barriers, Obstacles, and Mine Warfare for Joint Operations.*

w. JP 3-15.1, *Counter-Improvised Explosive Device Operations.*

x. JP 3-16, *Multinational Operations.*

y. JP 3-22, *Foreign Internal Defense.*

z. JP 3-28, *Defense Support of Civil Authorities.*

aa. JP 3-33, *Joint Task Force Headquarters.*

bb. JP 3-34, *Joint Engineer Operations.*

cc. JP 3-35, *Deployment and Redeployment Operations.*

dd. JP 3-41, *Chemical, Biological, Radiological, and Nuclear Consequence Management.*

ee. JP 3-50, *Personnel Recovery.*

ff. JP 3-57, *Civil-Military Operations.*

gg. JP 3-61, *Public Affairs.*

hh. JP 3-63, *Detainee Operations.*

ii. JP 3-68, *Noncombatant Evacuation Operations.*

jj. JP 4-0, *Joint Logistics.*

kk. JP 4-01.6, *Joint Logistics Over-the-Shore.*

ll. JP 4-02, *Health Services.*

mm. JP 4-06, *Mortuary Affairs.*

nn. JP 4-08, *Logistics Support of Multinational Operations.*

oo. JP 4-09, *Distribution Operations.*

pp. JP 4-10, *Operational Contract Support.*

qq. JP 5-0, *Joint Operation Planning.*

rr. JP 6-0, *Joint Communications System.*

6. Service and Other Military Publications

a. Air Force Handbook 10-222, Volume 22, *Camp Planning for Displaced Persons.*

b. DSCA H-1, *DSCA Handbook for Foreign Assistance Act (FAA) Drawdown of Defense Articles and Services.*

c. DTRA, *Foreign Consequence Management Legal Deskbook.*

d. FM 3-57, *Civil-Military Operations.*

e. FM 4-20.147, Technical Manual 4-48.14, *Airdrop of Supplies and Equipment: Humanitarian Airdrop.*

f. FM 27-10, *The Law of Land Warfare.*

g. Graphic Training Aid (GTA) 41-01-003, *Civil Affairs Foreign Humanitarian Assistance Planning Guide.*

h. GTA 41-01-006, *Working with the Office of US Foreign Disaster Assistance.*

i. GTA 90-01-030, *Department of Defense Support to Foreign Disaster Relief (Handbook for JTF Commanders and Below).*

j. *Joint Task Force Commander's Handbook for Peace Operations,* Joint Warfighting Center.

k. NTTP 4-02.4, *Expeditionary Medical Facilities.*

l. NTTP 4-02.6, *Hospital Ships.*

m. NTTP 4-02.8, *Forward Deployable Preventive Medicine Unit.*

n. NWP 1-14M, *The Commander's Handbook on the Law of Naval Operations.*

o. NWP 3-29, *Disaster Response Operations.*

p. *Operational Law Handbook, The Judge Advocate General's Legal Center and School.*

q. *DOD Support to Foreign Disaster Relief (FDR) Handbook for Joint Task Force Commanders and Below, US Army Test and Evaluation Command.*

7. United States Government Publications

a. *Federal Acquisition Regulation.*

b. Field Operations Guide for Disaster Assessment and Response, Version 4.0, *Office of Foreign Disaster Assistance, Bureau for Democracy, Conflict, and Humanitarian Assistance, US Agency for International Development.*

c. *Guidelines for Relations Between US Armed Forces and Nongovernmental Humanitarian Organizations in Hostile or Potentially Hostile Environments,* US Institute of Peace.

d. US Department of State Foreign Affairs Manual, Volume 11, *Political Affairs.*

e. *USAID Primer.*

f. *USAID's Strategy for Sustainable Development: an Overview.*

8. United Nations Publications

a. *Handbook for Emergencies, UN High Commissioner for Refugees.*

b. *Civil-Military Relationship in Complex Emergencies—an IASC Reference Paper, UN Office for the Coordination of Humanitarian Affairs.*

c. *Convention on the Safety of United Nations and Associated Personnel.*

d. Emergency Field Handbook: *A Guide for UNICEF Staff, United Nations Children's Fund.*

e. General guidance for interaction between United Nations personnel and military and other representatives of the belligerent parties in the context of the crisis in Iraq, *UN Office for the Coordination of Humanitarian Affairs.*

f. Guidance Note on Using the Cluster Approach to Strengthen Humanitarian Response, *Inter-Agency Standing Committee.*

g. Guidelines for Assessment in Emergencies, *Inter-Agency Standing Committee Emergency Shelter Cluster.*

h. Guidelines for HIV/AIDS Interventions in Emergency Settings, *Inter-Agency Standing Committee.*

i. Guidelines for Humanitarian Organisations on Interacting with Military and Other Security Actors in Iraq, *UN Assistance Mission for Iraq.*

j. Guidelines on the Use of Military and Civil Defence Assets in Disaster Relief, — "Oslo Guidelines," *UN Office for the Coordination of Humanitarian Affairs.*

k. Guidelines on the Use of Military and Civil Defence Assets to Support United Nations Humanitarian Activities in Complex Emergencies, *UN Office for the Coordination of Humanitarian Affairs.*

l. Glossary of Humanitarian Terms in Relation to the Protection of Civilians in Armed Conflict, *UN Office for the Coordination of Humanitarian Affairs.*

m. Essentials for Emergencies, *World Health Organization.*

n. Handbook for Emergency Field Operations, *World Health Organization.*

o. Office for the Coordination of Humanitarian Affairs (OCHA) Orientation Handbook, *UN Office for the Coordination of Humanitarian Affairs.*

p. Operational Protection in Camps and Settlements; A Reference Guide of Good Practices in the Protection of Refugees and Other Persons of Concern, *UN High Commissioner for Refugees.*

q. Partnership: an Operations Management Handbook for UNHCR's Partners, *UN High Commissioner for Refugees.*

r. Protecting Persons Affected by Natural Disasters; IASC Operational Guidelines on Human Rights and Natural Disasters, *Inter-Agency Standing Committee.*

s. Relationships with Military Forces in Afghanistan—Guidelines for UNAMA Area Coordinators and other UN personnel, *UN Assistance Mission for Afghanistan.*

t. Sanctions Assessment Handbook; Assessing the Humanitarian Implications of Sanctions, *UN Office for the Coordination of Humanitarian Affairs.*

u. United Nations Disaster Assessment and Coordination (UNDAC) Handbook, *UN Office for the Coordination of Humanitarian Affairs.*

v. Use of Military or Armed Escorts for Humanitarian Convoys (Discussion Paper and Non-binding Guidelines), *UN Office for the Coordination of Humanitarian Affairs.*

9. North Atlantic Treaty Organization Publications

a. AJP-3.4.9, *Allied Joint Doctrine for Civil-Military Cooperation.*

b. *NATO Military Assistance to International Disaster Relief Operations.*

c. *Standing Operating Procedures for the Euro-Atlantic Disaster Response Coordination Centre.*

10. Other Selected Publications

a. *The Code of Conduct for the International Red Cross and Red Crescent Movement and NGOs in Disaster Relief.*

b. *Humanitarian Assistance in Disaster Situations: A Guide for Effective Aid,* Pan American Health Organization.

c. *Humanitarian Charter and Minimum Standards in Disaster Response,* the Sphere Project.

d. *Humanitarian Supply Management and Logistics in the Health Sector,* Pan American Health Organization.

e. *Worldwide Humanitarian Assistance Logistics System Handbook,* Institute for Defense Analysis.

APPENDIX H
ADMINISTRATIVE INSTRUCTIONS

1. User Comments

Users in the field are highly encouraged to submit comments on this publication to: Joint Staff J-7, Deputy Director, Joint Education and Doctrine, ATTN: Joint Doctrine Analysis Division, 116 Lake View Parkway, Suffolk, VA 23435-2697. These comments should address content (accuracy, usefulness, consistency, and organization), writing, and appearance.

2. Authorship

The lead agent for this publication is the US Army. The Joint Staff doctrine sponsor for this publication is the Joint Staff Logistics Directorate (J-4).

3. Supersession

This publication supersedes JP 3-29, 17 March 2009, *Foreign Humanitarian Assistance.*

4. Change Recommendations

a. Recommendations for urgent changes to this publication should be submitted:

TO: JOINT STAFF WASHINGTON DC//J7-JE&D

b. Routine changes should be submitted electronically to the Deputy Director, Joint Education and Doctrine, ATTN: Joint Doctrine Analysis Division, 116 Lake View Parkway, Suffolk, VA 23435-2697, and info the lead agent and the Director for Joint Force Development, J-7/JE&D.

c. When a Joint Staff directorate submits a proposal to the CJCS that would change source document information reflected in this publication, that directorate will include a proposed change to this publication as an enclosure to its proposal. The Services and other organizations are requested to notify the Joint Staff J-7 when changes to source documents reflected in this publication are initiated.

5. Distribution of Publications

Local reproduction is authorized, and access to unclassified publications is unrestricted. However, access to and reproduction authorization for classified JPs must be IAW DOD Manual 5200.01, Volume 1, *DOD Information Security Program: Overview, Classification, and Declassification,* and DOD Manual 5200.01, Volume 3, *DOD Information Security Program: Protection of Classified Information.*

6. Distribution of Electronic Publications

a. Joint Staff J-7 will not print copies of JPs for distribution. Electronic versions are available on JDEIS at https://jdeis.js.mil (NIPRNET) and http://jdeis.js.smil.mil (SIPRNET), and on the JEL at http://www.dtic.mil/doctrine (NIPRNET).

b. Only approved JPs are releasable outside the CCMDs, Services, and Joint Staff. Release of any classified JP to foreign governments or foreign nationals must be requested through the local embassy (Defense Attaché Office) to DIA, Defense Foreign Liaison/IE-3, 200 MacDill Blvd., Joint Base Anacostia-Bolling, Washington, DC 20340-5100.

c. JEL CD-ROM. Upon request of a joint doctrine development community member, the Joint Staff J-7 will produce and deliver one CD-ROM with current JPs. This JEL CD-ROM will be updated not less than semi-annually and when received can be locally reproduced for use within the CCMDs, Services, and combat support agencies.

GLOSSARY
PART I–ABBREVIATIONS AND ACRONYMS

AC	Active Component
AOI	area of interest
AOR	area of responsibility
APAN	All Partners Access Network
APEX	Adaptive Planning and Execution
ARG	amphibious ready group
ASD(SO/LIC)	Assistant Secretary of Defense (Special Operations and Low-Intensity Conflict)
BOS	base operating support
C2	command and control
CA	civil affairs
CAO	civil affairs operations
CAP	crisis action planning
CBRN	chemical, biological, radiological, and nuclear
CBRN CM	chemical, biological, radiological, and nuclear consequence management
CCDR	combatant commander
CCMD	combatant command
CDEMA	Caribbean Disaster Emergency Management Agency
CDHAM	Center for Disaster and Humanitarian Assistance Medicine
CFST	coalition forces support team
CI	counterintelligence
CIE	collaborative information environment
CIM	civil information management
CJCS	Chairman of the Joint Chiefs of Staff
CJCSI	Chairman of the Joint Chiefs of Staff instruction
CJCSM	Chairman of the Joint Chiefs of Staff manual
CJTF	commander, joint task force
CMAT	consequence management advisory team
CMC	Office of Civilian-Military Cooperation (USAID)
CMO	civil-military operations
CMOC	civil-military operations center
COA	course of action
COEDMHA	Center for Excellence in Disaster Management and Humanitarian Assistance (USPACOM)
COM	chief of mission
CONOPS	concept of operations
CONPLAN	concept plan
CONUS	continental United States
CRC	Civilian Response Corps (DOS)

CSO	Bureau of Conflict and Stabilization Operations (DOS)
CTS	commodity tracking system
DALIS	Disaster Assistance Logistics Information System
DART	disaster assistance response team
DCHA	Bureau for Democracy, Conflict, and Humanitarian Assistance (USAID)
DDA	deputy development advisor
DDOC	Deployment and Distribution Operations Center (USTRANSCOM)
DIA	Defense Intelligence Agency
DLA	Defense Logistics Agency
DMT	disaster management team (UN)
DNBI	disease and nonbattle injury
DOD	Department of Defense
DODD	Department of Defense directive
DODI	Department of Defense instruction
DOS	Department of State
DSCA	Defense Security Cooperation Agency
DSPD	defense support to public diplomacy
DTRA	Defense Threat Reduction Agency
EADRU	Euro-Atlantic disaster response unit
EAPC	Euro-Atlantic Partnership Council
ECHO	European Commission Directorate General for Humanitarian Aid and Civil Protection
EMEDS	expeditionary medical support
EMF	expeditionary medical facility
EMU	expeditionary medical unit
EP	excess property
ERC	emergency relief coordinator
ERU	emergency response unit
ERW	explosive remnants of war
FAA	Foreign Assistance Act
FACT	field assessment and coordination team
FAO	Food and Agriculture Organization (UN)
FCM	foreign consequence management
FDPMU	forward-deployable preventive medicine unit
FDR	foreign disaster relief
FEST	foreign emergency support team
FFP	Office of Food for Peace (DOS)
FGS	final governing standard
FHA	foreign humanitarian assistance
FHP	force health protection
FID	foreign internal defense

FM	field manual (Army)
FY	fiscal year
GARS	Global Area Reference System
GCC	geographic combatant commander
GFM	global force management
GTA	graphic training aid
HA	humanitarian assistance
HACC	humanitarian assistance coordination center
HAST	humanitarian assistance survey team
HCA	humanitarian and civic assistance
HDR	humanitarian daily ration
HDTC	Humanitarian Demining Training Center
HEWSweb	Humanitarian Early Warning Service
HIC	humanitarian information center
HIU	humanitarian information unit (DOS)
HMA	humanitarian mine action
HN	host nation
HOC	humanitarian operations center
HQ	headquarters
HRT	health response team
HUMINT	human intelligence
IASC	Inter-Agency Standing Committee (UN)
ICC	International Criminal Court
ICRC	International Committee of the Red Cross
IDP	internally displaced person
IED	improvised explosive device
IFRC	International Federation of Red Cross and Red Crescent Societies
IGC	Integrated Data Environment/Global Transportation Network Convergence
IGO	intergovernmental organization
IHS	international health specialist
INSARAG	International Search and Rescue Advisory Group
InterAction	American Council for Voluntary International Action
IO	information operations
IOM	International Organization for Migration
IPC	interagency policy committee
IPI	indigenous populations and institutions
ISN	Bureau of International Security and Nonproliferation (DOS)
J-2	intelligence directorate of a joint staff
J-3	operations directorate of a joint staff
J-4	logistics directorate of a joint staff

JCMOTF	joint civil-military operations task force
JDDOC	joint deployment and distribution operations center
JECC	joint enabling capabilities command
JEMB	joint environmental management board
JFC	joint force commander
JFCH	joint force chaplain
JFUB	joint facilities utilization board
JIACG	joint interagency coordination group
JIOC	joint intelligence operations center
JIPOE	joint intelligence preparation of the operational environment
JISE	joint intelligence support element
JLOC	joint logistics operations center
JMAO	joint mortuary affairs office
JMC	joint movement center
JMISTF	joint military information support task force
JNCC	joint network operations control center
JOA	joint operations area
JOPES	Joint Operation Planning and Execution System
JOPP	joint operation planning process
JP	joint publication
JPASE	Joint Public Affairs Support Element (USTRANSCOM)
JRSOI	joint reception, staging, onward movement, and integration
JSOTF	joint special operations task force
JTF	joint task force
LFA	lead federal agency
LNO	liaison officer
LOC	line of communications
LSS	logistics support system
MA	mortuary affairs
MAGTF	Marine air-ground task force
MARO	mass atrocity response operations
MDRO	mission disaster response officer
METL	mission-essential task list
MEU	Marine expeditionary unit
MIS	military information support
MISO	military information support operations
MITAM	mission tasking matrix
MOC	media operations center
MOE	measure of effectiveness
MOP	measure of performance
MPF	maritime pre-positioning force
MTF	medical treatment facility

NA	nation assistance
NATO	North Atlantic Treaty Organization
NAVELSG	Navy expeditionary logistic support group
NEO	noncombatant evacuation operation
NG	National Guard
NGA	National Geospatial-Intelligence Agency
NGO	nongovernmental organization
NSC	National Security Council
NTTP	Navy tactics, techniques, and procedures
NWP	Navy warfare publication
OAS	Organization of American States
OCONUS	outside the continental United States
OCS	operational contract support
OE	operational environment
OEBGD	Overseas Environmental Baseline Guidance Document
OFDA	Office of United States Foreign Disaster Assistance (USAID)
OHDACA	Overseas Humanitarian, Disaster, and Civic Aid (DSCA)
OHDM	Office of Humanitarian Assistance, Disaster Relief, and Mine Action
OPCON	operational control
OPLAN	operation plan
OPORD	operation order
OPSEC	operations security
OSC	on-site commander
OSCE	Organization for Security and Cooperation in Europe
OSOCC	on-site operations coordination center
OTI	Office of Transition Initiatives (USAID)
OUSD(C)	Office of the Under Secretary of Defense (Comptroller)
PA	public affairs
PAM	preventive and aerospace medicine
PAO	public affairs officer
PCC	policy coordination committee
PDC	Pacific Disaster Center
PIR	priority intelligence requirement
PM	Bureau of Political-Military Affairs (DOS)
PN	partner nation
PO	peace operations
POLAD	policy advisor
PR	personnel recovery
PRC	populace and resources control
PRM	Bureau of Population, Refugees, and Migration (DOS)
RC	Reserve Component
RCA	riot control agent

RFA	request for assistance
RMT	response management team
ROE	rules of engagement
SAR	search and rescue
SDA	senior development advisor
SecDef	Secretary of Defense
SJA	staff judge advocate
SOF	special operations forces
SOFA	status-of-forces agreement
SPP	State Partnership Program (NG)
SROE	standing rules of engagement
SRUF	standing rules for the use of force
TACON	tactical control
TCP	theater campaign plan
TIP	trafficking in persons
UN	United Nations
UNCLOS	United Nations Convention on the Law of the Sea
UNDAC	United Nations disaster assessment and coordination
UNDP	United Nations development programme
UNEP	United Nations environment programme
UNHAS	United Nations Humanitarian Air Service
UNHCR	United Nations Office of the High Commissioner for Refugees
UNICEF	United Nations Children's Fund
UNOCHA	United Nations Office for the Coordination of Humanitarian Affairs
USAID	United States Agency for International Development
USC	United States Code
USD(P)	Under Secretary of Defense for Policy
USG	United States Government
USNS	United States naval ship
USPACOM	United States Pacific Command
USSOCOM	United States Special Operations Command
USTRANSCOM	United States Transportation Command
UTC	unit type code
VI	visual information
WFP	World Food Programme (UN)
WHO	World Health Organization (UN)
WMD	weapons of mass destruction
WRA	Office of Weapons Removal and Abatement (DOS)

PART II–TERMS AND DEFINITIONS

dislocated civilian. A broad term primarily used by the Department of Defense that includes a displaced person, an evacuee, an internally displaced person, a migrant, a refugee, or a stateless person. Also called **DC.** (JP 1-02. SOURCE: JP 3-29)

displaced person. A broad term used to refer to internally and externally displaced persons collectively. (JP 1-02. SOURCE: JP 3-29)

foreign assistance. Assistance to foreign nations ranging from the sale of military equipment to donations of food and medical supplies to aid survivors of natural and man-made disasters; that may be provided through development assistance, humanitarian assistance, and security assistance. (Approved for incorporation into JP 1-02.)

foreign disaster. A calamitous situation or event that occurs naturally or through human activities, which threatens or inflicts human suffering on a scale that may warrant emergency relief assistance from the United States Government or from foreign partners. (Approved for incorporation into JP 1-02.)

foreign disaster relief. Assistance that can be used immediately to alleviate the suffering of foreign disaster victims that normally includes services and commodities as well as the rescue and evacuation of victims; the provision and transportation of food, water, clothing, medicines, beds, bedding, and temporary shelter; the furnishing of medical equipment, medical and technical personnel; and making repairs to essential services. Also called **FDR.** (Approved for incorporation into JP 1-02.)

foreign humanitarian assistance. Department of Defense activities conducted outside the United States and its territories to directly relieve or reduce human suffering, disease, hunger, or privation. Also called **FHA.** (Approved for incorporation into JP 1-02.)

humanitarian and civic assistance. Assistance to the local populace, specifically authorized by Title 10, United States Code, Section 401, and funded under separate authorities, provided by predominantly United States forces in conjunction with military operations. Also called **HCA.** (Approved for incorporation into JP 1-02.)

humanitarian assistance coordination center. A temporary center established by a geographic combatant commander to assist with interagency coordination and planning during the early planning and coordination stages of foreign humanitarian assistance operations. Also called **HACC.** (Approved for incorporation into JP 1-02.)

humanitarian demining assistance. The activities related to the furnishing of education, training, and technical assistance with respect to the detection and clearance of land mines and other explosive remnants of war. (JP 1-02. SOURCE: JP 3-29)

humanitarian operations center. An international and interagency body that coordinates the overall relief strategy and unity of effort among all participants in a large foreign humanitarian assistance operation. Also called **HOC.** (Approved for incorporation into JP 1-02.)

internally displaced person. Any person who has been forced or obliged to flee or to leave their home or places of habitual residence, in particular as a result of or in order to avoid the effects of armed conflict, situations of generalized violence, violations of human rights or natural or human-made disasters, and who have not crossed an internationally recognized state border. Also called **IDP.** (Approved for incorporation into JP 1-02.)

migrant. A person who (1) belongs to a normally migratory culture who may cross national boundaries, or (2) has fled his or her native country for economic reasons rather than fear of political or ethnic persecution. (JP 1-02. SOURCE: JP 3-29)

natural disaster. An emergency situation posing significant danger to life and property that results from a natural cause. (JP 1-02. SOURCE: JP 3-29)

refugee. A person who, owing to a well-founded fear of being persecuted for reasons of race, religion, nationality, membership of a particular social group, or political opinion, is outside the country of his or her nationality and is unable or, owing to such fear, is unwilling to avail himself or herself of the protection of that country. (Approved for incorporation into JP 1-02.)

resettled person. A refugee or an internally displaced person wishing to return somewhere other than his or her previous home or land within the country or area of original displacement. (JP 1-02. SOURCE: JP 3-29)

returnee. A displaced person who has returned voluntarily to his or her former place of residence. (JP 1-02. SOURCE: JP 3-29)

stateless person. A person who is not considered as a national by any state under the operation of its law. (JP 1-02. SOURCE: JP 3-29)